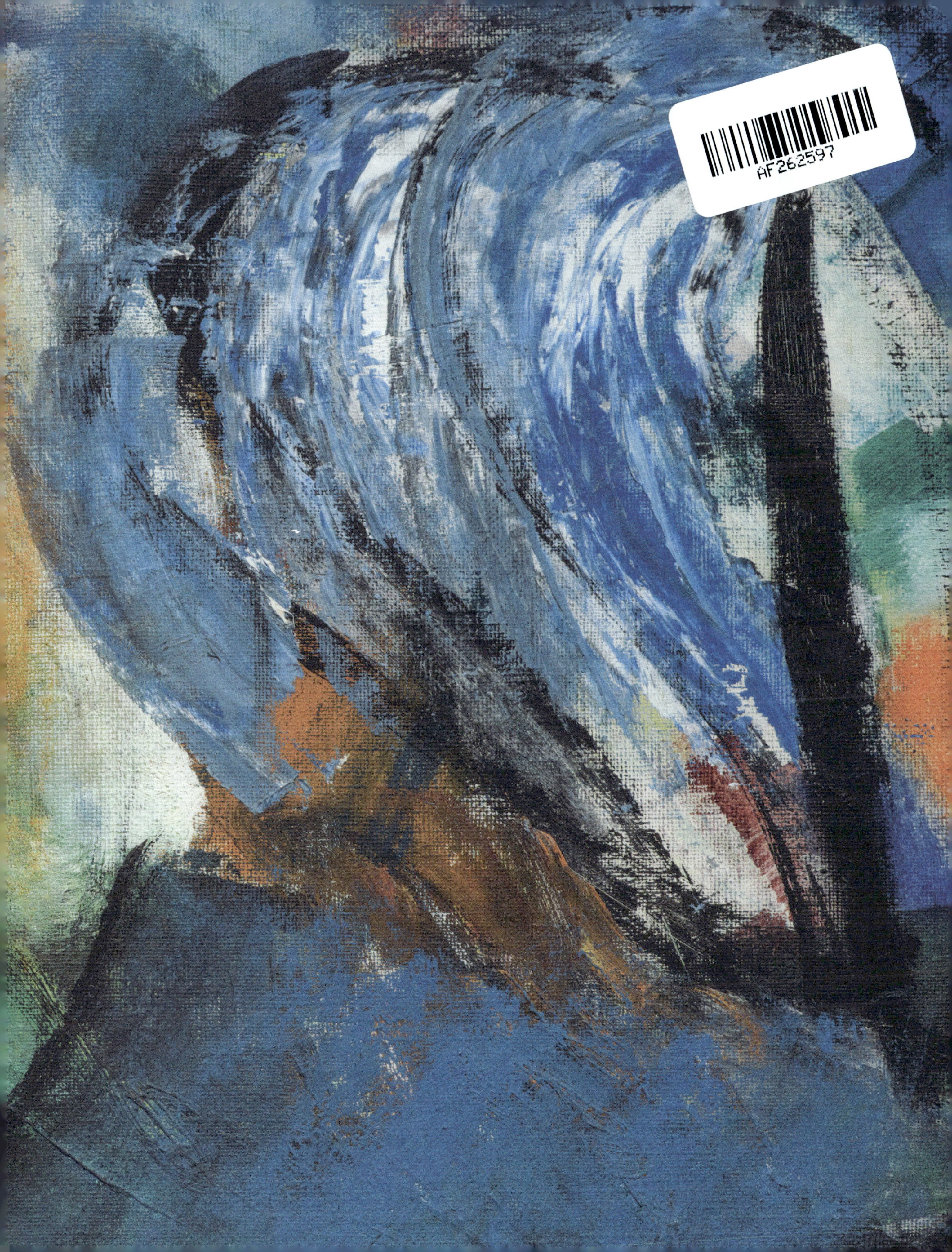

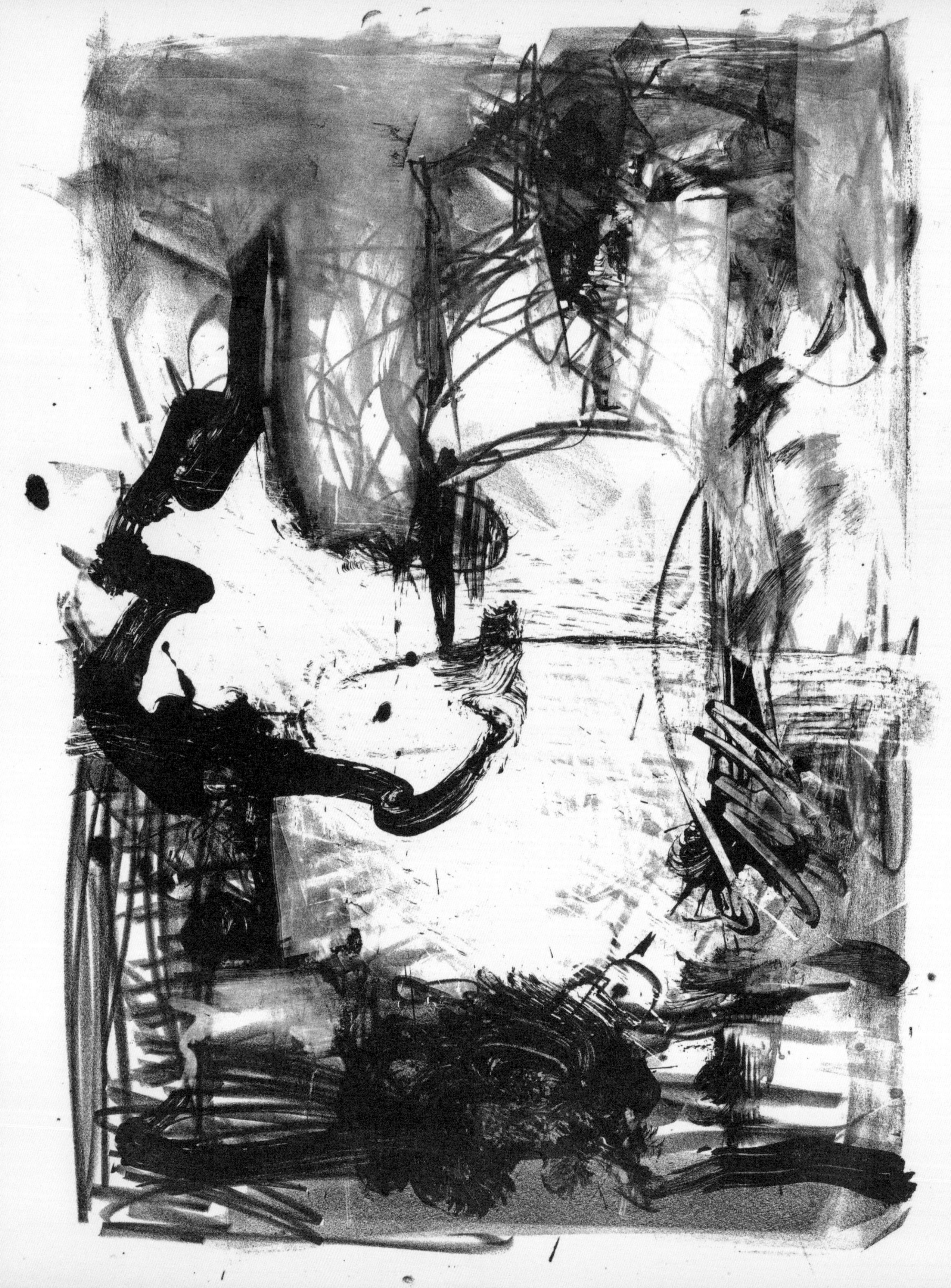

GRACE HARTIGAN

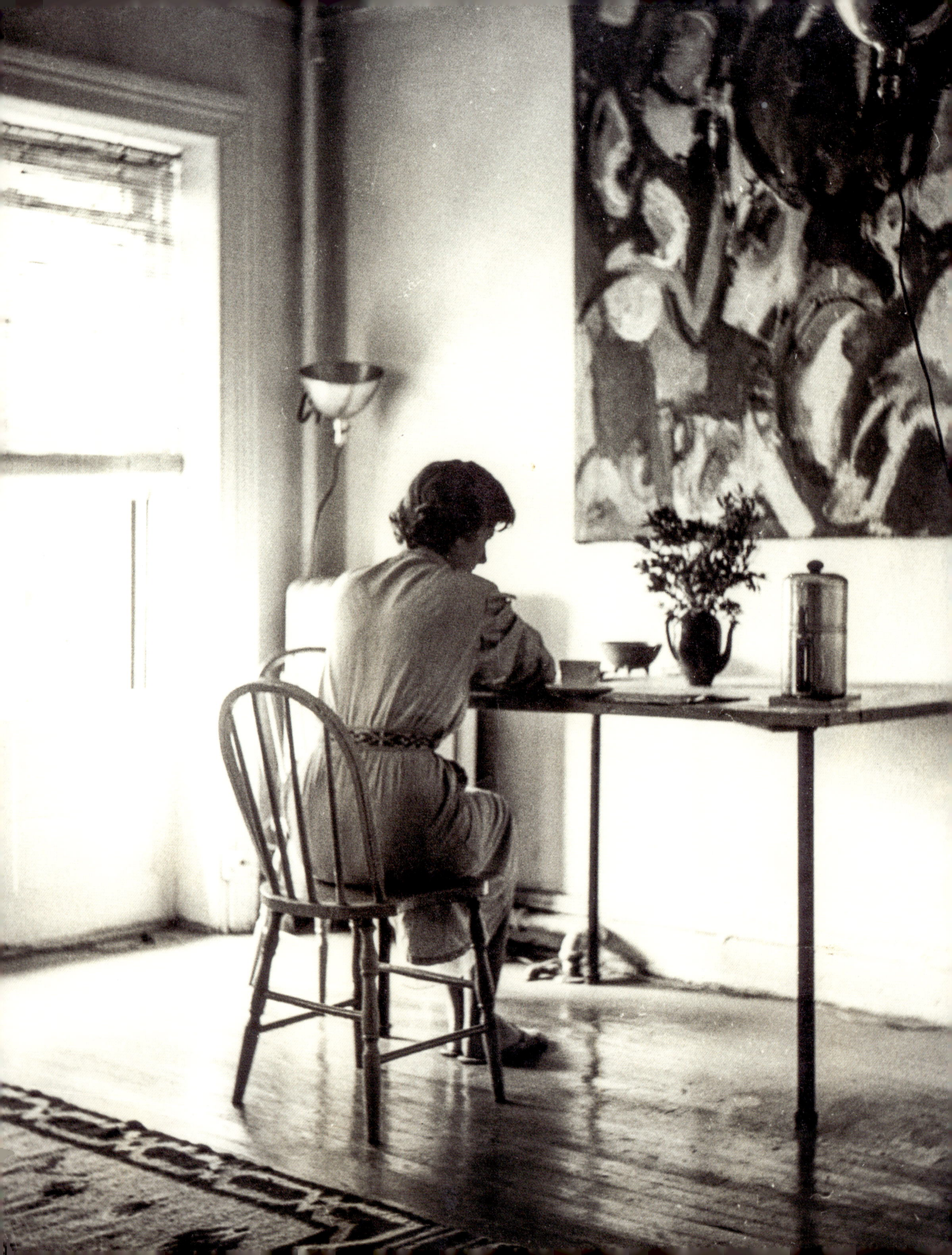

JARED LEDESMA

Contributions by
Terence Diggory
Rachel Blau DuPlessis
Frances Lazare

GRACE HARTIGAN

The Gift of Attention

North Carolina Museum of Art, Raleigh, North Carolina,
in association with D Giles Limited

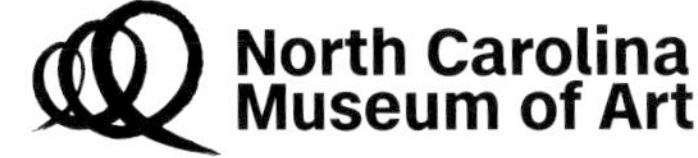

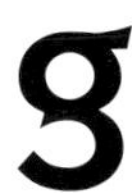

This catalogue accompanies the exhibition *Grace Hartigan: The Gift of Attention* on display at the North Carolina Museum of Art, Raleigh, April 12–August 10, 2025; Portland Museum of Art, Portland, ME, October 10, 2025–January 11, 2026; and Sheldon Museum of Art, University of Nebraska, Lincoln, NE, August 13–December 31, 2026.

Organized by the North Carolina Museum of Art

In Raleigh support is provided, in part, by the North Carolina Department of Natural and Cultural Resources; the North Carolina Museum of Art Foundation, Inc.; and the William R. Kenan Jr. Endowment for Educational Exhibitions. Research for this exhibition was made possible by Ann and Jim Goodnight/The Andrew W. Mellon Foundation Fund for Curatorial and Conservation Research and Travel.

© 2025 North Carolina Museum of Art

First published in 2025 by GILES
An imprint of D Giles Limited
66 High Street
Lewes, BN7 1XG, UK
gilesltd.com

ISBN: 978-1-913875-88-6
All rights reserved

No part of the contents of this book may be reproduced, stored in a retrieval system, or transmitted in any form or by any means electronic, mechanical, photocopying, recording, or otherwise, without the written permission of the North Carolina Museum of Art and D Giles Limited. Inquiries should be addressed to Manager of Book Publishing, North Carolina Museum of Art, 4630 Mail Service Center, Raleigh, NC 27699-4630.

North Carolina Museum of Art
2110 Blue Ridge Road
Raleigh, North Carolina
ncartmuseum.org

The North Carolina Museum of Art is an agency of the North Carolina Department of Natural and Cultural Resources, D. Reid Wilson, secretary. Operating support is provided through state appropriations and generous contributions from individuals, foundations, and businesses.

For the North Carolina Museum of Art:
Meghan Olis, Director of Collections and Exhibitions Management
Lee Nisbet, Manager of Exhibitions
Laura Napolitano, Editor and Manager of Book Publishing
Dan Ruccia, Senior Graphic Designer
Sean Livingstone, Photo Editor

For D Giles Limited:
Jodi Simpson, Proofreader
Produced by GILES, an imprint of D Giles Limited
Printed and bound in Italy

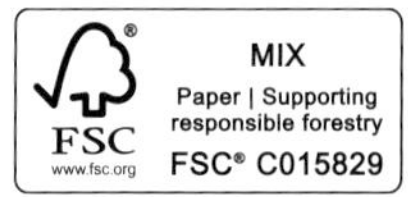

All measurements are in inches; height precedes width precedes depth.

Library of Congress
Cataloging-in-Publication Data

Names: Ledesma, Jared, 1982- contributor. | Diggory, Terence, 1951- contributor. | DuPlessis, Rachel Blau, contributor. | Lazare, Frances, contributor. | North Carolina Museum of Art organizer, host institution. | Portland Museum (Portland, Me.), host institution. | Sheldon Museum of Art, host institution.
Title: Grace Hartigan : the gift of attention / Jared Ledesma ; contributions by Terence Diggory, Rachel Blau DuPlessis, Frances Lazare.
Description: Raleigh, North Carolina : North Carolina Museum of Art ; Lewes : in association with D Giles Limited, 2025. | Includes bibliographical references and index. | Summary: "This exhibition catalogue explores the impact midcentury American poets and poetry had on painter Grace Hartigan's early career during the 1950s and 1960s. Through dialogue, prose, patronage, and, for some, their bold expression of sexuality, these poets collectively transformed Hartigan's outlook on art and life" -- Provided by publisher.
Identifiers: LCCN 2024030303 | ISBN 9781913875886 (hardcover)
Subjects: LCSH: Hartigan, Grace--Exhibitions.
Classification: LCC N6537.H3632 A4 2025 | DDC 759.13--dc23/eng/20240815
LC record available at https://lccn.loc.gov/2024030303

Front cover Grace Hartigan, *East Side Sunday*, 1956, oil on canvas, 80 × 82 in., Brooklyn Museum, Gift of James I. Merrill, 56.180

Back cover Unidentified photographer [Walter Silver?], Grace Hartigan seated in front of *River Bathers*, circa 1953

Endpaper details Plates 15, 18, and 24

Frontispiece Walter Silver, Grace Hartigan at a table in her Essex Street Studio, with *Months and Moons* on the wall, circa 1950

Contents

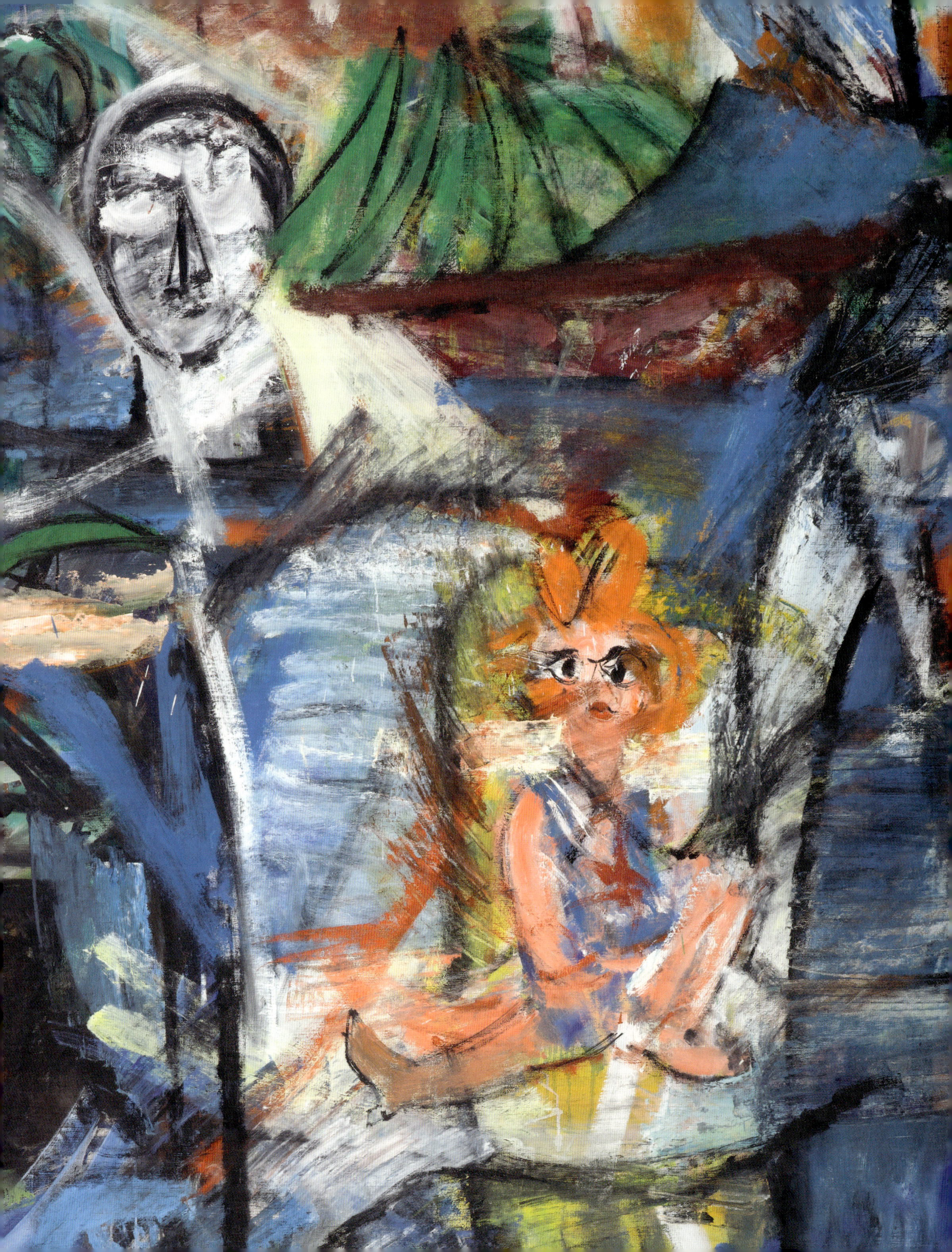

Director's Foreword

Grace Hartigan's *Interior with Mexican Doll* (1955) has been part of the North Carolina Museum of Art's collection for over sixty-five years, generously gifted by the renowned American poet James Merrill. Within the picture Hartigan's distinctive blend of broad abstraction and subtle figuration offers a dynamic view of her studio. Today, beyond its significance as a hallmark of the NCMA's collection of mid-20th-century art, *Interior with Mexican Doll* serves as a source of inspiration for *Grace Hartigan: The Gift of Attention*.

Featuring over three dozen works, including several rarely displayed paintings, this exhibition seeks to illuminate the extraordinary influence midcentury New York poets and poetry had on Hartigan's early career. Organized by Jared Ledesma, the NCMA's curator of 20th-century art and contemporary art, *Grace Hartigan: The Gift of Attention* is one of the most ambitious investigations of Hartigan's career in over two decades. Ledesma's discerning eye and exhaustive scholarship has led to the assemblage of an inspired selection of her artworks, whose significance is elucidated both in the show and by this publication.

I would like to extend my deepest gratitude to Ledesma, NCMA staff from across the institution, lenders, the staffs of the Special Collections Research Center at the Syracuse University Libraries and the Beinecke Rare Book and Manuscript Library at Yale University, and other supporters, who made this important and timely project possible. *Grace Hartigan: The Gift of Attention* embodies the North Carolina Museum of Art's commitment to amplifying overlooked artistic voices and sharing them with our communities. Taken together, the exhibition and the catalogue exemplify the NCMA's dedication to offering an ever-expansive view of the history of art.

Valerie Hillings, PhD
Director and CEO
North Carolina Museum of Art

Acknowledgments

It is a pleasure to acknowledge all who contributed to the success of *Grace Hartigan: The Gift of Attention*. Over the course of three years, I have had the privilege of working with esteemed colleagues across various institutions and within the NCMA family as well as received unfaltering support from my family.

Firstly, I am deeply grateful to Rex Stevens, executor of the estate of Grace Hartigan, for his unequivocal support of this exhibition.

I extend my heartfelt appreciation to the essayists in this catalogue: Terence Diggory, Rachel Blau DuPlessis, and Frances Lazare, for their insightful contributions that expand our knowledge of Hartigan and the influential writers who played a role in shaping her career. I owe a special thanks to Terence Diggory, whose pioneering 1993 exhibition *Grace Hartigan and the Poets: Paintings and Prints* at Skidmore College was a key starting point for our exhibition. Terry's steadfast scholarship on Hartigan's engagement with poetry has been invaluable.

I am immensely thankful to the staff at the Syracuse University Special Collections Research Center, where Hartigan's papers are preserved, especially Julia Dudley, access services supervisor, who facilitated my research with tremendous ease. I also appreciate the Beinecke Rare Book and Manuscript Library at Yale University for preserving the papers of poets Daisy Aldan and Barbara Guest, leading to phenomenal findings. Joel Minor, curator of modern literature collection/manuscripts, and Steven Vance, curatorial assistant, at the Washington University in St. Louis libraries were instrumental in my review of James Merrill's papers.

My deepest gratitude goes to the generous staff at various art and history institutions who assisted in my research. This includes Indira Abiskaroon, curatorial assistant, Modern and Contemporary Art, Brooklyn Museum; Eric Crosby, Henry J. Heinz II Director, and Elizabeth Tufts Brown, associate registrar, Carnegie Museum of Art; Mary-Kay Lombino, deputy director and the Emily Hargroves Fisher '57 and Richard B. Fisher Curator, the Frances Lehman Loeb Art Center, Vassar College; Willard Spiegelman, James Merrill House; Lily Goldberg, collection specialist, Department of Painting and Sculpture, the Museum of Modern Art; and Majida Mugharbel, permanent collection documentation manager, Whitney Museum of American Art.

I also appreciate the support from individuals at auction houses, galleries, and firms who assisted in pursuing artworks by Hartigan, facilitated conversations with collectors, and provided instrumental connections. This includes Mikaela Sardo Lamarche, ACA Galleries; Christine Berry, Berry Campbell Gallery; Emily Bivins, department coordinator, and Rachael White Young, senior specialist, vice president, Post-War and Contemporary Art, Christie's; Neal Meltzer, Neal Meltzer Fine Art; Andrew Arnot, Tibor de Nagy Gallery; Liz Sterling, art consultant and dealer; and Allison Whiting, principal, Allison Whiting LLC.

Many thanks go to Daniel Belasco, executive director, Al Held Foundation, whose scan of a now-lost letter exchanged between poet Barbara Guest and Grace Hartigan was invaluable. I am also grateful to the formidable poet Stephen Yenser, distinguished professor emeritus at UCLA, for his insights on James Merrill's history. I'm indebted to Jenni Quilter, executive director of the Expository Writing Program and assistant vice dean of General Education at New York University, for her insightful application of the phrase "the gift of attention" in describing the creative relationship between Grace Hartigan and Frank O'Hara. This phrase serves as the subtitle of both the exhibition and catalogue but is applied here more broadly in respect to several poets and players who bestowed Hartigan with attention.

To the collectors who have entrusted their Hartigan works to us for this exhibition, I extend my sincere thanks. Your willingness to include these important works—some of which have rarely been seen by the public—is incredibly appreciated. Thank you for supporting Hartigan's legacy.

I drafted a large portion of my catalogue essay at the Weymouth Center for the Arts & Humanities in Southern Pines, NC, when I took part in their writers-in-residence program. Thanks very much to Weymouth's staff for ensuring that my stay was comfortable and productive and for creating such a stimulating environment in which to write.

This exhibition and publication could not have achieved its scope without the expertise and dedication of the North Carolina Museum of Art team. I am especially grateful to Valerie Hillings, director and CEO, and Linda Johnson Dougherty, chief curator and senior curator of contemporary art, for their unwavering faith in this project. My curatorial colleagues have also contributed significantly, each in their unique way, lending a supportive ear and insightful input.

A big thank you goes out to the exhibitions team, whose hard work made this dream exhibition and publication a reality. Meghan Olis, director of collections and exhibitions management, provided invaluable guidance and management, while Lee Nisbet, manager of exhibitions, brought enthusiasm and tenacity that propelled this project forward. Project associate Sean

Livingstone diligently gathered images for the publication, and Denice Celley, curatorial and exhibitions assistant, stepped in with optimal support when needed. Associate registrar Angie Bell-Morris ensured seamless national and international loans, and Ian Larson, chief art handler, and Rand Esser, head preparator, executed an exceptional installation. Megan Salazar-Walsh, exhibitions conservator, provided astute oversight throughout.

To the NCMA's exhibition design and publications teams, I extend my heartfelt thanks. Kathryn Briggs, senior exhibition designer, whose passion for Grace Hartigan and her work is palpable, created a key design for the exhibition. Dan Ruccia, senior graphic designer, demonstrated exceptional talent in the design of this stunning publication, and Laura Napolitano, editor and manager of book publishing, contributed with her keen eye and patience.

Thanks go to the NCMA's advancement team, especially Rob Linens, gift officer, and Margaret Nelson, major gift officer, for their enthusiastic campaigning of the exhibition and to Jamie Powell, institutional gift officer, for her incomparable insight and organization.

Felicia Knise, manager of interpretation, brought creativity to the exhibition's content and media, and Lizzie Newton, director of marketing and communications, along with her team, promoted the exhibition and publication relentlessly.

I am grateful to those who personally offered exceptional guidance and support throughout this project—Suzanne Field, my closest friend and number one cheerleader, and Alison Ferris, my mentor, whose intelligent feedback greatly strengthened my essay in this publication.

My family's unwavering support for my career and passion for art means the world to me. To my late father, Tomas (Tommy) Ledesma, your loving, heartfelt pride was always felt. And to my mother, Georgianna Ledesma, your steadfast confidence and constant encouragement have been a tremendous source of empowerment and inspiration.

Lastly, and most important, I give thanks to the poet in my life: my husband, Jon. If it wasn't for you, this exhibition would not have come to fruition. Your presence is felt in every facet of this project. Thank you for your invaluable input, for encouraging me when I doubted myself, and for being my inspiration, strength, and motivation. I love you deeply and dedicate this to you.

Jared Ledesma
Curator of 20th-Century Art and Contemporary Art
North Carolina Museum of Art

Lenders to the Exhibition

Albert and Shirley Small Special Collections Library, University of Virginia
Baltimore Museum of Art
Brooklyn Museum
Carnegie Museum of Art
Paul Fingersh and Brenda Althouse
The Frances Lehman Loeb Art Center, Vassar College
James Merrill House & Writer-In-Residence Program
Lizbeth and George Krupp
The Levett Collection
The McNay Art Museum
The Museum of Modern Art
National Gallery of Art
The Nelson-Atkins Museum of Art
Steven and Beverly Newborn
Hart Perry
Private collections
The Raymond Danowski Poetry Library, Emory University
Smithsonian American Art Museum
Special Collections Research Center, Syracuse University Libraries
Rex R. Stevens and the Grace Hartigan Estate
The University of Arizona Museum of Art
University at Buffalo Art Galleries
Whitney Museum of American Art

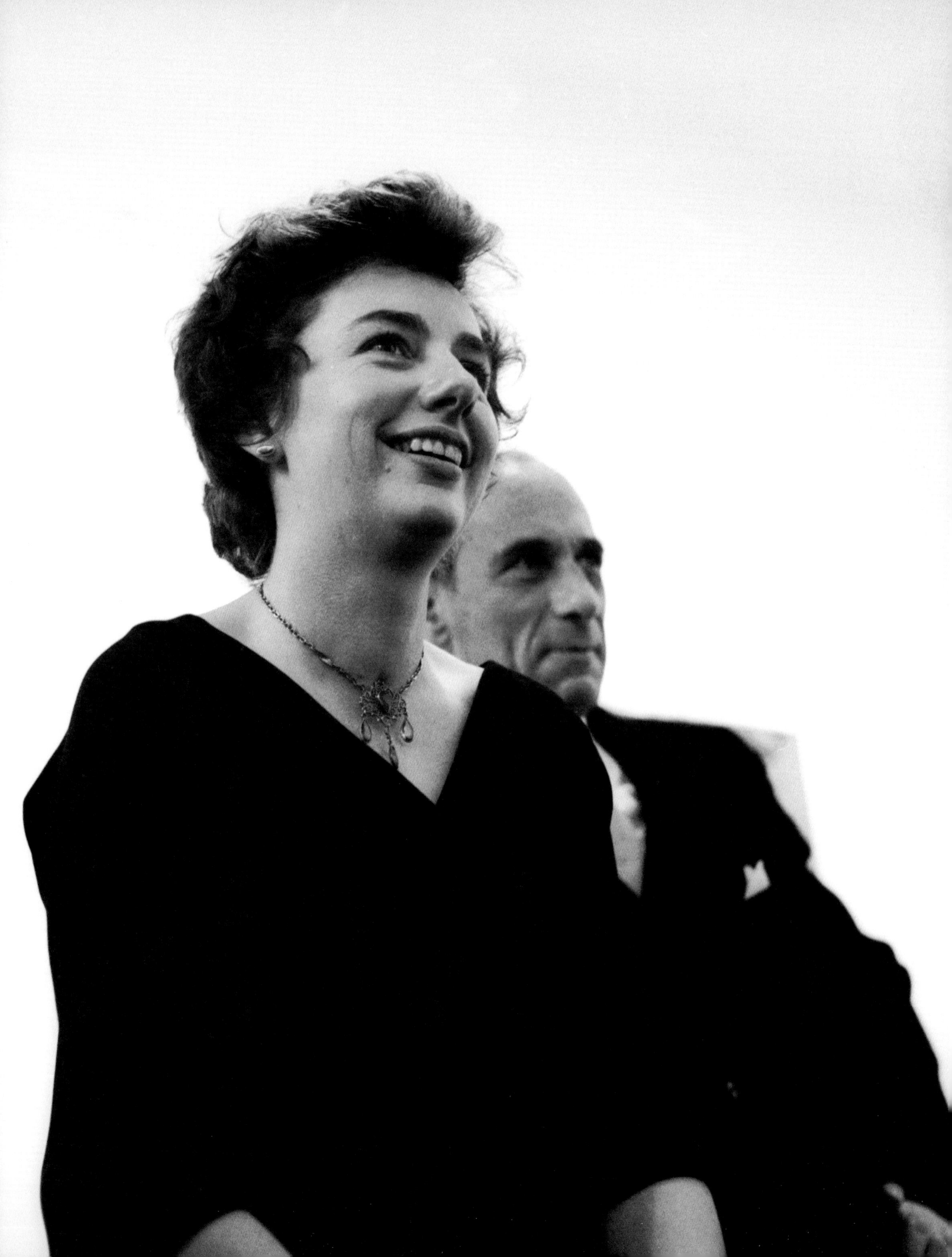

Grace Hartigan: Image Maker

An Introduction

TERENCE DIGGORY

If the "New York School" label sounds too narrow, try *The New American Painting*, the title of the major exhibition that New York's Museum of Modern Art (MoMA) sent traveling through Europe in 1959, with work by Jackson Pollock and Willem de Kooning leading the way. Grace Hartigan (1922–2008) was the youngest artist and the only woman represented. The following year Hartigan's poet friends Frank O'Hara and Barbara Guest were included in the groundbreaking anthology *The New American Poetry*, announcing "new conceptions of the poem" parallel to the advances in the new painting.[1] If we question whether the "newness" claimed in these titles remains relevant today, we can apply the test proposed by an acknowledged forerunner, Ezra Pound: "Literature is news that STAYS news."[2] The same goes for visual art.

Parallels between literature and visual art that we may take for granted today were the subject of much controversy when a group of young artists, including Hartigan, lured a group of poets into the caldron of experimentation stirred by John Bernard Myers at the Tibor de Nagy Gallery, founded in New York City in 1950. Although Myers chose many of his artists from a list drawn up by the critic Clement Greenberg, the culture of "no rules" that Myers promoted

Fig. 1 Fred W. McDarrah, Grace Hartigan with Tibor de Nagy at the opening of an exhibition of her works at his gallery, New York, April 28, 1959

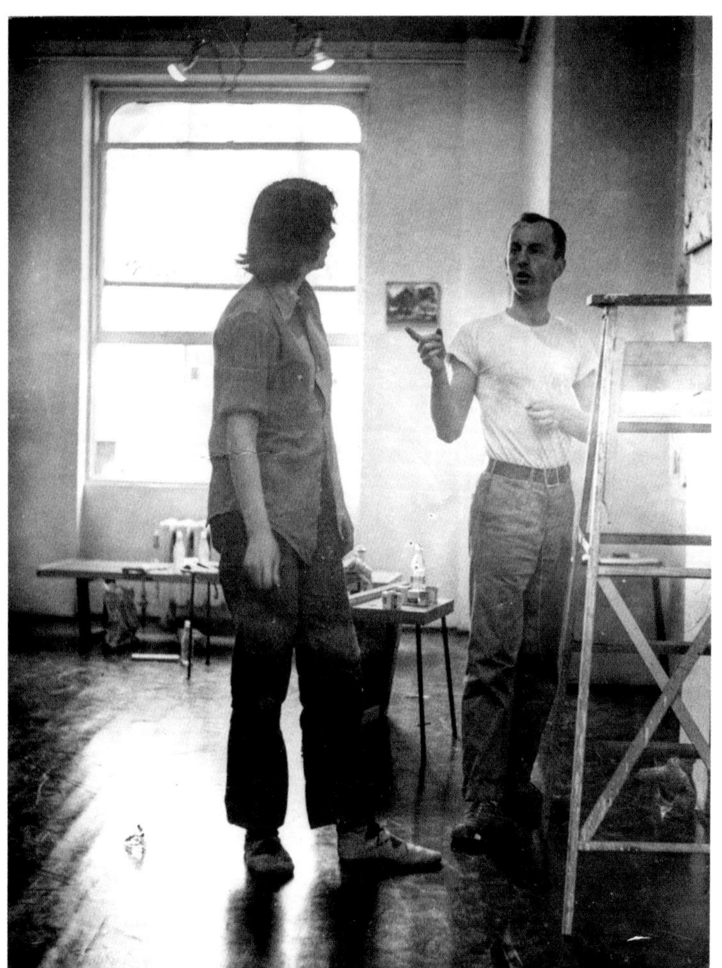

at his gallery was very different from Greenberg's dogmatic approach to art criticism.[3] Greenberg had made it a point of principle that "pure" painting must avoid the taint of "literature"—that is, subject matter.[4] Through the process of abstraction—a historically inevitable process, according to Greenberg—we are left to see forms or shapes on a canvas but not figures or images. Against such orthodoxy the painters of the Tibor de Nagy Gallery deliberately sought an "impure" style, as Hartigan declared in her journal.[5] And if they needed images, they had the poets to supply them. Hartigan's *Oranges* series (1952, plate 2), based on poems by O'Hara, "coincided with a time when I was moving out of completely abstract work into imagery," she recalled. "So he was handing me image after image after image in these things."[6]

Images are not symbols. In a 1952 panel titled "The Image in Poetry and Painting" at the informal artist organization the Club, O'Hara dismissed the reigning neo-symbolist mode, personified by T. S. Eliot, in favor of Ezra Pound, "the father of modern poets" and spokesperson for imagism.[7] The meaning of a symbol stands behind what the poem, or painting, presents to the senses. The meaning of an image is immediately present, on the surface—a position of great importance to both O'Hara and Hartigan. In his poem "Second Avenue" (1953), O'Hara "consciously intended to keep the surface of the poem high and dry, not wet, reflective and self-conscious."[8] A few years later, in her statement for the 12 *Americans* show at MoMA (1956), Hartigan declared, "I no longer invite the spectator to walk into my canvases. I want a surface that resists, like a wall, not opens, like a gate."[9] In the *Oranges*, images maintain the surface by crowding in on each other—"image after image after image"—so that no single image becomes the center of meaning, a foreground against a background. Moreover, by including the words of the poems in the space of the images, Hartigan reinforced the flatness of the surface as a writing space. Her images are to be read as well as seen.

It might seem that Hartigan has invited us to probe behind the surface in paintings that display masks (*The Masker*, plate 16; *Masquerade*, plate 14), costumes (*The Persian Jacket*, plate 1; *Two Women*, plate 12), or a combination of both (*Grand Street Brides*, plate 13; *Interior with Mexican Doll*, plate 15). However, Hartigan's poet friends, many of whom posed for the paintings and most of whom were gay, would have read these images in the spirit of camp.

 Grace Hartigan: The Gift of Attention

"This is not the familiar split-level construction of a literal meaning, on the one hand, and a symbolic meaning, on the other," Susan Sontag explained in her famous "Notes on 'Camp.'" Rather, the camp image vacillates between "meaning something" and existing as "pure artifice."[10] O'Hara saw pure artifice, and once again asserted the value of surface, in Hartigan's *Grand Street Brides* (1954), "who face without bitterness the glassy shallowness of American life which is their showcase."[11]

Images such as the store window mannequins of *Grand Street Brides* have been read as precursors of pop art, but the "tender feeling" that animates camp is very different from pop's cool detachment.[12] Hartigan, who found "permission" to use images from popular culture in O'Hara's poetry, employed them to evoke "an emotional state, expressive, metaphoric, not dead pan."[13] The images might start out dead, like the artificial flowers Hartigan found (similar to the bridal mannequins) in store windows, but her goal was to make them come alive. "Like a good witch," she explained, "if I can make a wonderful painting, then I can make those flowers, which are plastic, alive and real and wonderful."[14] Consider *Artificial Flowers and Apples* (1952, plate 4) in the current exhibition.

Throughout her career Hartigan identified her creative power as an artist with the power of witchcraft, starting with *Secuda Esa Bruja* (1949), "The Witch Is Stirring Things Up."[15] It cannot be just an accident that Hartigan used the reverse of this canvas to paint *Frank O'Hara and the Demons* (1952, plate 3). Those demons are not tormenting O'Hara but rather emanating from him, as visible manifestations of the poet's power to generate images. Similarly, the poet Barbara Guest seems to have stirred up in Hartigan associations with angels (*Snow Angel*, plate 28), goddesses (*Pallas Athena*, plates 34 and 35), *The Hero* (plate 23), or heroines (*Dido*, plate 22; Atalanta). Such figures do not represent Guest but again, like O'Hara's demons, express creative power. In fact, the paintings and prints associated with Guest seem more abstract than representational, less distinct images and more "image-in-the-making," as critics referred to Hartigan's early work.[16] Like all of Hartigan's images, they exhibit—because they are produced by—the power that Hartigan claimed for herself as "image-maker."[17]

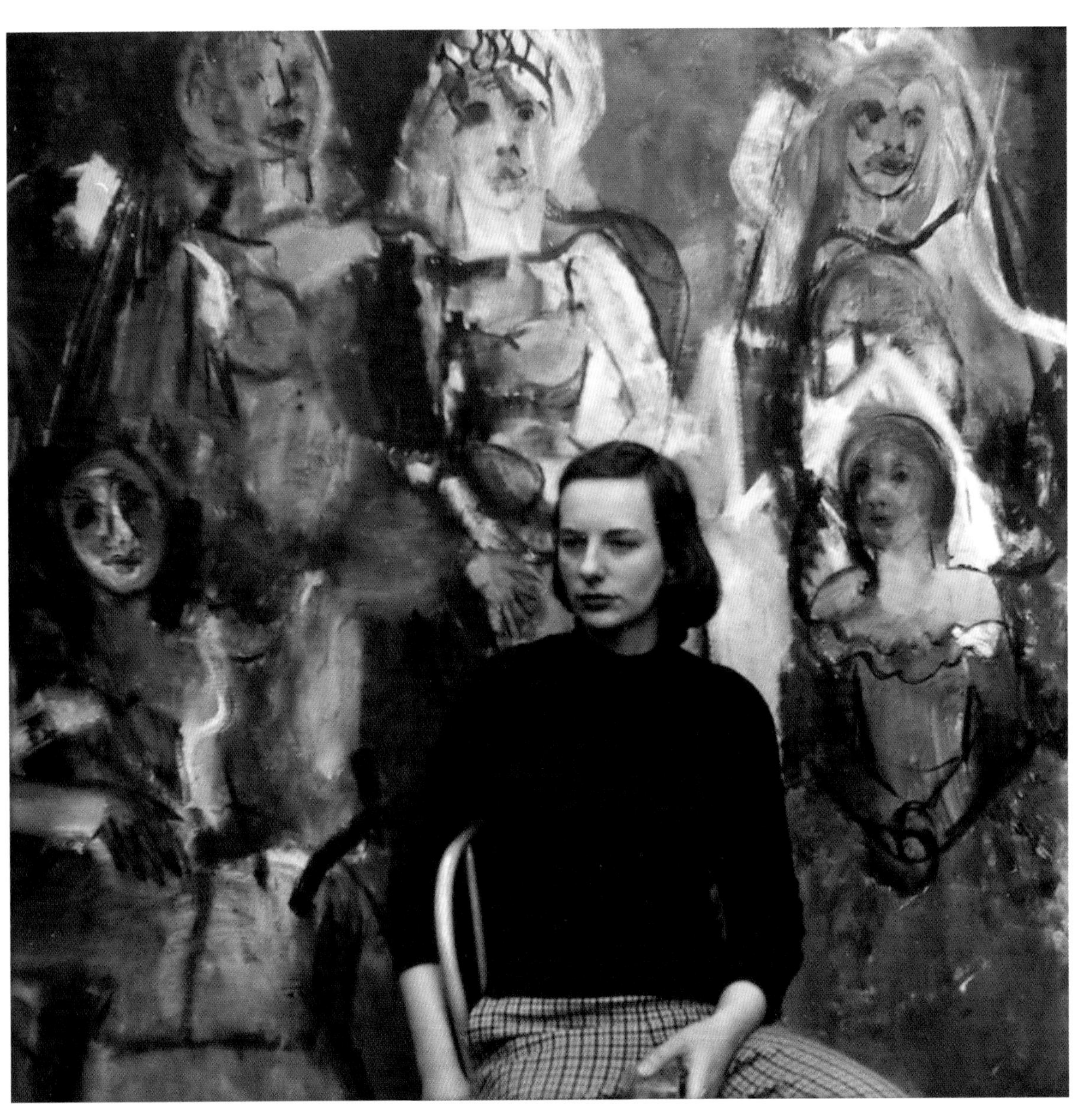

"The Basis of My Own Creation"

Grace Hartigan and Poetic Exchange

JARED LEDESMA

It only reached thirty-three degrees on March 26, 1960, in Bridgehampton, New York. Painter Grace Hartigan, along with her then husband, Robert Keene, had purchased a home and studio there the previous year. The cold, dreary day may have drawn Hartigan to the comforts of poetry, especially drafts of poems her close friend and collaborator Barbara Guest had recently sent. "Dearest Barbara," Hartigan wrote, "Your poems have lived with me so constantly and with such rapport that I almost forgot that they are not you—so I write!"[1] While their correspondence between the late 1950s and early 1960s reveals a deeply shared faith in each other's creativity, Hartigan's simpatico relationship with Guest was not singular.

Many New York poets and painters of the era banded together to become a defining force that challenged literary and visual conventions. Their constant conversations, experimental collaborations, and convivial critiques became the framework that evolved into the touchstones of modernist American poetry and visual art. More important, these interactions assisted the foundation of several careers, including Hartigan's.

Beginning in the early 1950s, New York poets Daisy Aldan (1923–2001), Barbara Guest (1920–2006), James Merrill (1926–1995), Frank O'Hara (1926–1966),

Fig. 3 Walter Silver, Grace Hartigan posing in front of *Grand Street Brides*, circa 1954

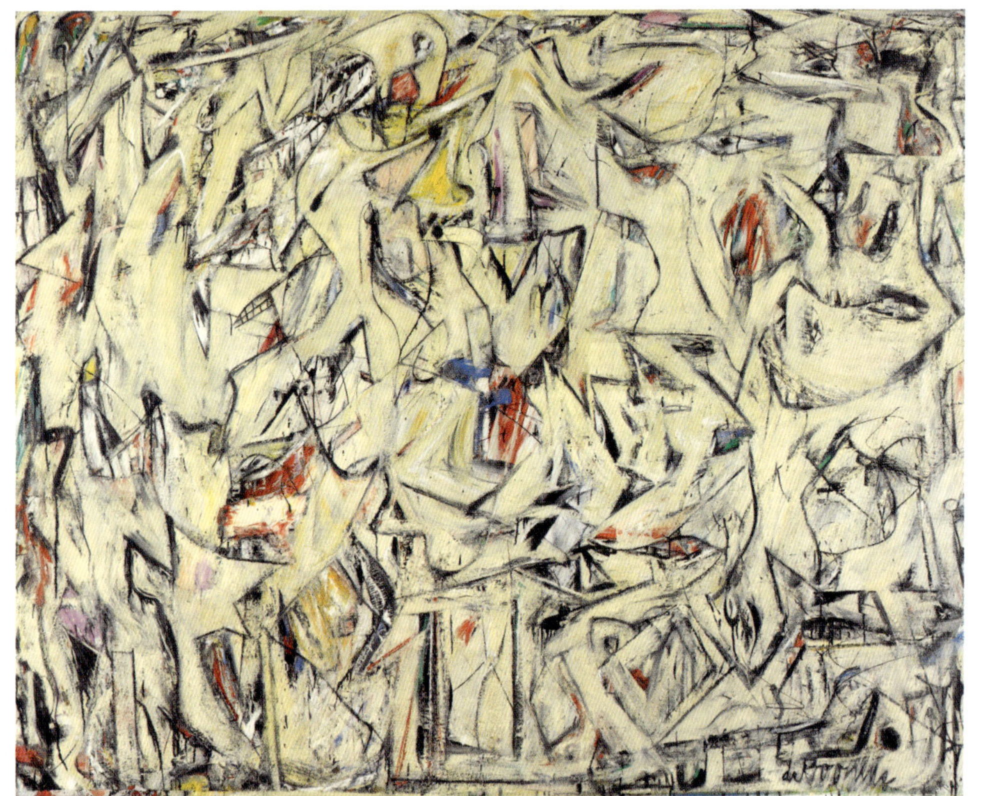

and James Schuyler (1923–1991) fervently encouraged Hartigan's creative pursuits. While this engagement between a painter and group of poets was not unique for the time, in this case it greatly influenced Hartigan's shift between pure abstraction and figuration and equally contributed toward the rise of her success. These poets supported her through creative exchange, serving as subjects in career-defining paintings, as critical champions, and as artistic and financial patrons. Given that by 1957 Hartigan was "selling every single thing" she painted, had been included in the Museum of Modern Art's landmark exhibition *12 Americans* (1956), and would go on to participate in MoMA's global traveling show *New American Painting* (1958–59), her artwork from this period can arguably be considered the most significant of her decades-long career.[2] This would not have materialized without the New York poets and their genuine, multifaceted support.

BECOMING HER OWN

When Hartigan left New Jersey for New York City in 1945 at the age of twenty-three, she entered a vibrant milieu of burgeoning art and literary movements that heralded the rise of abstract expressionism. Inspired by the revolutionary techniques and experimentation of European modernist styles such as surrealism and in reaction to prevailing conservative trends in American art during the Great Depression, the abstract expressionists aimed to push visual art in radical new directions. Artists such as Willem de Kooning and Jackson Pollock emerged as influential figures within this loosely affiliated group in New York.

Pollock, known for his monumental, action-oriented paintings, "mesmerized and fascinated" Hartigan with his method of dripping, pouring, and splattering industrial enamel and aluminum paint onto vast canvases.[3] His technique, in which he tapped the inner psyche, left a lasting impression on her. Hartigan also witnessed de Kooning's physical art-making process as he executed works such as *Excavation* (1950; fig. 4), observing how he applied layers of paint onto canvas only to scrape them away to reveal intricate anatomical subtleties.[4] This new cadre of painters, many of whom received acclaim from American art critic

Grace Hartigan: The Gift of Attention

Clement Greenberg for their narrative-free works, significantly impacted Hartigan's early experimentation with abstract art.

In her paintings such as *King of the Hill* (1950) and *Six by Six* (1951; fig. 5), Hartigan's debt to Pollock is palpable through her combination of patches of color with swirling, varied marks—embracing the democratic all-over painting trend of the era. Moreover, art historian Robert Mattison has argued that the "curving black brush marks" in *Months and Moons* (1950; fig. 6) are suggestive of "human anatomy," nodding to de Kooning's incorporation of bodily forms in pictures like *Excavation*.[5] In assimilating stylistic techniques from her predecessors, Hartigan, alongside other emerging artists at the time—many of them women—found herself labeled part of the "second generation" of abstract expressionists. She would later reject and even mock this classification, asserting her independence within the movement.[6]

While the abstract expressionists worked toward expanding the limits of modern art, New York poets were simultaneously challenging the limits of lyricism. Taking inspiration from predecessors such as Hart Crane and Ezra Pound—who desired to free poetry from the bondage of nineteenth-century conventions—Aldan, Guest, O'Hara, and Schuyler boldly prioritized the abstract interpretation of everyday life in their work. Reflecting in 1968, poet John Ashbery, an important participant and chronicler of the period, declared that at the time "there was in fact almost no experimental poetry being written in this country."[7] Participating in this rebellion, Ashbery conceded, not only felt as if "one was poised on some outermost brink" but also that "if one wanted to depart, even moderately, from the norm, one was taking one's life—one's life as an artist—into one's hand."[8] Partly through Ashbery's introductions but mostly due to his own infectious, affable demeanor, O'Hara quickly became the anchor of this liberal yet exclusive network of New York poets, which came to discover a new style of poetics that left rhyming meter and formal structures like sonnets and sextets behind.

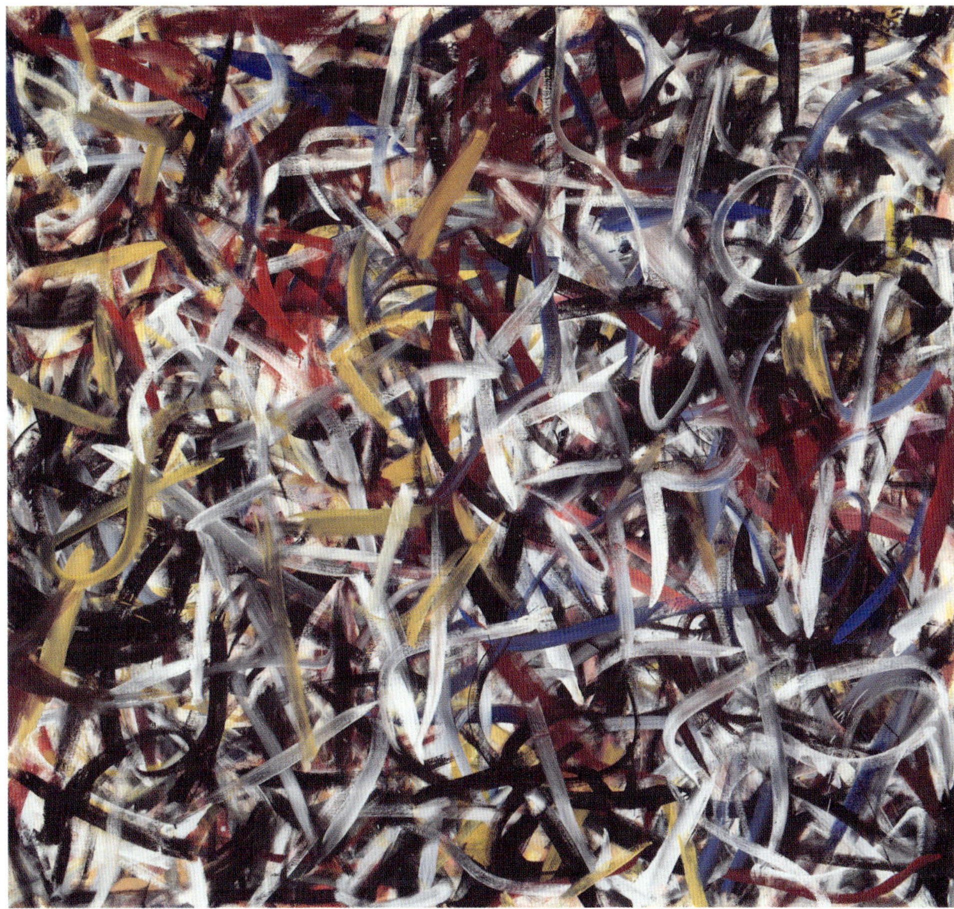

Fig. 5 Grace Hartigan, *Six by Six*, 1951, oil on canvas, 59¹³⁄₁₆ × 64⁹⁄₁₆ in., The Frances Lehman Loeb Art Center, Vassar College, Bequest of Agnes Rindge Claflin

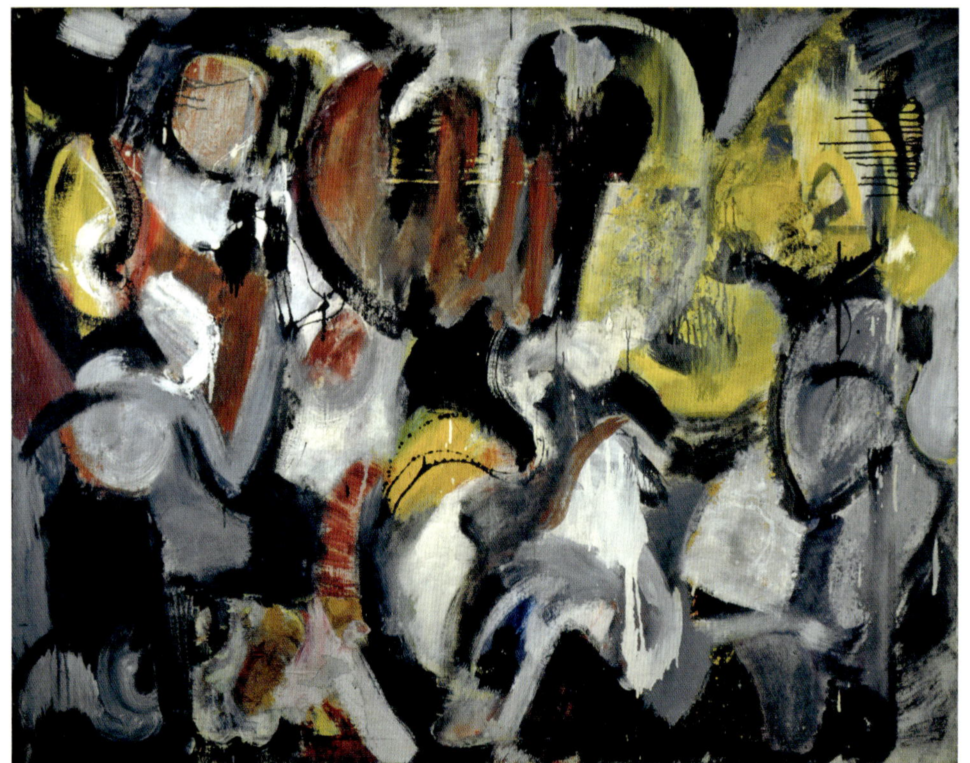

As these evolving trends took shape in post–World War II New York, the city hastily overtook Paris as the art capital of the Western world. Among the key players in this landscape was gay impresario John Bernard Myers, a "colorful and disputatious presence in the art world."[9] Born in Buffalo, Myers landed in New York City in 1944 to work as managing editor at the surrealist art and literary magazine *View*.[10] In 1950 Myers and Hungarian immigrant and banker Tibor de Nagy co-founded the Tibor de Nagy Gallery. Largely funded by gay English American collector Dwight Ripley, the gallery took as its mission organizing "shows that nobody else would do."[11] Myers set out in search of artists for his new endeavor, guided largely by a list passed along by Greenberg. Among the names on this list was Hartigan. Upon witnessing Hartigan's fresh take on abstraction, he was sold.[12] As a signed member of the newly minted gallery, Hartigan not only had representation but became part of the growing Tibor de Nagy family.

Critically, Hartigan found a sense of creative liberation within Myers's circle of gay peers and, later, queer poets. "I came from a middle-class family," she explained, "where my brilliance and imagination had been encouraged." But as she grew, Hartigan experienced the pressures of adulthood—and likely the demands of womanhood—with her dreams feeling "squashed." "Meeting homosexuals in New York in 1950 was a revelation ... their wit, 'secret' life and courage appealed to everything in me that the bourgeoisie had tried to repress."[13] The playful, subversive negotiations of gender roles exhibited by Hartigan's gay peers relieved the weight of tradition she experienced as a middle-class white woman in 1950s America. Without encountering these gay men, Hartigan may never have been inspired to play with her artistic identity as a painter of pictures that uneasily vacillate between abstraction and representation.

Hartigan herself partook in the manipulation of gender roles when she adopted the pseudonym George around 1951.[14] This choice has often been misunderstood as the artist attempting to overcome the sexist confinements of the mid-twentieth-century art world, which likely did motivate her to entrust

  Grace Hartigan: The Gift of Attention

her young son, Jeffrey, to his grandparents in the late 1940s so she could pursue painting.[15] However, Hartigan later clarified that her choosing George sprang from pure jealousy of her gay friends who had camp names, playful nicknames given as acts of affection that often exaggerate sexual identity while challenging gender norms. "I wanted one too," Hartigan disclosed, confirming she and her art dealer Myers "hit" on George: "The same initial as Grace ('Darling, you won't have to change your [monogrammed] linens!')."[16] More than Myers's pithy excuse, Hartigan landed on George as an ode to the pen names of nineteenth-century women novelists and poets George Eliot and George Sand. In January 1951 Tibor de Nagy opened its doors with the inaugural exhibition *Paintings by George Hartigan*.

Even before its inaugural exhibition and for years afterward, thanks in large part to Myers, the Tibor de Nagy Gallery was recognized as a nexus of genre-bending art and avant-garde poetry. In fostering the convergence of artists and writers, Myers was likely motivated by a mutual benefit—one that furthered the exploration of uncharted territories by this new coterie of defiant thinkers *and* solidified Tibor de Nagy as a hive of artistic innovation. "It was like being back at *View* magazine," Myers explained, "when poets and painters were invariably making collaborations."[17] His encouragement led the gallery to invest in multiple avenues, including the short-lived *Semicolon*, a four-page newspaper of poetry and prose, and the Artist's Theater, a drama program that commissioned poets to write plays and painters to create backdrops. Through attending gatherings at the gallery and Thursday-night salons at Myers's apartment and by frequenting the Cedar Tavern—a Greenwich Village haunt where artists mingled and debated new trends—Hartigan befriended poets O'Hara, Guest, and Schuyler. In her journal she likened this newly formed, tight-knit, synaptic circle to "a concentration of a nucleus."[18] Soon, they would become subjects in Hartigan's artworks that emphatically indicate the apotheosis of a risk-taking style.

POET AS SUBJECT

Over the next several years, Hartigan engaged in artistic dialogue with this cohort of poets, resulting in the creation of artworks that sharply defined her style of the period. Her intimate relationship with Frank O'Hara has often been the focus of this exchange, which initially took shape in February 1952. Theirs was a queer affair. "We fell in love," recalled Hartigan to O'Hara's biographer Brad Gooch. "If a homosexual and heterosexual could be in love, it was a falling in love."[19] O'Hara and Hartigan spoke daily and openly shared work in progress for critique.[20] O'Hara first appears in Hartigan's journals in early March 1952, when she lovingly responded to *Poem for a Painter*, a "tender" work obliquely dedicated to her.[21] Furthering this attention, O'Hara visited Hartigan's studio later that month to see new work that would soon be on view at her second Tibor de Nagy exhibition. The day was "magic," Hartigan wrote, due to their "real rapport."[22] This rapport may refer to O'Hara's ability

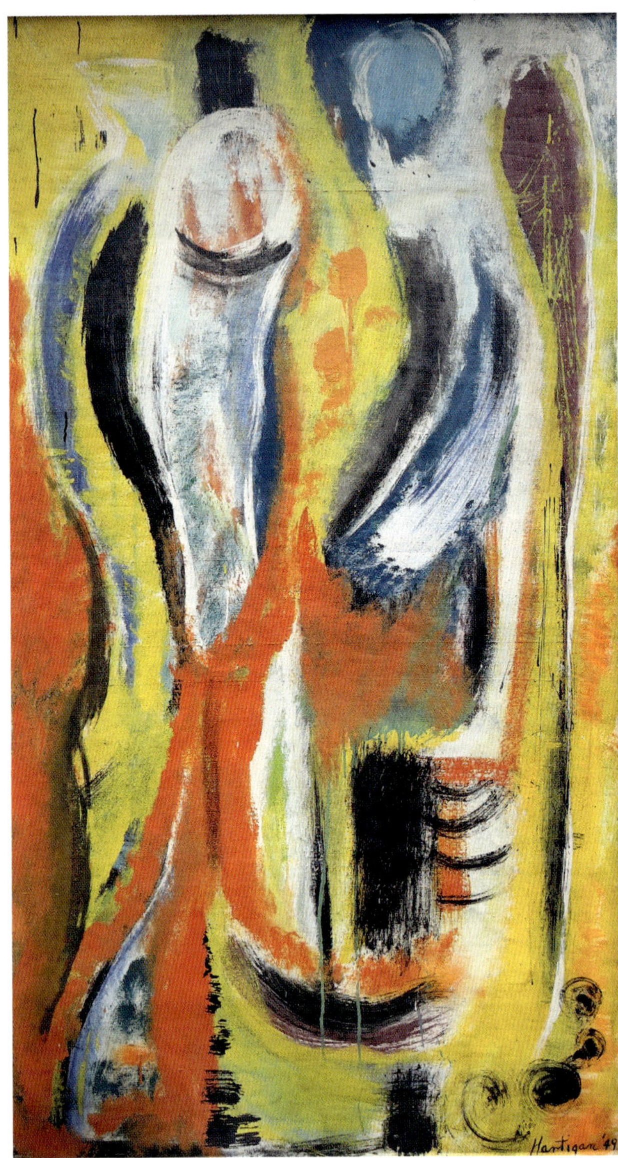

Fig. 7 Grace Hartigan, *Secuda Esa Bruja*, 1949, oil on canvas, 72 × 36 in., Rex R. Stevens and the Grace Hartigan Estate

Fig. 8 Plate 16, *The Masker* (detail)

Fig. 9 Walter Silver, Frank O'Hara posing at Grace Hartigan's studio, circa 1954

Fig. 10 Unidentified photographer [Walter Silver?], Olga Petroff posing at 743 Madison Ave., New York, with Grace Hartigan's *Two Women* on the wall behind her, 1950s

to "articulate Hartigan to herself," noted Gooch, adding poet Kenneth Koch once observed that O'Hara served as Hartigan's "wings of language."[23] It's no surprise, then, that the earliest artworks by Hartigan featuring poet likenesses depict O'Hara, "the man in her life."[24]

Frank O'Hara and the Demons (1952; plate 3) was painted shortly after O'Hara dashed off "Portrait of Grace" ("This poem makes me have an existence," Hartigan later praised). The picture depicts the nude poet with a bowed head and, according to its title, red, devilish figures attached at his left hip.[25] Initially inspired by sketches of O'Hara, the painting came to Hartigan in a memorable vision during a sleepless night. To find the rightsized canvas to realize her vision, she turned over *Secuda Esa Bruja* (1949; fig. 7), a painting created while visiting Mexico characterized by vertical, curving marks that coalesce into an abstract, fiery-colored picture. In *Demons* O'Hara's elongated body emerges from a translucent white ground amid Hartigan's application of jet black, blues, and grays.

Frank O'Hara and the Demons marks a critical moment, which Hartigan later described as a period of "re discovery."[26] Her portrayal of a partially rendered O'Hara pinpoints an early abandonment of pure abstraction while navigating the presence of a figure. Composing the poet's body from simplistic vertical marks and a mindful negotiation of positive and negative space, Hartigan channeled her understanding of abstraction into creating an image derived from reality. If "Portrait of Grace" is O'Hara's attempt at portraiture, where one must rummage through indirect syntax to decipher an image, then Hartigan's *Demons* is its match and a fundamental element of the duo's flirtatious conversation.[27]

Hartigan painted O'Hara a second time in *The Masker* (1954; fig. 8, plate 16), composed from a modeling session and photograph captured by her then partner, Walter Silver (fig. 9).[28] The picture implicitly comments on sexuality, while offering a more overt portrayal of O'Hara. Hartigan presented the poet costumed in a Persian jacket, surrounded by sections of subdued color. While O'Hara's figure distinctly jumps from the painting, Hartigan's use of broadswept black lines produces the illusion of glass panes, imparting a feeling that O'Hara is confined yet also visible through multiple lenses. Further, by assigning O'Hara the archetype of masker, Hartigan seems to have been influenced by his 1954 poem "Homosexuality," which opens "So we are taking off our masks, are we, and keeping / our mouths shut? as if we'd been pierced by a glance!"

Grace Hartigan: The Gift of Attention

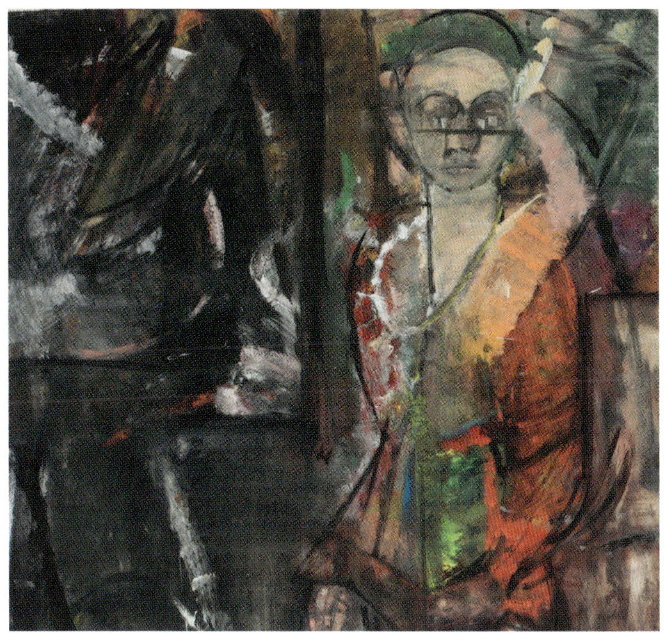

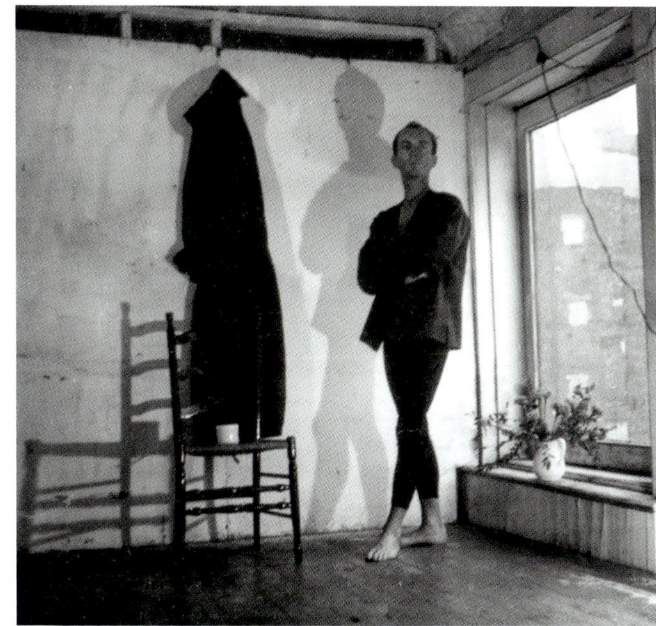

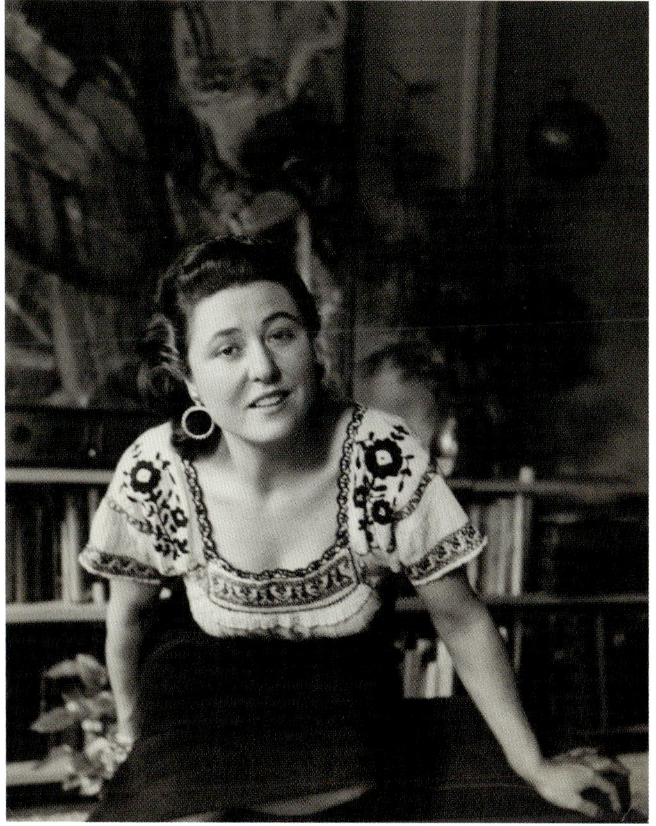

Notably, the poem later describes the protagonist as standing on "delicate feet," a detail mirrored in O'Hara's barefoot pose in Silver's photograph and Hartigan's painting.

The theme of masking reappears in a group portrait titled *Masquerade* (1954; plate 14), featuring key members of Hartigan's circle. Vaguely rooted in reality, Aldan, Ashbery, painter Jane Freilicher, O'Hara, Olga Petroff (Aldan's lover), Floriano Vecchi, and Hartigan—seen in the upper right donning a hooded black cloak and mask—are grouped in what O'Hara referred to as a "tragic" picture, where "individual identities are being destroyed by costumes which imprison them."[29] By concealing the identity of the models and herself, Hartigan indeed critiqued the act of masking oneself in society. Moreover, by including her likeness in the work, she aligned herself with these influential figures, marking her solidarity with their courageous undertakings.

Hartigan's final attempt at depicting her coterie of poets is *Two Women* (1954; plate 12), a double portrait of Daisy Aldan and Olga Petroff.[30] The picture stands out as Hartigan's sole portrait of a couple. The artist portrayed the lovers in ornate, folk-inspired attire (fig. 10). Considering sensitive depictions of female same-sex partners of this period are rare, Hartigan's documentation of their relationship is significant.[31] Writing about this work in her journal, Hartigan boldly declared "painting is not putting on a mask, but taking it off,"

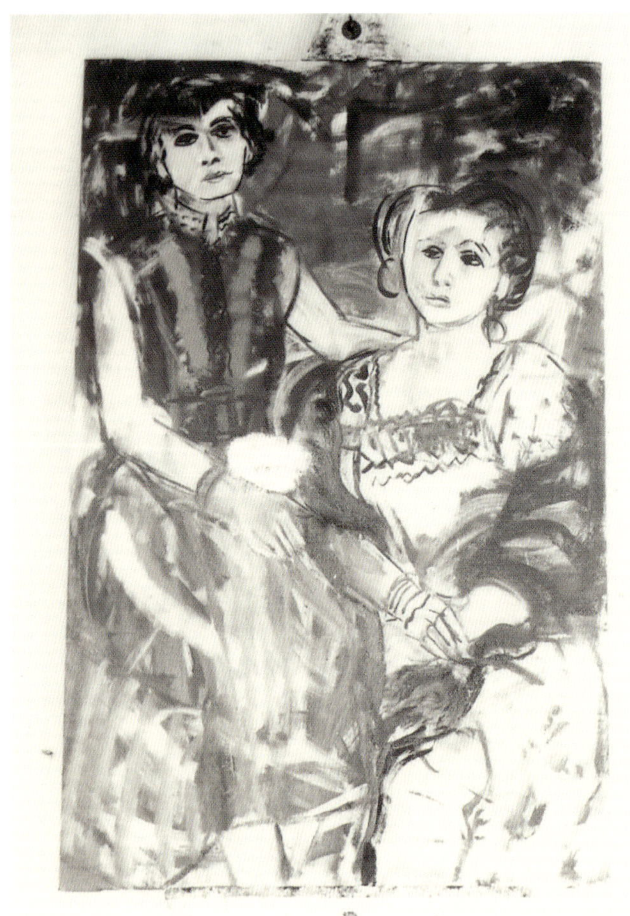 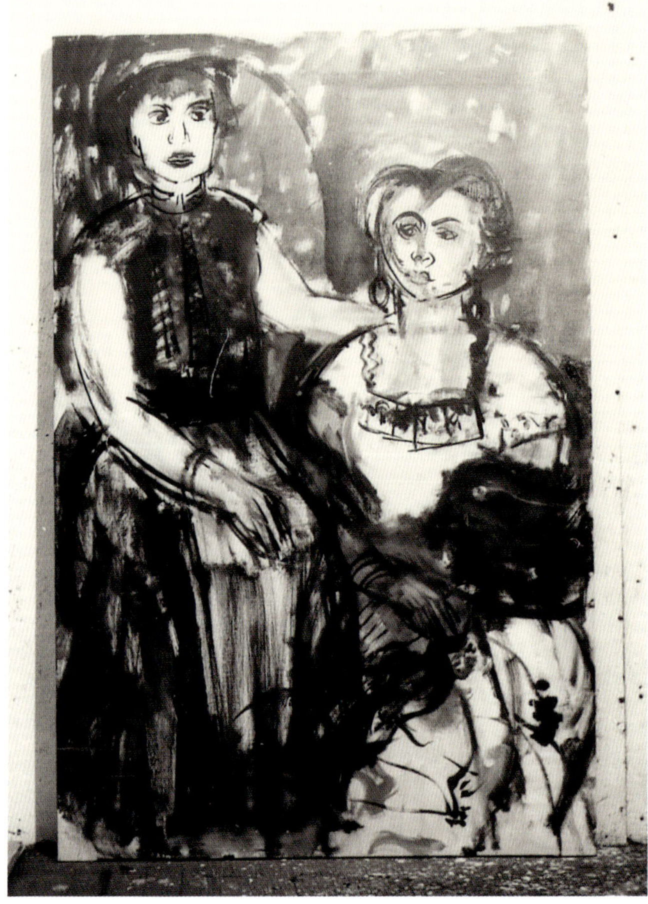

a statement that speaks to her philosophy as a painter of inner emotion.[32] It is intriguing to note her deliberate use of the term *mask*, drawing connections between the double portrait and her other works *The Masker* and *Masquerade*, which also feature queer subjects adorned in costume. Further, in referring to *Two Women*, Hartigan might be alluding to Aldan and Petroff's sexual unmasking. *Two Women* was acquired by its sitters for $300 (equivalent to just over $3,000 today), a substantial sum at the time, especially for Hartigan, who was just beginning to sustain herself through her art.[33]

By examining *The Masker*, *Masquerade*, and *Two Women* at once, a throughline is apparent in the artist working as both abstract and figurative artist. In reviewing in-progress photographs of *Two Women* in particular (fig. 11), we see the work in its initial stages as featuring recognizable likenesses of Aldan and Petroff. Hartigan later shrouds their half-formed visages behind a veil of translucent paint and settles on mere line and suggestive form for the lower half of their bodies. These three works importantly sustain Hartigan's successful "stage between 'realism' and 'abstraction,'" furthering an equilibrium where "both things speak fully and with meaning."[34]

It's worth pausing here to consider Hartigan working between two pillars of style—abstraction and representation—and how this resonates with a queer effort to explore tension within a binary system. While Hartigan herself was

Grace Hartigan: The Gift of Attention

not queer, her friendships with gay and lesbian artists and poets stimulated a rebellious urge to push the limits of societal norms. It also set the stage for challenging the dominant narrative of abstract expressionism that promoted the movement as quintessentially masculine, white, and heterosexual.[35]

Hartigan's straying from her initial abstract mode garnered criticism from within avant-garde circles, including that of Clement Greenberg. A proponent of absolute form over the metaphorical, Greenberg rebuked Hartigan when she first began inserting figurative elements into her abstractions in 1952.[36] One can argue that Hartigan, in defiance, undermined the strict binaries of style by playfully smuggling recognizable forms into her work. As she once coyly deflected, "I want an art that is not 'abstract' and not 'realistic'—I cannot describe the look of this art, but I think I will know it when I see it."[37]

Similarly, O'Hara slipped between social spheres, embodying what his longtime friend and occasional lover Joe LeSueur described as "a homo-sexuality that was gracefully assimilated into straight society without being closeted."[38] O'Hara managed a delicate balancing act in the performance of his sexuality. Further, the innovative style of his poetry has been likened to the impenetrable, action-oriented, and physical "surface" of abstract painting: "The *surface* of the painting," scholar Marjorie Perloff has written, "and by analogy the *surface* of the poem, must, then, be regarded as a field upon which the physical energies of the artist can operate, without mediation of metaphor or symbol."[39] The poem itself, according to Perloff—its structure, pace, and appearance on the page—becomes the subject, regardless of its content.

However, O'Hara's (and to an extent Ashbery's and Schuyler's) incorpo-ration of everyday references into poetry, theorist Maggie Nelson has argued, can be considered "not-macho" due to its "mixture of high/low sensibilities ... the repeated use of localized names, dates, and places, along with a positive focus on the detritus of 'everyday life.'"[40] This mixture is both queer and subver-sive in its glorification of the quotidian. Hartigan's conflation of style between pure abstraction and figuration, which eventually includes her incorporation of everyday objects, can therefore be seen as a parallel queer endeavor. It mirrors the efforts of O'Hara and other queer writers at the time, such as Aldan, Ashbery, and Schuyler, in its playful deviation from dominant policy.[41]

COLLABORATION—A PAINTER RESPONDS

Between the 1950s and mid-1960s, Hartigan not only commemorated poets in pictures that bear her innovative style but also worked with them in translat-ing the existence of their mutual appreciation into tangible material. Among the collaborations they pursued, Hartigan's perceptive response to O'Hara's *Oranges* is the most widely known and has garnered much critical attention.[42] As an act of reverse ekphrasis—that is, responding to poetry through a work of art—Hartigan expressed interest in incorporating O'Hara's poems into her artwork in the fall of 1952. O'Hara responded with resounding wit: "How about oranges? I have a dozen."[43]

Written in 1949 during O'Hara's time as an undergraduate at Harvard University, the twelve *Oranges* poems satirize the pastoral tradition in poetry, which idealizes rural life. Extremely poor and with no oil or canvas on hand, Hartigan turned to house paint and newsprint to create her interpretation. She began *Black Crows (Oranges No. 1)* (1952; plate 2) by incorporating the entire poem onto one sheet of paper. She then "imaged all around it," applying expressionistic marks, where the impressions of figures echo the irregular flow of images in O'Hara's poem.[44] The palette, a muddy mixture of earth tones, closely mimics the poem's rural, sour mood in lines such as

> O pastures dotted with excremental discs, wheeling
> in interplanetary green, your brown eyes stare down our
> innocence, the brimstone odor of your stars sneers at
> our horoscope!

After completing *Oranges No. 1*, Hartigan professed it "set a model for the other eleven that I want to sustain."[45]

Hartigan's engagement with O'Hara's *Oranges* reached Daisy Aldan and Richard Miller, the co-founders of the imprint Tiber Press, who at the time were launching *Folder* magazine, a brief yet impactful poetry and visual arts publication.[46] Aldan and Miller not only admired Hartigan's work but also recognized its style as compatible with the poetry of *Folder*'s contributors, which included Aldan, Ashbery, O'Hara, Merrill, and Schuyler.

For the inaugural issue, Hartigan was asked to contribute screen prints. The resulting works—*The Persian Robe, Pastorale*, and *Still Life in Primary Colors* (1953; plates 7–9)—were her first foray into printmaking.[47] She produced the prints over the course of July and was especially proud of *The Persian Robe* due to its striking cherry red that for her translated an "emotional intensity."[48] The screen-printing process, involving multiple stencils to create a unified image, left a lasting impression on Hartigan as well. She candidly admitted it "may be of help in the future; the nature of the process has made me more analytic about my 'technique' or procedure in constructing a picture." Her keen observation of the relationship between screen printing and painting closely resonates with the fragmented construction of lines and stanzas that comprise poetry of the era. For example, the structure of Ashbery's "The Way They Took," published in the same issue of *Folder*, is composed of obscure, autonomous lines, beginning with

> The green bars on you grew soberer
> As I petted the lock, a crank
> In my specially built shoes.[49]

Hartigan's collaboration on *Folder* led to a technical epiphany, yet it was her affiliation with Barbara Guest and Guest's poetry that would later serve as both creative enlightenment and a source of empathy. Although Hartigan officially met Guest in the early 1950s, it wasn't until the end of the decade that their

Grace Hartigan: The Gift of Attention

relationship would transform into one of great influence. This was largely catalyzed by a pivotal moment for Hartigan in 1960 when she met Winston Price, an epidemiologist based in Baltimore. Despite both being married at the time, they quickly became deeply romantically involved, leading Hartigan to contemplate relocating to Maryland. Price's struggle to convince his current wife to divorce put a pause on Hartigan's move and steered her toward Guest's poetry for solace.

This moment of emotional turmoil also ushered in a transformation in Hartigan's painting style that had started in 1957. Drawing from "the expression of inner experience," Hartigan began to present subjects further enmeshed with abstract elements. This evolution seems to echo her style in *Frank O'Hara and the Demons*, where O'Hara's form barely materializes. The change in Hartigan's work also resonates with Guest's poetic sensibilities of the era. Guest believed that, in the act of composing a work, "the subject finds itself" rather than the artist starting work with a predetermined pictorial goal.[50]

At the time Guest was preparing *The Location of Things*, a book of poetry edited by Myers and published by Tibor de Nagy Gallery. Guest shared typescripts of poems with Hartigan, and these sincerely resonated with the artist's turbulent moment, igniting an intense friendship between the two. Hartigan admitted that Guest's poems were becoming "the basis of my own creation."[51]

Unofficially, their collaboration could be said to have begun with a brief squabble over the evolution of Hartigan's 1958 painting *Untitled* [or *New York*] (plate 18)—a work she eventually dedicated to Guest and gifted to the poet. Officially, the two first collaborated on the collected lithographs *The Hero Leaves His Ship* (1960; plates 24–27), a direct response to Guest's poem of the same title. "After the first line," Hartigan confessed to Guest, "the rest of the poem was read through a tear film."[52] Hartigan effectively conveyed the poem's idiom, which opens with the line "I wonder if this new reality is going to destroy

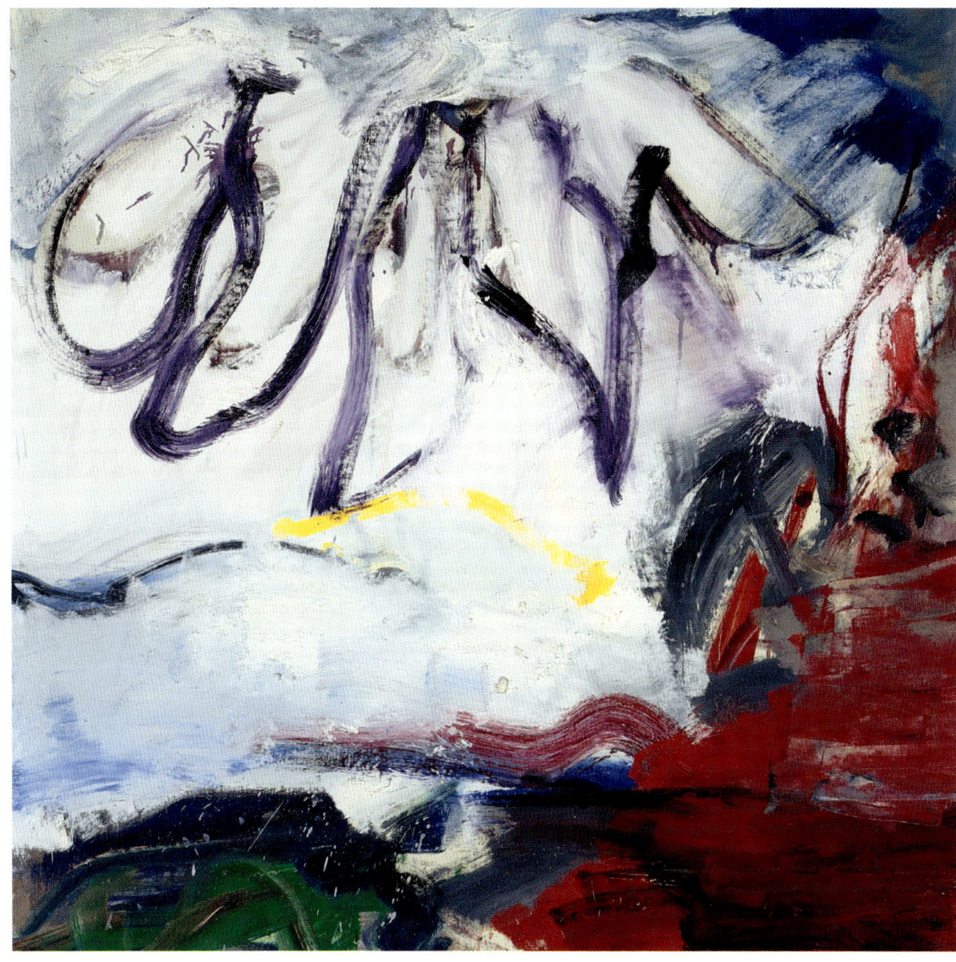

Fig. 12 Plate 28, *Snow Angel* (detail)

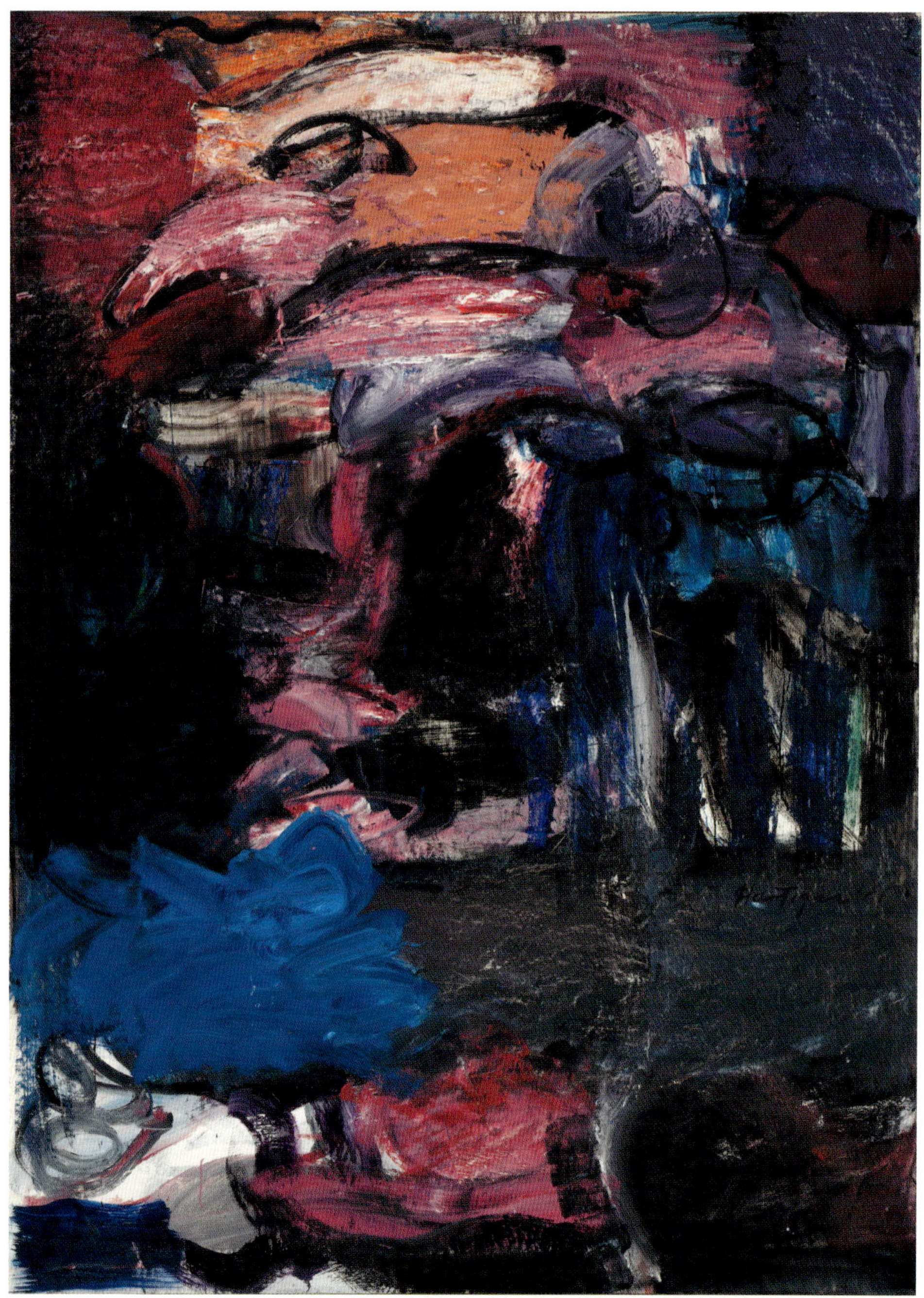

me," through spontaneous scribble and erasure (plates 24 and 25) and focused areas of black as the repercussions of one's past (plates 26 and 27). She would collaborate with Guest for a second suite of prints, entitled *The Archaics*, between 1962 and 1966 (plates 36–42).[53]

In addition to lithographs, Hartigan's execution of three paintings in 1960—*Dido* (plate 22), *Snow Angel* (fig. 12, plate 28), and *The Hero* (plate 23)—find her sustaining the interest in reverse ekphrasis that began with O'Hara's *Oranges*. The genesis of *Dido* stemmed from Guest sharing her poem "Dido to Aeneas." Initially hesitant due to her perception of relying too heavily on classical themes, Guest nevertheless encouraged Hartigan to produce her visual interpretation, remarking, "well if the painting comes, what does it matter."[54]

Both *Snow Angel* and *The Hero* took their titles from Guest's poems and, akin to *Dido*, were formed from a combination of spontaneous marks and contemplative zones of tempestuous, integrated color. When describing *Snow Angel* to Guest, Hartigan referenced the poem, pointing to the picture's "underground fires" evoked by blood-red paint at the lower right of the painting. She spoke of the angel's "violet wings," Hartigan's own poetic choice, and the "white grey snow," delineated between areas of white dirtied by blue and gray.[55]

Before her permanent departure from New York, Hartigan executed *The Hero*.[56] Its ominous color palette perhaps points to this critical moment, marking her physical separation from a circle of New York peers that nurtured her burgeoning career. Upon settling in Baltimore, Hartigan continued corresponding

     Grace Hartigan: The Gift of Attention

with Guest, who resided in Washington, DC. They maintained their creative exchange that, in addition to her *Archaics* prints, resulted in Hartigan producing a suite of paintings referencing the goddess Athena.

The Athena paintings were influenced by Hartigan's ongoing conversations with Guest on classical themes. Hartigan shared her exploration of Homer's descriptions of Athena, acknowledging that the goddess would be a "continuing theme" throughout a series of works. Among these, the expansive canvas *Pallas Athena—Fire* (1961; fig. 13, plate 34) features vibrant magentas and pinks disrupting the solemnity of blacks and midnight blue, causing a dynamic rupture that spills into a sky aglow with a fuchsia-pink hue.[57] Hartigan later revealed that the Athena paintings held personal significance, describing them as self-portraits. She explained, "I think I chose Athena for myself because she was full-blown from the head of Zeus. She'd had no nurturing, and she was an intellectual goddess."[58] With no formal artistic training behind her, the metaphor seems apt indeed. The *Athena* series thus becomes an expressive exploration of Hartigan's own identity fused with her intellectual pursuits.

ENDORSEMENT BY PATRONAGE

Embedded within the creative energy the New York poets bestowed upon Hartigan were moments of additional support, manifested through word of mouth, art criticism, and financial patronage. For instance, when Museum of Modern Art director Alfred Barr and curator Dorothy Miller pulled Hartigan's *The Persian Jacket* (1952; plate 1) off the walls of Tibor de Nagy and brought it to the museum in 1953, O'Hara was working at the museum's front desk. Overcome with joy, O'Hara reportedly phoned Hartigan, informing the artist that she had officially made it. After O'Hara rose through the ranks to become one of MoMA's most revolutionary curators, the painting hung at the poet's request.[59]

Many poets of the era, including James Schuyler and O'Hara, deeply intertwined with the contemporary art scene, wrote art criticism for magazines such as *ARTnews* and *Art in America*. In O'Hara's review of Hartigan's 1954 Tibor de Nagy exhibition, he singled out *Black Still Life* (1953; plate 5) for "pushing the limits of its structural capacity."[60] The picture is indeed one of a handful of still lifes from the period that showcase Hartigan's continued experimentation with distorting reality within paintings that exhibit a stiff formal architecture. In 1959 Schuyler astutely identified that Hartigan's recent bent toward creating more abstract pictures revealed a return to embracing pure form, including a "painstaking and original strength of structure." Additionally, Schuyler heralded *Bray* (1958; plate 19) for its bold, "chunky stroke of orange" and hints of pink, emphasizing these flourishes as integral components of the work rather than mere decorative embellishments.[61]

While O'Hara and Schuyler amplified Hartigan's reputation through written critique, the gay poet and writer James Merrill accomplished this through monetary means. His patronage remains a particular case, one that John Myers at Tibor de Nagy Gallery expertly cultivated but also found

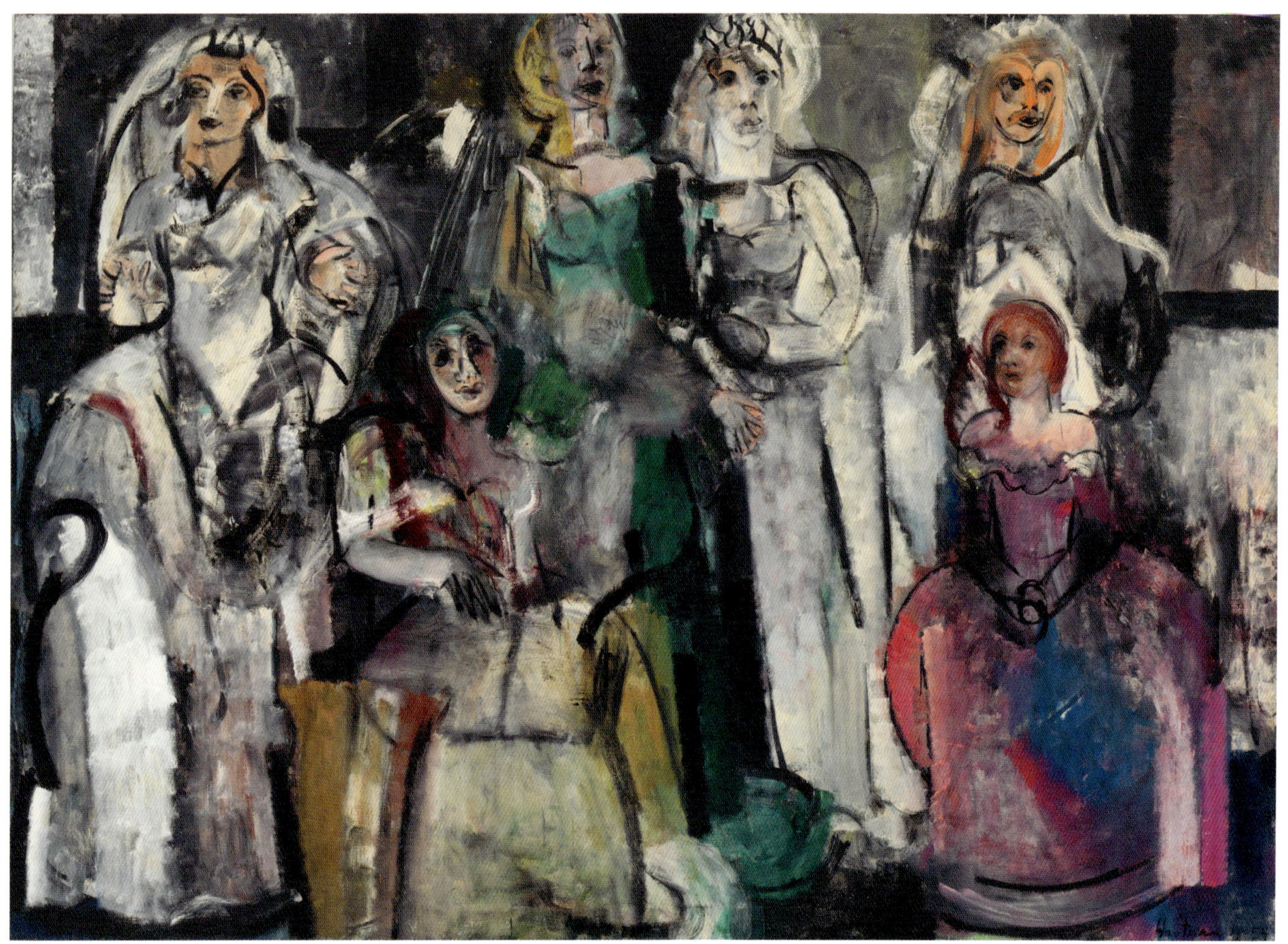

mysterious.[62] In addition to working as a poet and writer, Merrill—the son of Charles Merrill, the founder of Merrill, Lynch & Co.—was a discreet monetary supporter of the arts.[63] It's understood that as Hartigan's patron he funded the acquisition of works at the Brooklyn Museum (*East Side Sunday*, 1956; plate 17 and cover), Carnegie Museum of Art (*Orange Field*, 1958; plate 20), North Carolina Museum of Art (*Interior with Mexican Doll*, 1955; plate 15), and Whitney Museum of American Art (*Grand Street Brides*, 1954; fig. 14, plate 13), respectively.[64] "Each gift," Myers expressed to Hartigan, "was arrived at by relentless attention" from Merrill and his longtime romantic partner, David Jackson.[65] Besides a collage formed from fractured material that Hartigan lovingly gifted to Merrill and Jackson before they departed for Europe in 1959 (*It's a Farewell*, plate 21), there is little evidence of Hartigan and Merrill's friendship. Nevertheless, Merrill's patronage proved decisive in supporting the production and preservation of Hartigan's art.

Merrill's patronage included securing Hartigan's epic *Grand Street Brides* in 1955. Inspired by mannequins displayed in Lower East Side bridal shops, it features the veiling of figures also found in *The Masker, Masquerade,* and *Two Women.* The painting stands six feet tall, bringing the figures to life size. Their

   Grace Hartigan: The Gift of Attention

arrangement is rooted in the composition of Spanish artist Diego Velázquez's seventeenth-century work *Las Meninas*. Presenting a "strange combination of 'nature' and 'abstraction,'" as the artist once elucidated about her mid-1950s style, this particular approach "makes each area relate and 'jell,'" resulting in one of her most significant and largest works to date.[66]

Immediately following the Whitney's decision to acquire *Grand Street Brides*, Myers wrote to Merrill acknowledging that after "much talk and meetings" the museum had "agreed to accept Grace's adorable biggie."[67] Merrill gifted the museum $2,000 (the equivalent of over $23,000 today) so they in turn could pay Hartigan. The payoff from this exchange was instrumental for Hartigan, allowing her to paint without largely worrying about finances for most of the year. Or, as Myers emphatically explained to Merrill, Hartigan felt she "had been saved by the bell," adding with humor, "Now she will be able to get thru' the Spring & summer to paint without a sign of heart-burn."[68]

Two years later, Merrill funded the North Carolina Museum of Art's acquisition of *Interior with Mexican Doll*. The acquisition stemmed from Hartigan's role as a panelist for the NCMA's inaugural exhibition of contemporary art in 1957.[69] The exhibition was co-organized with Women's College in Greensboro (now the University of North Carolina, Greensboro), and besides Hartigan's painting *Giftwares* (1955, formerly *Shopwares*, Neuberger Museum of Art), it included works by Mary Abbott, Louise Bourgeois, Helen Frankenthaler, Elaine de Kooning, and Joan Mitchell.[70]

For many years *Interior with Mexican Doll* remained the sole example of Hartigan's painting in a public North Carolina collection.[71] In fact, when Hartigan was invited to lecture at the Weatherspoon Art Museum (then the Weatherspoon Art Gallery) in 1995, she requested that the NCMA's painting be on view.[72] Featuring expressionist marks skillfully applied that guide the viewer's gaze toward subtle renderings of a classical bust and a papier-mâché Mexican doll, it encapsulates the unparalleled lessons Hartigan gleaned from midcentury poets who integrated the transient aspects of everyday life. More significant, it forms part of Hartigan's own visual poetry that remains indebted to a kinship between the artist and her intimate few.

Hartigan later recalled that her growing success of the 1950s was because of her considerable involvement in pivotal exhibitions at the time.[73] Even so, without encountering Aldan, Guest, O'Hara, Merrill, and Schuyler, the work she produced at the time—characterized by an intelligently independent vision— may not have emerged, and her reputation would not have "mushroomed on and on and on."[74] Indeed, from her early years in New York to settling in Maryland, these faithful poets welcomed collaboration without hesitation, willingly bestowed their critical eye, and offered unequivocal endorsement—their gifts of attention. As Hartigan aptly put it, "the poets put into words the approximation of my emotional state," evolving into the basis of creation that would guide her realization of a consequential body of work eternally entwined in poetic exchange.[75]

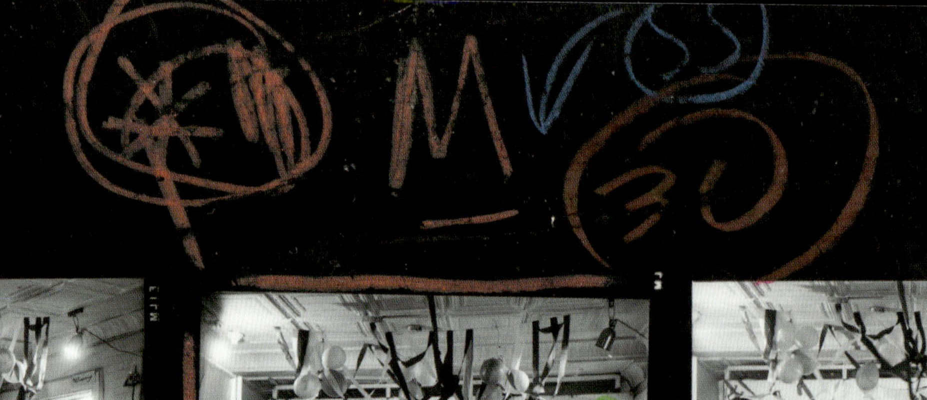
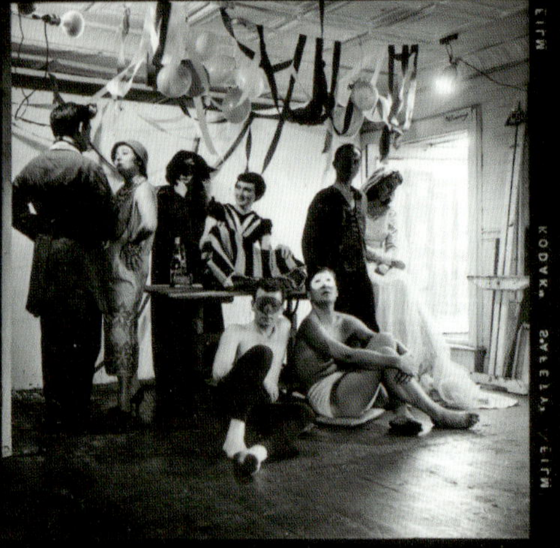
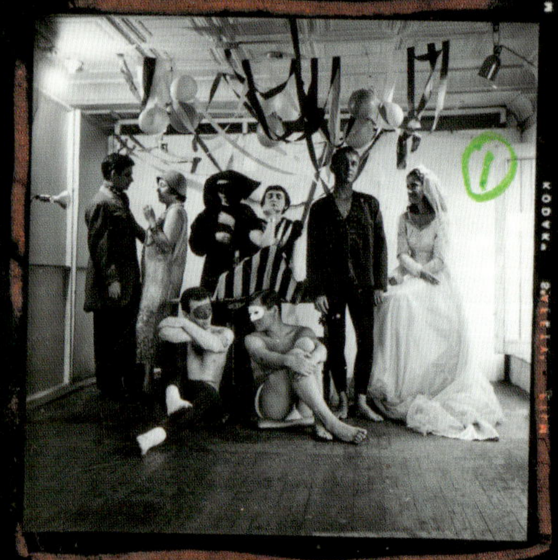
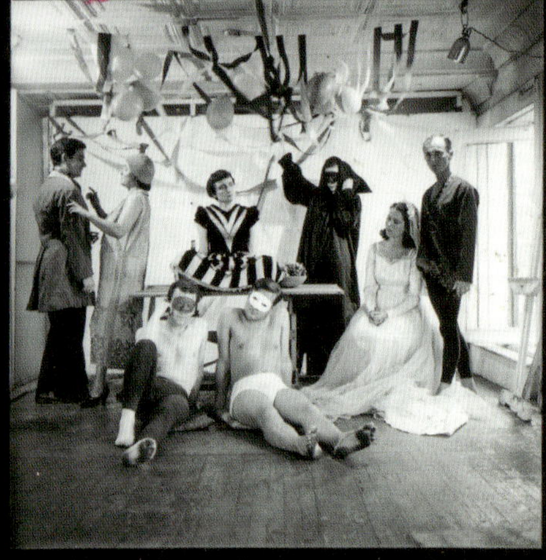
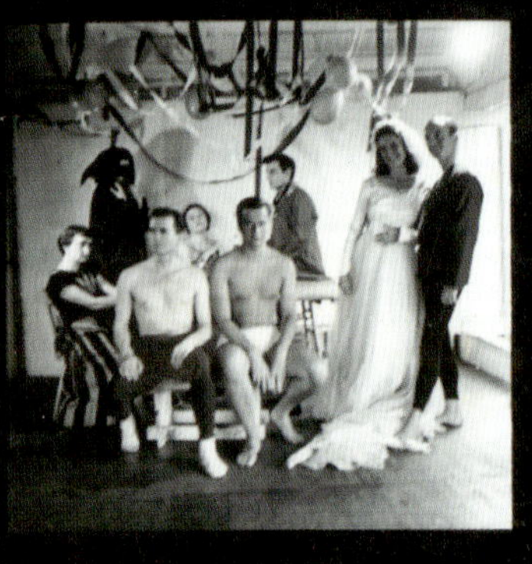
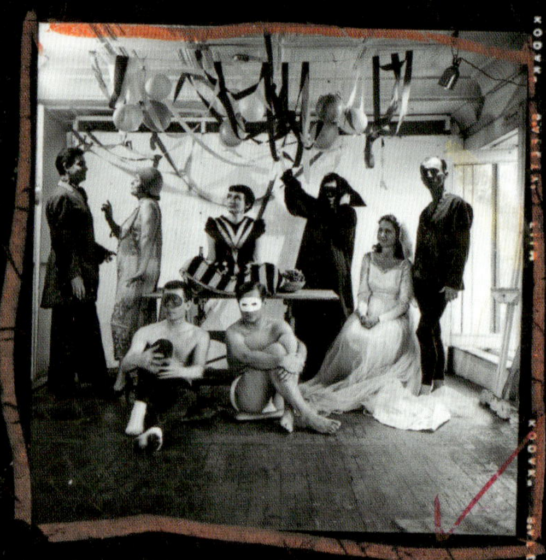
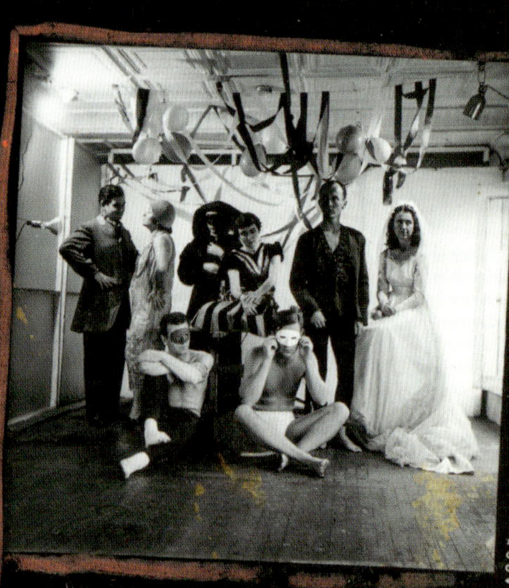
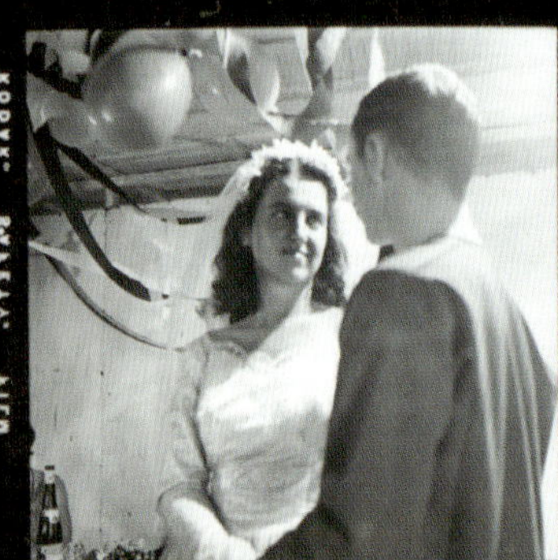
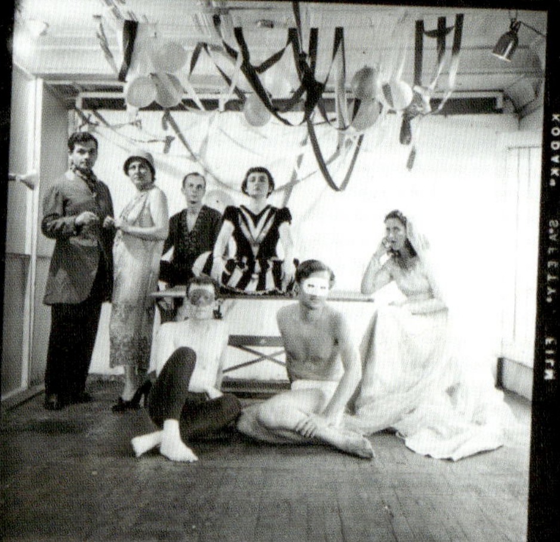
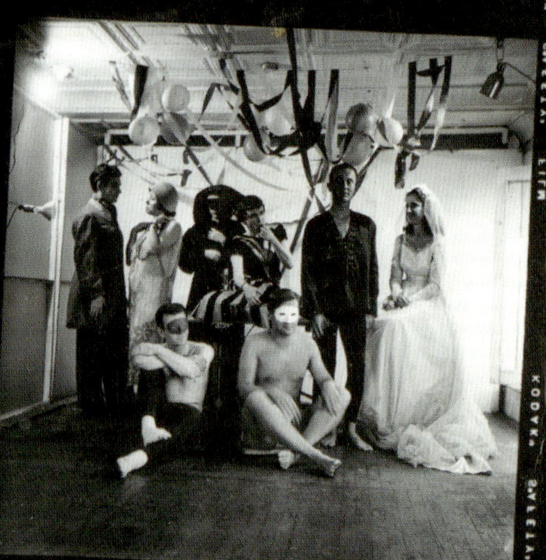
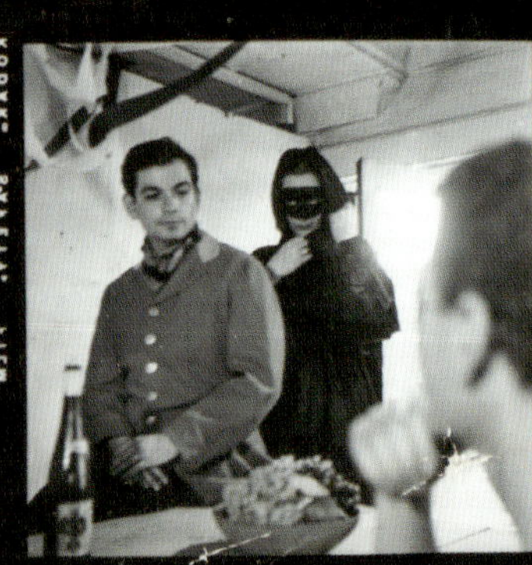

"Being Together in the World"

Grace Hartigan at the Tiber Press

FRANCES LAZARE

In 1954 Grace Hartigan gathered a group of her friends and collaborators—all affiliates of the avant-garde publishing studio Tiber Press—into her studio to pose for her. The group, including Hartigan and her then beau, photographer Walter Silver, who documented the event, donned masks and costumes and struck various postures against a set of streamers and balloons assembled by the artist. A contact sheet in Silver's archive reveals many staged configurations, including an ongoing face-off between those at the photograph's far left and a marital vignette, with painter Jane Freilicher and poet Frank O'Hara assuming the roles of bride and groom (fig. 15).

Hartigan used Silver's photographs of the merry scene as source material for her painting *Masquerade* (1954; fig. 16, plate 14), a large canvas that loosely though evocatively depicts the intimate group. Removing narrative and detail, the painter transformed her sitters into a mass of bright, interlocking strokes of paint. Individual figures emerge from this tangle of colorful gestures via a thin black outline, which Hartigan used to create stylized, masklike faces that suggest (but do not ultimately reveal) the identities of her models. Shuttling between abstraction and figuration, Hartigan married the energetic and expressive paint handling characteristic of abstract expressionism with figura-

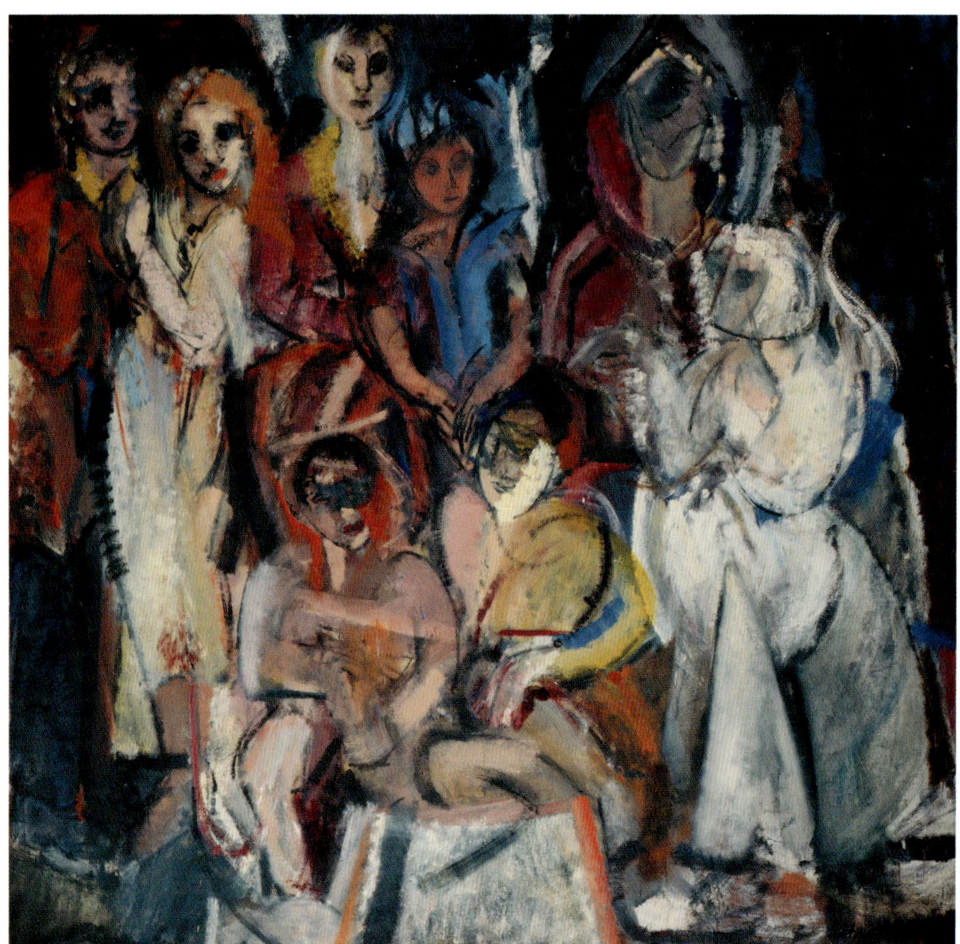

tive imagery drawn from her personal life, conveying the liveliness of the scene without representing it outright.

A few months after Hartigan completed the painting, O'Hara, her confidant, muse, and frequent collaborator, cited *Masquerade* directly in his essay "Nature and New Painting," which examines a neo-figurative turn in contemporary painting and argues that artists who turn away from abstraction are not more objective or real than those who pursue it.[1] Unlike painters who pursued "pure" and "unified" abstraction, Hartigan, O'Hara wrote, "had found that the great, beautiful, and solitary aim of abstract painting was not hers, she could not give enough to that art. Essentially a painter of heterogeneous pictures which bring together wildly discordant images through insight into their functional relationship (their 'being together in the world')."[2]

As represented in *Masquerade*, O'Hara and fellow affiliates of the Tiber Press comprised an intimate, inside audience that helped both produce and anchor Hartigan's semi-figural painterly address.[3] O'Hara's essay was published in the press's avant-garde literary magazine *Folder*, the very publication whose editors and contributors posed for the painting. Speaking to and about this creative community, the poet praised *Masquerade* for its nerve and sensuality and indicated his great pleasure not only with the "wildly discordant" variety of things from the world that made their way onto the canvas—including streamers, costumes, and masks—but also with the artist's range of gestures and paint handling. In a journal entry from the same period, Hartigan herself suggested that her paintings address the "wildly discordant" experience of "being together in the world": "The figures in my painting ask, 'what are we doing? what do we mean to each other?'"[4]

Following the painter's lead, the current essay explores how Hartigan's artworks facilitate and document the intimate conditions of being together in the world. In particular, I examine the screen prints Hartigan made at the

Tiber Press—an upstart printing studio run out of the shared apartment of two gay men and a lesbian poet—as documents of the overlapping creative and interpersonal intimacies that constituted its milieu. During her brief but meaningful stint at the press, Hartigan honed the tenets of figural expressionism—the "heterogenous" visual language for which she became most known. Her break with the more insistent abstraction of her early career was fundamentally shaped both by the medium of screen print, a collaborative art form that is predicated on contact between two distinct surfaces, and the coterie of the press itself, where the creative intimacies between the founders evade classification in the normalizing discourses of art history. In this new, mixed mode, Hartigan accumulated—rather than resolved—the tensions between abstraction and figuration, queer and straight, lovers and friends.

The Tiber Press was founded on April 21, 1953—the anniversary of the birth of Rome—by poet Daisy Aldan and art historian Richard Miller, who were joined in a marriage of mutual convenience. Together with Miller's lover, the Italian-born printmaker Floriano Vecchi whom Miller met at a life-drawing class while studying at the University of Rome, the unlikely couple established one of the first American print houses to publish poetry and literature directly alongside original art prints (fig. 17).[5]

At the time Aldan was completing a doctoral thesis on the influence of French surrealism in the US.[6] Much like the surrealists, who bridged the visual and literary arts, Aldan worked across creative categories. She supported her graduate work as a radio actress and simultaneously self-published poetry, crafting her first chapbook with wallpaper pasted to cardboard laundry sheets in a limited edition of five hundred. This venture whetted Aldan's desire to establish a dedicated venue for writers like herself, whose work was flouted by academic and prestige publishers on the basis of either politics or style or both. Indeed, Aldan recalled one rejection letter that read, "your poems are dynamic and beautiful ... but we regret we are unable to publish them because they are not political and do not reflect the current American scene."[7]

After Miller returned from abroad with his partner, Aldan, Miller, and Vecchi established the Tiber Press in a small walk-up on 59th Street. They were driven both by Aldan's want for a

Fig. 17 Unidentified photographer, Floriano Vecchi, Richard Miller, Olga Petroff, and Daisy Aldan, circa 1955

receptive audience and Vecchi's need for self-employment (due to his lack of a US work visa). Choosing the still new and relatively unpopular screen print—a stencil process of creating imagery atop a transparent mesh matrix—as their primary medium, the trio created a print studio "devoted solely to the work of young writers and artists."[8]

Vecchi, who studied agriculture at the University of Perugia, assumed the unlikely role of master printer at the fledgling press.[9] He began his training in the graphic arts in 1952, shortly after arriving in the United States, during a three-month apprenticeship at the Pippin Press, a small commercial printshop underwritten by art critic and co-founder of the New York City Ballet Lincoln Kirstein.[10] Pippin functioned as "an informal salon that served as a nexus for gay men in the arts."[11] At Pippin Vecchi screen-printed a wide variety of imagery, including reproductions of paintings by Paul Cadmus (known for his bawdy depictions of homosexual desire), collectible ballet designs, patterned greeting cards, and wallpaper. It was in this small and notably queer milieu that Vecchi first explored the expressive possibilities inherent to the process of pushing ink through a mesh screen. Later, within the context of his own (queer) workspace, alongside artists like Grace Hartigan and Andy Warhol, Vecchi pioneered the creative application of screen printing to produce a painterly effect in original (rather than reproductive) graphic artworks.[12]

Despite a meager budget and limited facilities—and, by Hartigan's account, a swelteringly hot workroom—between 1953 and 1960, the Tiber Press produced a pioneering series of collaborative periodicals, including the vanguard literary magazine *Folder*, in which O'Hara published his review of *Masquerade*, and a suite of limited edition *livres d'artiste*. Prefiguring developments in publishing associated with the "print renaissance" of the 1960s, the Tiber Press periodicals paired work from soon-to-be-canonical New York School poets, including V. R. "Bunny" Laing, John Ashbery, and Frank O'Hara, with bespoke prints by painters including Hartigan, Joan Mitchell, and Alfred Leslie, all of whom created their first-ever screen prints under Vecchi's guidance.[13] As an editor Aldan distinguished herself by emphasizing the importance of handling original graphic media such that "the visual became an important aspect of the total poem experience."[14]

At the same time that Aldan, Vecchi, and Miller were reimagining the relationship between text and image in the sphere of avant-garde publishing, Hartigan was reimagining the practice and possibilities of abstract painting. For Hartigan this reimagining was accompanied by significant turmoil. The painter's journals reveal anxiety about the influence of her immediate predecessors, including Jackson Pollock and Willem de Kooning, in her canvases up to that point. By her own account, her paintings of the late 1940s and early 1950s embrace the principles of entropy to produce an all-over effect mirroring the stylistic currents of abstract expressionism.[15]

By 1951 Hartigan began to doubt the efficacy of these techniques, and by the end of October 1952, she definitively declared that "the all over picture ha[d] died."[16] She expressed sustained apprehension about succumbing to a style that she termed "The Look," a canned and imitative version of abstract expressionism that critics including Irving Sandler and Leo Steinberg criticized as a "self-serving celebration of human invention" that failed to advance the history of painting.[17] In a particularly grueling journal entry, Hartigan addressed her critics, writing "If it is EXPRESSIONISM that is the pitfall, then I'm going to grapple with the monster, use it drain it, eat it, and eventually I know I'll throw it away."[18]

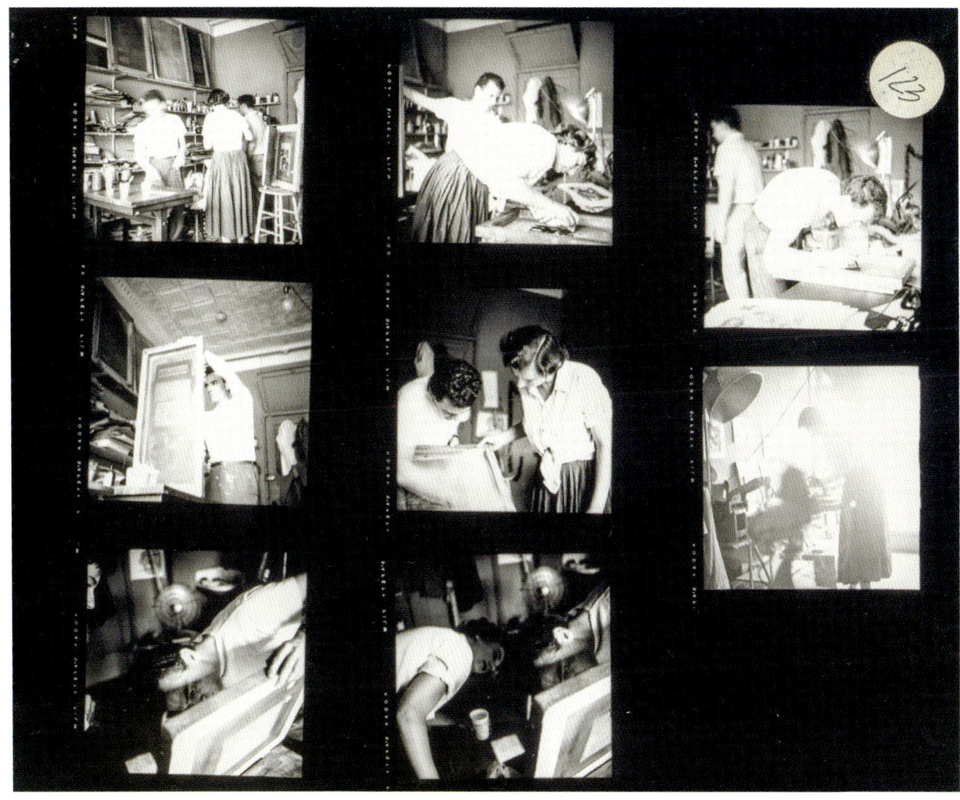

During this period of artistic turmoil, Hartigan was introduced to the milieu of the Tiber Press. In multiple journal entries, the painter recalled time spent with Vecchi and Miller as a respite from an overwhelming social life—made notorious by her intense, sometimes contentious and quasi-romantic friendship with O'Hara. She wrote, "I am being bitterly attacked, even by my 'friends.' Part of it is jealousy, part resentment of my willful attitudes & opinions. I am happier with people who admire me and don't challenge me, like ... Richard Miller, than I am with a group of my 'best friends' who can be vicious when they get together, knives drawn."[19] In another instance Hartigan recounted Miller coming to her assistance during a particularly hard financial season: "Richard came by Mon. evening with Floriano bringing violets, chartreuse, a gingerbread man, and a hundred dollar bill."[20] Violets, it can be noted, are a long-standing symbol of queer affection that had emerged in the early twentieth century.

In addition to providing comfort in the form of friendship and flowers, Hartigan's time at the Tiber Press was instrumental in carrying her through her battle with expressionism and "The Look." Though she was unexperienced in the art of printmaking, in July 1953 Vecchi and Aldan invited Hartigan to make an edition of screen prints for inclusion in the first issue of *Folder* alongside verse by O'Hara and Ashbery, among others. Silver—fellow contributor to *Folder* and later producer of the source photographs for *Masquerade*—documented the collaboration between Vecchi, Aldan, and Hartigan in a series of photographs that captures the physical intimacy of the work (fig. 18).

In one image Hartigan and Vecchi peer through the screen at opposing angles, their bodies hunched in contemplation. In another Hartigan works directly on the matrix, while Vecchi gazes over her. In still another Vecchi lifts the screen so that he and Hartigan might examine its image from its back side. Of the physical strain of producing the edition, Hartigan recalled in her journal, "the print process is interesting. I'm making 600 and my arm aches so I can hardly move it—and I've only pulled 2 colors."[21] Among the three prints she created during this initial collaboration with the Tiber Press is an abstracted version of her painting *River Bathers* (1953), inspired by Paul Cézanne's and Henri Matisse's paintings of nude bathers, in vivid color (*Pastorale*, 1953; plate 8). Many years later, Hartigan proudly recalled mixing the pigments herself.[22]

The second print Hartigan and Vecchi created side by side is a version of another recent painting, *The Persian Jacket* (1952; fig. 20, plate 1). The oil on canvas, drawn from a female model, depicts an ambiguously sexed figure in slashing brushstrokes and bold colors. The figure's masklike face and hollowed eyes are rendered in quick gray strokes that contrast with its vivid orange jacket. The painting marked a pivotal moment in Hartigan's career: in 1953 MoMA acquired it, marking the moment that the painter no longer needed to live on "oatmeal and bacon ends."[23]

At Tiber Hartigan created a comparatively bright and highly saturated print version titled *The Persian Robe* (fig. 21, plate 7). The painter proclaimed the print a success in her journal: "*The Persian Robe* is quite full and successful. It has an emotional intensity that I wasn't sure I could get in that medium, so am really pleased."[24] Unlike *The Persian Jacket*, where deep blues and blacks are concentrated at the center of the composition, the almost neon red of the garment in *The Persian Robe* dominates the foreground of the print. Next to the curve of the robe wearer's left shoulder, a block of the same red ink extends backward in space, creating the impression of an arm that reaches from the background and rests on the sitter's left knee. This specter, and the suggestion of two bodies compressed into one space, recall the very nature of printing alongside Vecchi, in which their two bodies pressed together above the shared space of the screen.

The mask seen in both *The Persian Jacket* and *The Persian Robe* was a recurring motif in Hartigan's paintings in the early 1950s— including *Masquerade*. Masks may refer to Hartigan's own desire to obfuscate professionally. For example, in exhibitions and publications of the first half of the 1950s, including the first issues of *Folder* magazine, Hartigan

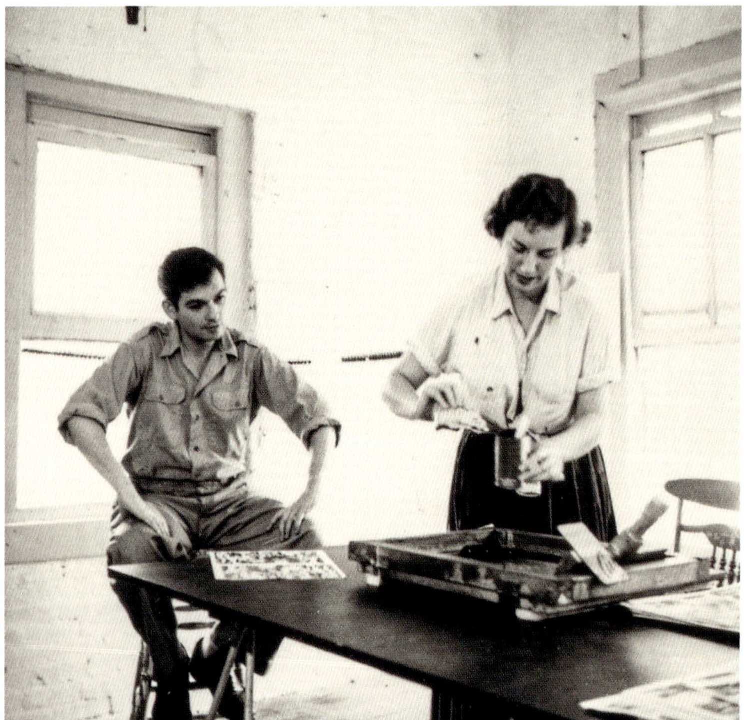

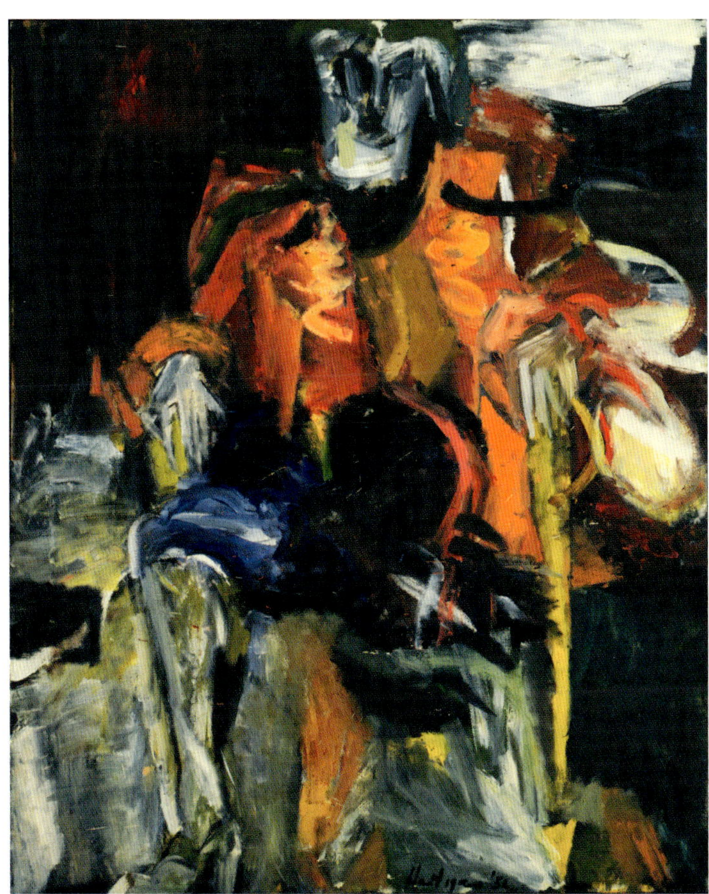

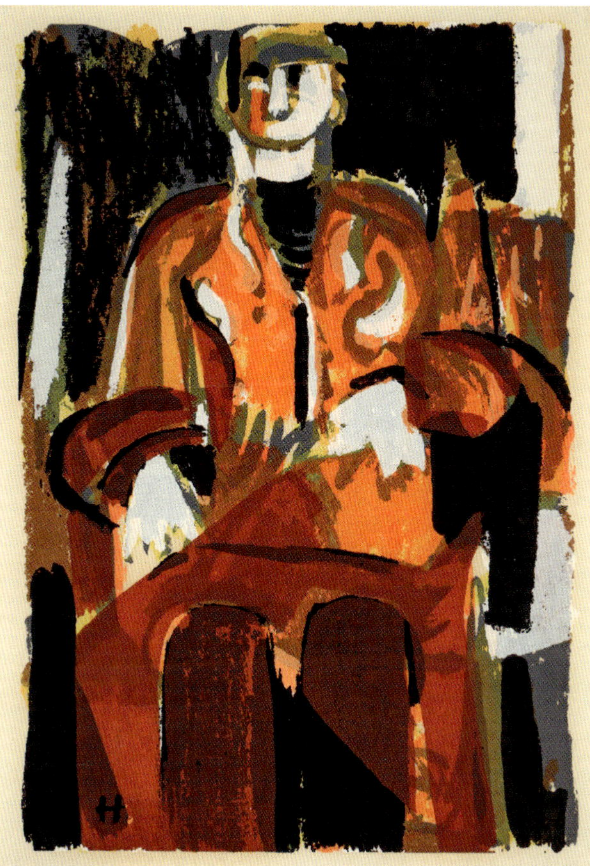

used the name George rather than Grace. Aldan recalled making this decision because "women's work was rarely published or accepted in major galleries."[25] Scholars, including Terence Diggory and Marjorie Rawle, see this masking (both literal and figurative) as an allegory not only of gender bias but also of the complicated and interwoven private lives of Hartigan's many queer friends and collaborators, including Aldan, O'Hara, Vecchi, and Miller. Indeed, as Amelia Jones has argued of the historical performance of (homo)sexuality, the field of visibility for queer postwar artists was "riven and contradictory" amid early Cold War anxieties about hidden and covert sexual behaviors.[26] Within this "culture of suspicion," as Gavin Butt termed it, same-sex desire was somewhat invisible (albeit widely stereotyped) and became legible through gossip and other kinds of fugitive language that functioned as a kind of mask or code.[27]

In the case of the Tiber Press, direct references to Aldan's status as either a lesbian or woman poet are almost always masked—though her personal correspondence suggests that the question of female desire and sexual difference fundamentally shaped the reception of her work. In the only article dedicated to the history of the Tiber Press, the author refers to Aldan as Miller's "childhood friend."[28] A less-than-delicate letter from poet James Schuyler to O'Hara evidences the lack of suitable language for Aldan's sexuality during the period itself and the sexism of the New York School's male-centric queer

Fig. 20 Plate 1, *The Persian Jacket*

Fig. 21 Plate 7, *The Persian Robe*

Fig. 22 Plate 12, *Two Women*

Fig. 23 Walter Silver?, Daisy Aldan (left) and Olga Petroff (right) posing for Grace Hartigan's *Two Women*, circa 1954

poetry scene. After taking digs at the quality of her writing, Schuyler made a series of crass allusions about Aldan's sexuality and her longtime partner Olga Petroff, comparing Petroff's genitalia to "a Dutch Maid Copper Scouring Pad."[29] There is even less archival record of Vecchi and Miller's relationship, the details of which endure primarily in secondhand accounts, including Cathy Curtis's biography of Hartigan. A single surviving photograph of Vecchi, Miller, Aldan, and Petroff standing side by side, arms linked, captures the particular arrangement of queer relationships at the heart of the Tiber Press.

Still masked by history, this web of relationships is captured both by the screen prints that Hartigan made at the Tiber Press and the paintings she created in the following years. Among these canvases is *Two Women* (1954; fig. 22, plate 12), for which Aldan and Petroff posed together in embroidered costumes. Captured by Silver, the source photographs for the painting show the two women angled toward one another wearing blank expressions (fig. 23). Although their bodies overlap and touch one another, the women do not meet eyes; Aldan looks directly at the camera, while Petroff gazes to the left of the frame. In Hartigan's oil on canvas, their vacant expressions have been rendered as stylized, flattened faces that recall the faces of the figures in the other Hartigan portrait Aldan and Petroff sat for, *Masquerade*.

Often read through the lens of camp as theatricalized performances of gender or the tawdry splendor of consumer culture, these images can also be

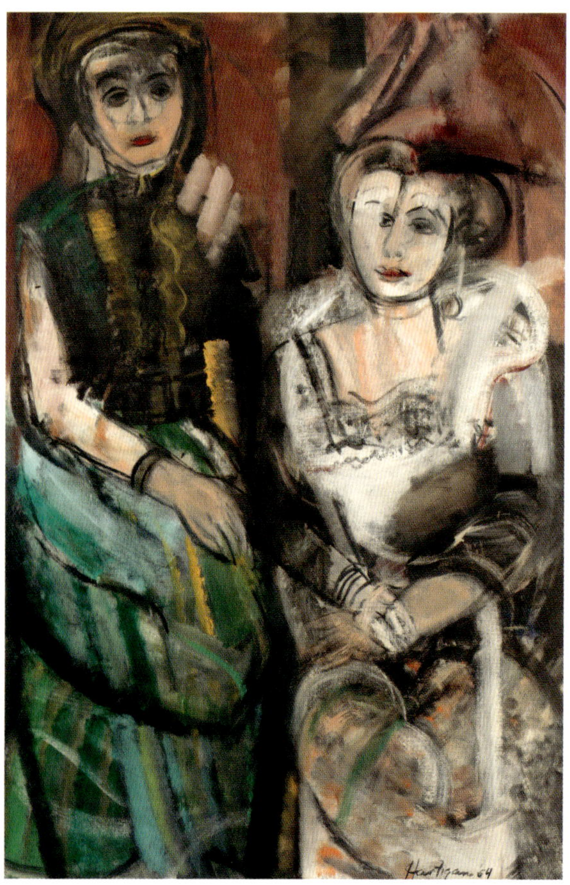

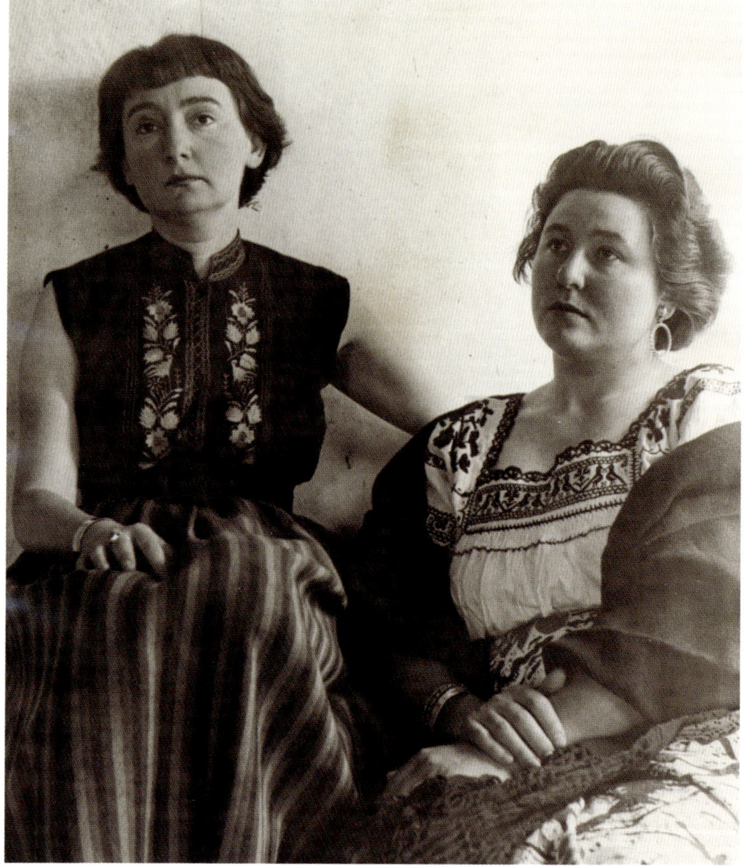

Grace Hartigan: The Gift of Attention

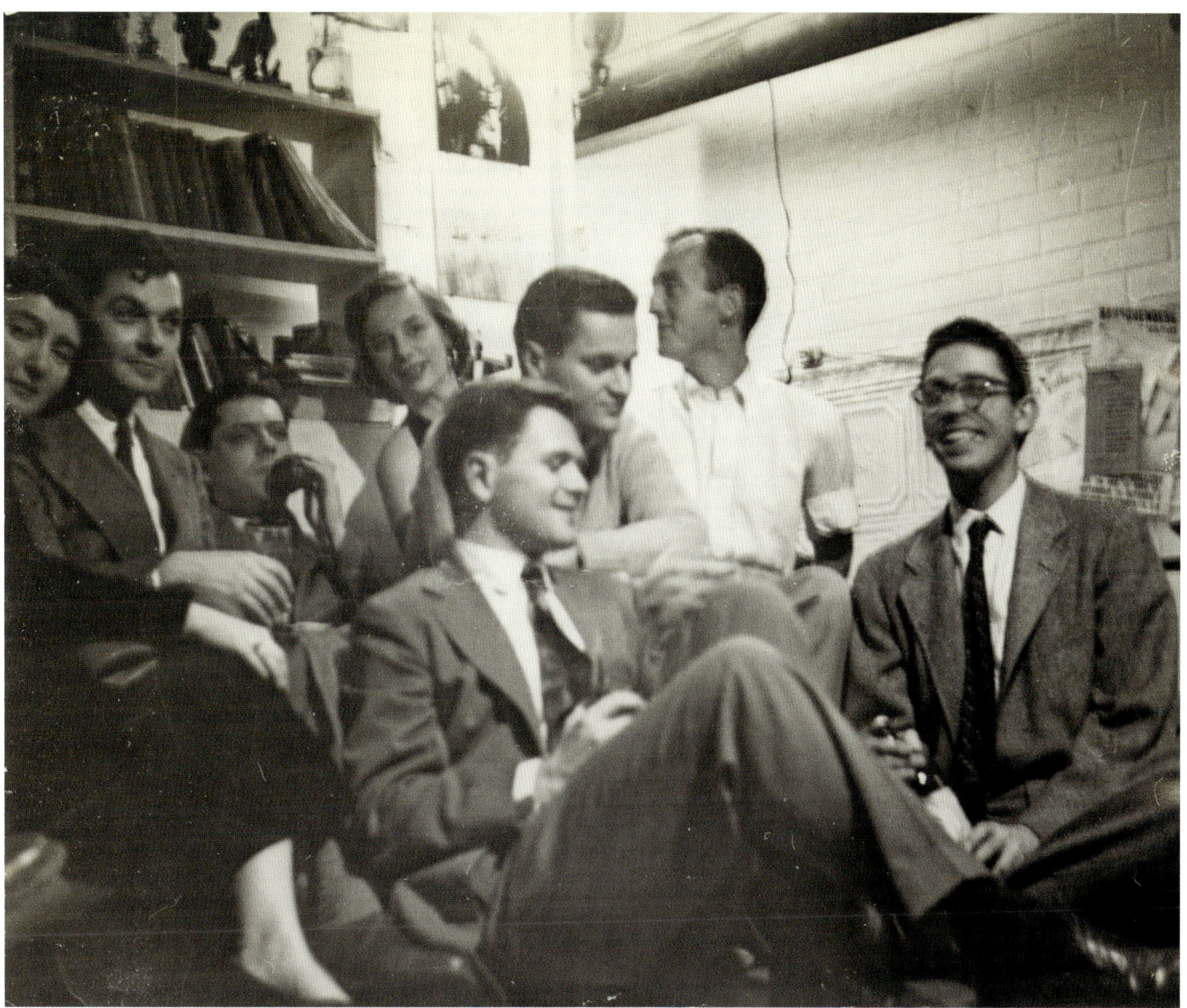

understood within the context of Hartigan's relationship with the founders of the Tiber Press. Indeed, her works featuring masks might be read as proffering a more subtle and nuanced notion of the self. The heterogenous visual language she honed in this series, including *Two Women*, *Masquerade*, and *The Persian Robe*, brings the vigorous paint handling of earlier expressionist movements to the depiction of close friends and colleagues who navigated the simultaneous experiences of masking and disclosure for gay men and women in the New York art world in the 1950s. In dialogue with peers including Aldan, Vecchi, and Miller, Hartigan articulated a fundamentally open approach to abstraction and figuration that captures the indeterminacy and multiple valences of the partnerships that unfolded among them—their particular way of being together in the world.

Fig. 24 Unidentified photographer, Celebration for *Folder* magazine, 1955; top row: Daisy Aldan, Richard Miller, William Fense Weaver, Grace Hartigan, John Ashbery, Frank O'Hara; bottom row: James Schuyler, Kenneth Koch

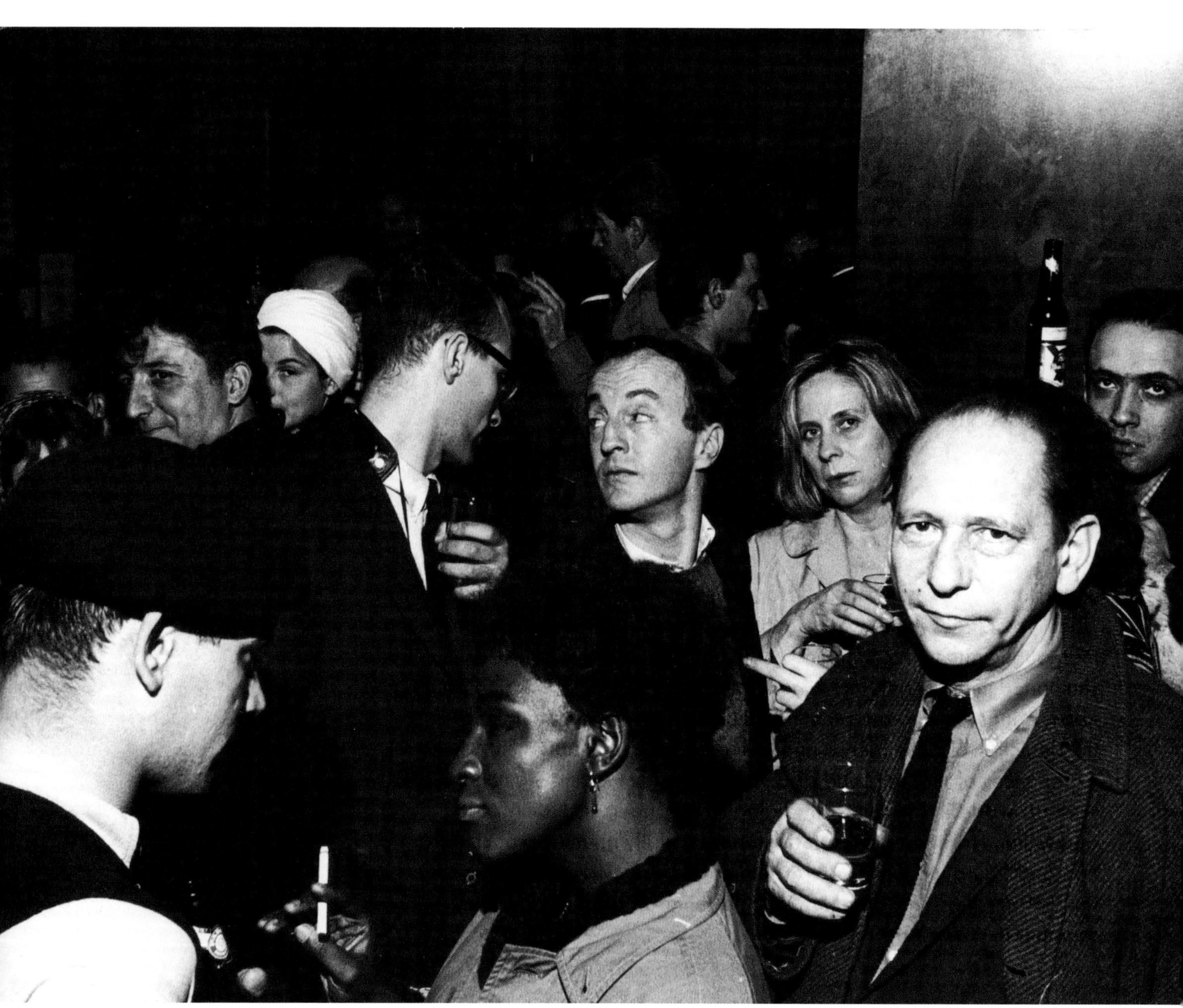

A Gestural Eros of Poesis
Hartigan Responds to Guest and O'Hara

RACHEL BLAU DUPLESSIS

As a woman filled with creative possibilities and powers in cultural scenes sometimes ambivalent to such trajectories, Grace Hartigan was ambitious, sexually open, and defiant in that high-stakes oil-paint world she struggled for and achieved a striking early success in bold statements of color, figuratively suggestive abstraction, and proud aesthetic scale. Hartigan's driven complexity, enormous semi-schooled powers, and combined vulnerability and ruthlessness contributed to her absolutist claim to not notice, shrug off, and eventually fiercely attack any ascription by anyone of aspects of *her* career to femaleness, involving choices made (about children—not raising her son), to sex-gender clichés (e.g., a "sensuous" brushstroke?), to "the" feminine character (sweetness? women are indeed "competitive," she averred). "I lived like the men," she said, "... I had no choice." Interesting formulation. Neither her exceptionalist stances, nor identifications with maleness as power, nor her critical observations about the relationship of Jackson Pollock and Lee Krasner ignore gender. Class, lower-middle-class limits of the time, seems to have affected her as well. Her formal education ended without university but with drafting skills. Her art education she herself pursued.

Fig. 25 Fred W. McDarrah, View of the crowded interior of the Cedar Street Tavern (24 University Place) on its closing night, with Frank O'Hara (center) and Barbara Guest (right, looking at camera), New York, March 30, 1963

Seriously bonded with fellow poets such as James Schuyler and Frank O'Hara and deeply fond of painters in their orbit, Barbara Guest showed a supportive admiration for Hartigan, expressed in warm letters (1959–61) that praise Hartigan's aura and power. Guest's characterization of her own social/ maternal and artistic responsibilities emerged in the challenges of her "do it all well" ethos, which did have relative economic security. This in a quiet remark in a letter to Hartigan saying it's hard to be a woman both doing what you have to do and what you want to do—an unmistakable comment on social role expectations and their strained meshing with serious artistic ambition.[1] By the mid-1960s, married for a third time—to Trumbull Higgins, with children and a serious poetic career, Guest was able to travel up to New York, to enjoy serious travel abroad, to share household management with a maid, a cook (Guest also cooked), and perhaps a nanny, to mother her children, Hadley and Jonathan, *and* to write poetry, surrealist plays, and reviews. Guest's articulate empathy, witty charm, and hard-won elegance were appealing to Hartigan.

I'd frame the fervent and much-debated poetics and personal relation ships of those years—among painters, among poets, and between them—as striking examples of the "eros of poesis," flaring up as both cause and effect of a period of passionate creative work among poets and painters. To have an ideal (if vulnerable) friendship, to admire each other's commitments, to enjoy the subtle differences and insights of another mind/spirit friendly to yours, to seek the intimacies of friendship as sustaining—all create an eros of poesis, a powerful and buoyant connection idealizing artistic *making*. These connections, often homosocial, mainly nonsexual, involved mutuality, mentor ship, struggles, mercurial emotions, and real impacts on artistic careers. Such eager enthusiasms and mutual mentoring might leave complex residues, not all positive (senses of betrayal, rupture, bitterness). Hartigan, other ambitious women—Guest, painter Helen Frankenthaler—and a related gay male cohort (O'Hara, Schuyler) became committed to their charmed gender- and sexually labile world, sometimes trying to sidestep, with their own artful claims, the powerful (dubbed "macho") forces of other artistic careers. An attempt to sustain social formations featuring nonhierarchical uses of power and respect for mastery were possible, sometimes plausible outcomes of these relationships.

Being seriously admired by your fellow artist, respected, wondered at, encouraged with friendly intimacy were characteristics of the relationships Hartigan enjoyed with both Guest and O'Hara, who was both fickle and expansive in and with his considerable charisma. Both these relationships ended or eroded after about 1966, with O'Hara's shocking accidental death and with Guest's growing concern about how poorly Hartigan treated herself by overusing alcohol. (Guest also thought that Hartigan's move to Baltimore with her third husband, Winston Price, isolated her from New York scenes, although Guest also lived during some of this time in nearby Washington, DC.)

Not only was the "eros of poesis" at play between each poet and the painter but each also had rich idealizations of the medium of the other.

   Grace Hartigan: The Gift of Attention

Hartigan simply saw poetry as "pure"—not materialist, since one could not, with poetry, earn that money beginning to be possible in the emerging art market context; nor did a poet need the often expensive materials of oil paint and canvas and the swathes of large time (purchased by intermittent jobs and by her surviving in an elemental, chosen poverty). In short, Hartigan claimed that the "nonutilitarian" stance of poetry was purifying, clarifying, given that poetry did not grant poets "power, prestige or money." However true, partially true, or overstated, Hartigan's idealization had an impact even in relation to her more interesting admiration of the emotional and existential suggestiveness, the dramatic ability to pose questions that she also attributed to poetry.

Parallel idealizing remarks by Guest about painters and painting, articulated years later, affirm the impact on her of early abstract expressionist aesthetics. Guest "envied" painters' "freedom," and she proposed for her continuing poetics "vision and plasticity," terms striking for their heft and torque from visual arts.[2] Further, "We admired the work of painters breaking rules of art performing [their concealed emotions and desires] on the canvas ...," so art feels "freed by action." Even more, this art is also well regarded—"applauded by their market" for "leaping boundaries of experiment."[3] This remark was intended as a dour contrast to rewards tendered only to academic poets, not to experimenters. Besides plasticity, these painters encouraged accident, spontaneity, play, exploratory curiosity.[4] That mode for a poem often began with "no fixed subject"—Guest's protest against topos-based activities of "developing" a poem in linear argument toward a singular mot or quasi-moralized conclusion.

The aesthetic thinking shared between Hartigan and "her" poets—Guest, O'Hara—involved fascination with a poetics of movement, a dramatic capture of the spontaneity of a force constantly moving, a tonal and visual plasticity, and diction glissades in which poetry or art were special and fraught acts expressing pulse and embodied attentiveness. ("Anthology of transit," a William Carlos Williams phrase on Marianne Moore, was a key structural idea, later called "projective" by Charles Olson). So, for Hartigan, Guest, and O'Hara, the two art forms—painting and writing—were on an aesthetic continuum, involving a dynamic spontaneity mutually responsive to each other's medium.

Among the interactions with or responses to another's work, one might identify citation and imitation, appropriation, editing, provocative distortion, and writing/painting yourself inside or around another work. Familiar in music is the cadenza—opening a work at a near terminal juncture and offering homage by intelligent elaboration (as Beethoven did for Mozart's Piano Concerto no. 20 in D Minor, K. 466). The deeply learned and informed spontaneity of jazz performance offers another example of homage to prior musicians' work. With your response you enter a nexus of connection making your expressive acts generated in your relationship with a person and with that person's art. The works talked of here—Hartigan with O'Hara and with

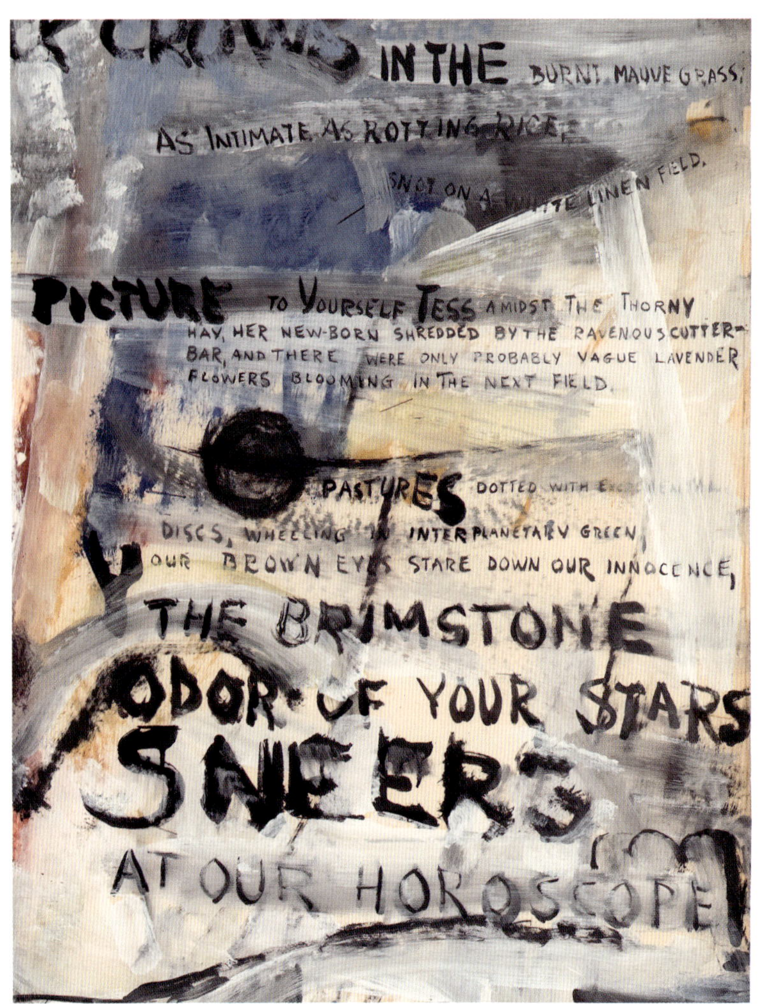

Guest—are not collaborations done together, though they were mutually agreed on and carried out variously by Hartigan responding to the poets' works.

These responses offer more than the aesthetic stances implied by *ekphrasis*—a poet writing a poem "about" or meditating on an existing artwork—or by *illustration*—a painter drawing something that represents a scene in a poem. Although with one poem of Guest's ("Palm Trees") Hartigan illustrates (plate 40), and with two with titles about a hero in a boat, one finds the boats (plates 26–27), still, in the *Oranges* and *Archaics* series, Hartigan engaged with the mercurial mutabilities, the physical trace, deploying line or stroke in motion as her response to the graphic, pictorial, or gestural aspects of language, as if something about language itself as a pure essence and pure gesture had to enter her works' visual syntax to respond to poetry. Different poets, different series, different gestures. But what these serial sets have in common are gestures drawing upon the lettristic trace—that idealized practice of literary "purity" as Hartigan had conjured it.

In the response of Hartigan to O'Hara's series of twelve *Oranges* poems, a dozen paintings (ten extant; see fig. 26, plate 2) from 1952, she was "excited" to "illustrate" the poems, but that word *illustrate* meant interestingly that "the printing [lettering] done by myself [is] an integral part of the picture."[5] She seemed enraptured with an evocation of the power of handwriting (as if a painterly, individuated typography)—the letter-gesture as a poetic/visual collaboration becomes an embodiment of poem elements, neither illustration nor copy of the O'Hara series. Some parts and words of the poems are presented in large letters, some words and phrases smaller, some almost effaced. She used a palette of a page quite blue—light and dark, sometimes with white, and with the odd saturations of oil on paper, including newsprint. Hartigan lettered her selected lines of O'Hara's poems in large mode or small within a swirl and foam of brushstrokes. Mysterious, sexually marked but angelic, light figures also emerge in this mobile conjunction of words and paint. This set most clearly represents the words of poems with brushed letters, not trying either to make neat typographical clarity of statement—not imitating "print"—or to deliver a copy of the whole poem but presenting figures, activities, brushwork, and letters stroked together as a total texture. Since both figures and letters

Fig. 26 Plate 2, *Black Crows (Oranges No. 1)* (detail)

Grace Hartigan: The Gift of Attention

are done with parallel gestural panache, it's as if this collaboration constructed a third poetic/visual mode: neither illustrative nor ekphrastic but gestural—an action of synthesis and merging of painterly forms and lettered poem-bits.

The emphasis on the gestural continued with Hartigan's uses of Guest's poems to generate visual responses. Hartigan's visual attention to Guest depended on two media, lithograph and collage. Four lithographs from 1960 responded to Guest's poem of the hero from her book *The Location of Things*. In two of the four, a viewer certainly can discern an abstract boat form (fig. 27, plate 26); these lithographs are more like drawing-units (plates 24–27). In the second set, *The Archaics* (1962–66; plates 36–42), each lithograph is strikingly divided into six pradelle-like gestural probes. Working from these writings of Guest seems to have encouraged Hartigan not because of the interestingly scenic and color-filled descriptions, nor their "Greek mythology," although one can always read relationships between poem and form, but rather, for me, as the attribution of emotional changes and odd, inexplicable images/events stoking a desire for change-up gesture, of alphabetic and letter-like evocations.

What Hartigan again showed, especially with the lithographs of *The Archaics* (with Guest's poems named in each of the eleven titles), was her desire for a dynamic presentation of making signage, having blocks of black pre-page or "slate" frames in some, with writing in a scribbled, pre-alpha-bet mode. These lithographs are hardly to be designated "pure" or anti-materialistic (or even poetic) but boldly gestural, teeming with matter, and filled with evocations of the materiality of visual making. Hartigan made untoward gestures on the stone, even strokes that look like finger painting. The series is like a dictionary of prewriting gestures combined with imposing black shapes.

Hartigan said she had never made lithographs before these, wasn't even sure what they were, nor how to proceed. Perhaps. Again proud of her partly schooled paths, she herself was mythologizing her risk-taking pride in direct treat-ment of the gestural and physical matter of making. Hartigan is described as accosting the large stones, spreading the tusche (a greasy crayon-like stick sat-urated with blackness) with apparent abandon, making bold scribbles, dark patches, and other dramatic marks,

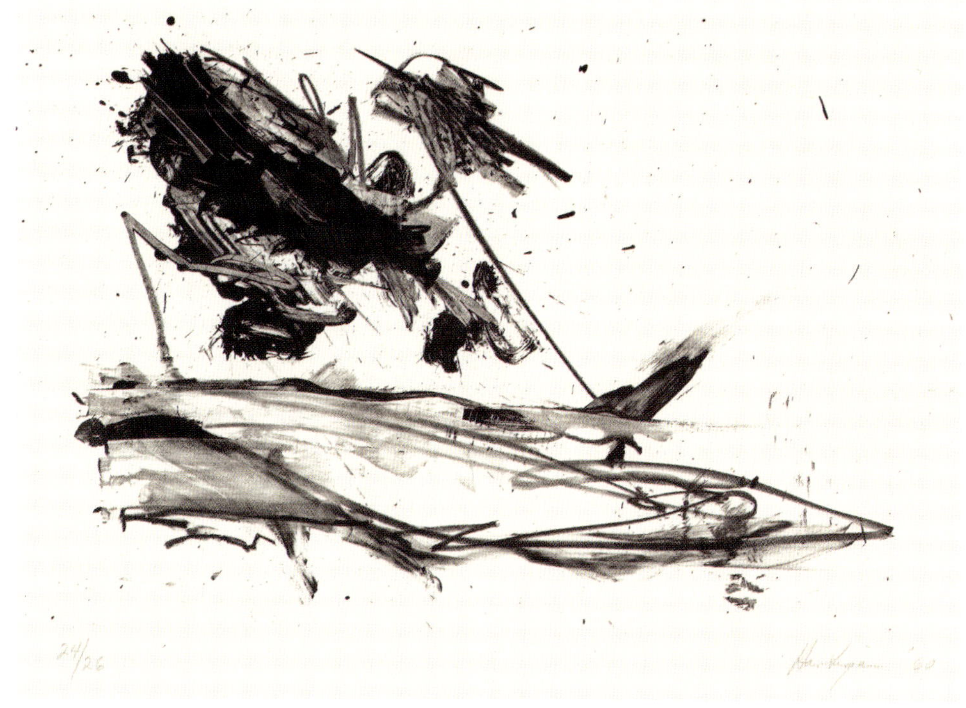

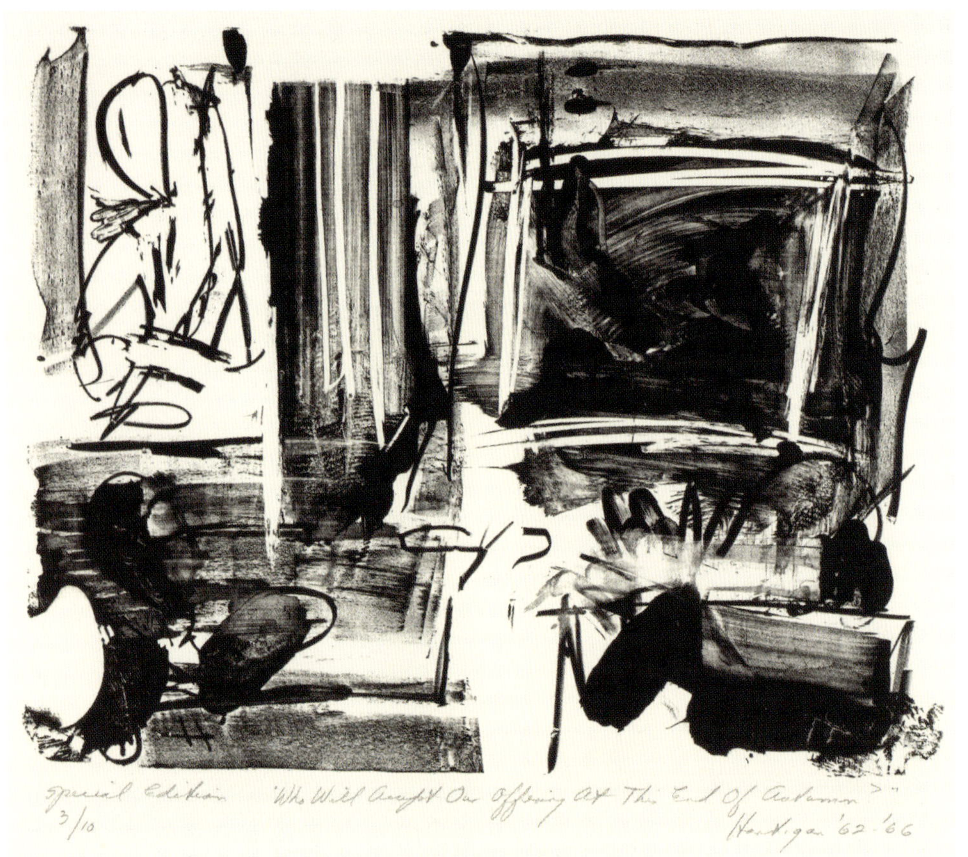

and to sum up, inventing a nonillustrative, strong surface almost the opposite of Guest's charming, even dainty, elegant poems. Hartigan's work is dense with emotion expressed as gesture, pre-letters, incisions, scribbles, and various dissimilar touches and textures in specific zones, each with a different look and density of blackness.

The unconventionality of *The Archaics* as they were being made shocked and stunned Tatyana Grossman, head of Universal Limited Art Editions (an anecdote Hartigan told with satisfaction and glee years later). She also gave an amused satisfaction to the lithograph master printer Robert Blackburn as being a challenge to his ability to handle that gestural insouciance.[6] The later several collages, from 1968 (plates 43 and 44), are also distinguished by small, page-like divisions with, on one, the striking use of an unreadable alphabetic-style written "comment."

Hartigan's use of Guest showcased gestures that might have led to writing but were, in effect, prewriting, a grab into the zone of what Hartigan saw as the materiality of emotional gesture. The final lithograph of the *Archaics* series (*Who Will Accept Our Offering at the End of Autumn?*; fig. 28, plate 42) even includes two patches of (unreadable) proto-writing. Aside from the palm tree as abstract palm tree in one "representational" lithograph, what Hartigan seems to have sought was to respond to Guest's poems by investing in the glamour and dynamic of gestural matter itself, to achieve a fundamental or root bond with not the prettiness of these poems, nor with their colorful adjectives, nor much with the plots or topoi of the retold classical stories—many involving a compromised female agency—but rather the forcefulness of marking and of spontaneous construction itself.

Fig. 28 Plate 42, *Who Will Accept Our Offering at the End of Autumn?* from *The Archaics*

Grace Hartigan: The Gift of Attention

This contribution draws on the following texts, including my existing analysis of the "eros of poesis" in *Purple Passages: Pound, Eliot, Zukofsky, Olson, Creeley, and the Ends of Patriarchal Poetry* (Iowa City: University of Iowa Press, 2012), 23. This book also tracks individual relations, mainly between countercultural male poets in poetic dyads. Sara Lundquist has already made a rich literary historical and thematic analysis of heroism and quest in the work Hartigan did with *The Archaics*. Lundquist, "Another Poet among Painters: Barbara Guest with Grace Hartigan and Mary Abbott," in *The Scene of My Selves: New Work on New York School Poets*, ed. Terence Diggory and Stephen Paul Miller (Orono, ME: National Poetry Foundation, 2001), 245–64. The edition of Guest consulted is *The Collected Poems of Barbara Guest*, ed. Hadley Haden Guest (Middletown, CT: Wesleyan University Press, 2008). Hartigan's gender opinions appear in an interview published in Cindy Nemser, *Art Talk: Conversations with 15 Women Artists* (New York: Icon Editions, 1995), 127–53; extrapolated citations are from Nemser, 134, 146, 130, and 129. Guest's letters to Hartigan are housed at the Special Collections Research Center, Syracuse University Libraries; seen in pdfs from Terence Diggory.

For Hartigan on poetry, see Terence Diggory, *Grace Hartigan and the Poets: Paintings and Prints* (Saratoga Springs, NY: Skidmore College, 1993). Her interpretation emerges in a 1976 gallery statement cited in Diggory's lecture for the Skidmore College exhibition he curated, which took place between March and April 1993. For Guest on painting, see Barbara Guest, *Forces of Imagination: Writing on Writing* (Berkeley, CA: Kelsey St. Press, 2003). The general poetics of motion and gesture are found in William Carlos Williams, "Marianne Moore [1925]," in *Selected Essays* (New York: Random House, 1954).

Plates of Hartigan's Frank O'Hara response are reproduced in Robert Saltonstall Mattison, *Grace Hartigan: A Painter's World* (New York: Hudson Hills Press, 1990) and Diggory, *Grace Hartigan and the Poets*. Plates of the Guest poems with the Hartigan lithographs appear in Diggory, *Grace Hartigan and the Poets*. I am grateful to Terence Diggory for the gift of this key catalogue. For the story of the lithographs, see Cathy Curtis, *Restless Ambition: Grace Hartigan, Painter* (New York: Oxford University Press, 2015).

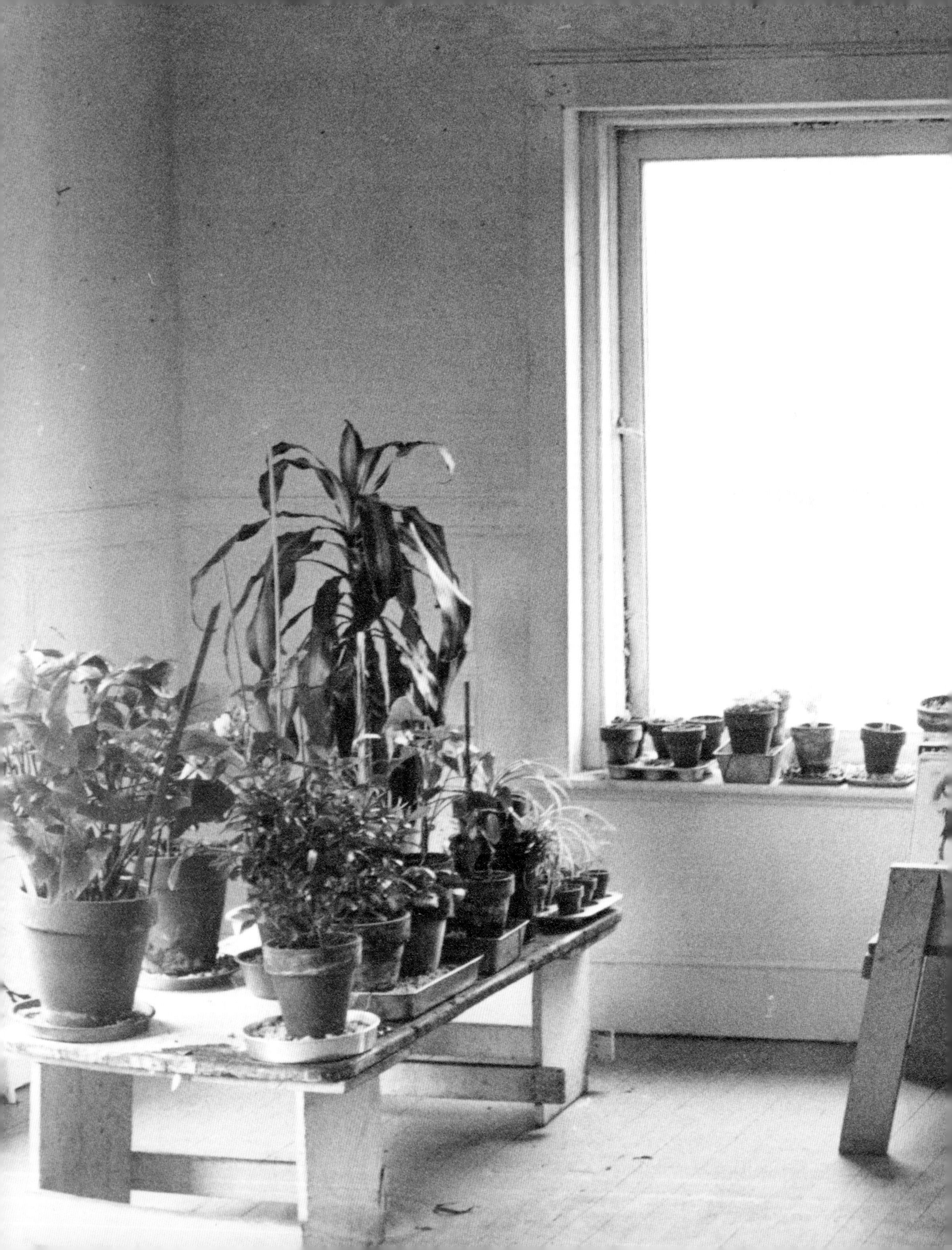

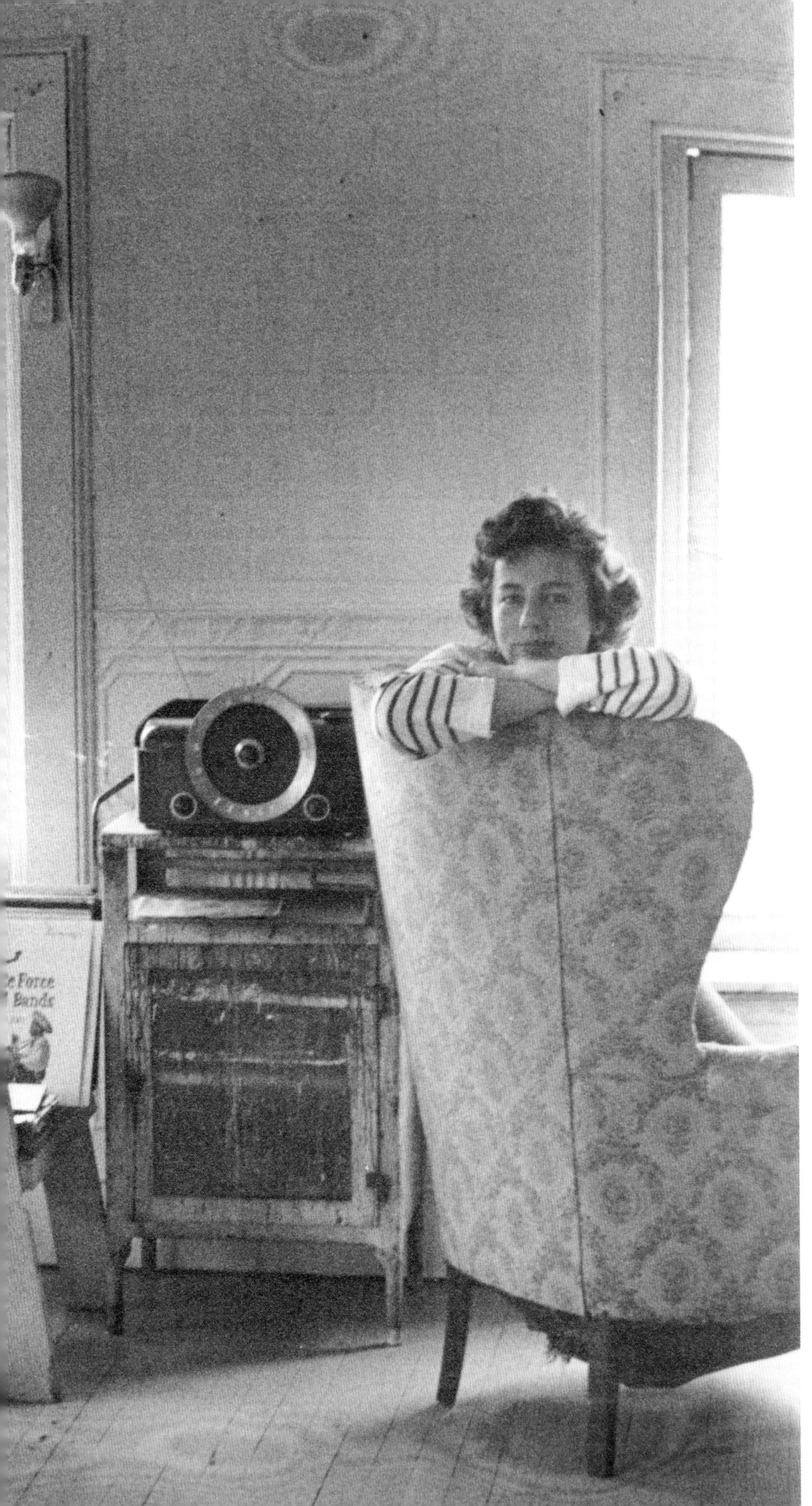

Plates, Poems, and Reviews

Fig. 29 Unidentified photographer, Grace Hartigan in her Essex Street Studio, 1958–59

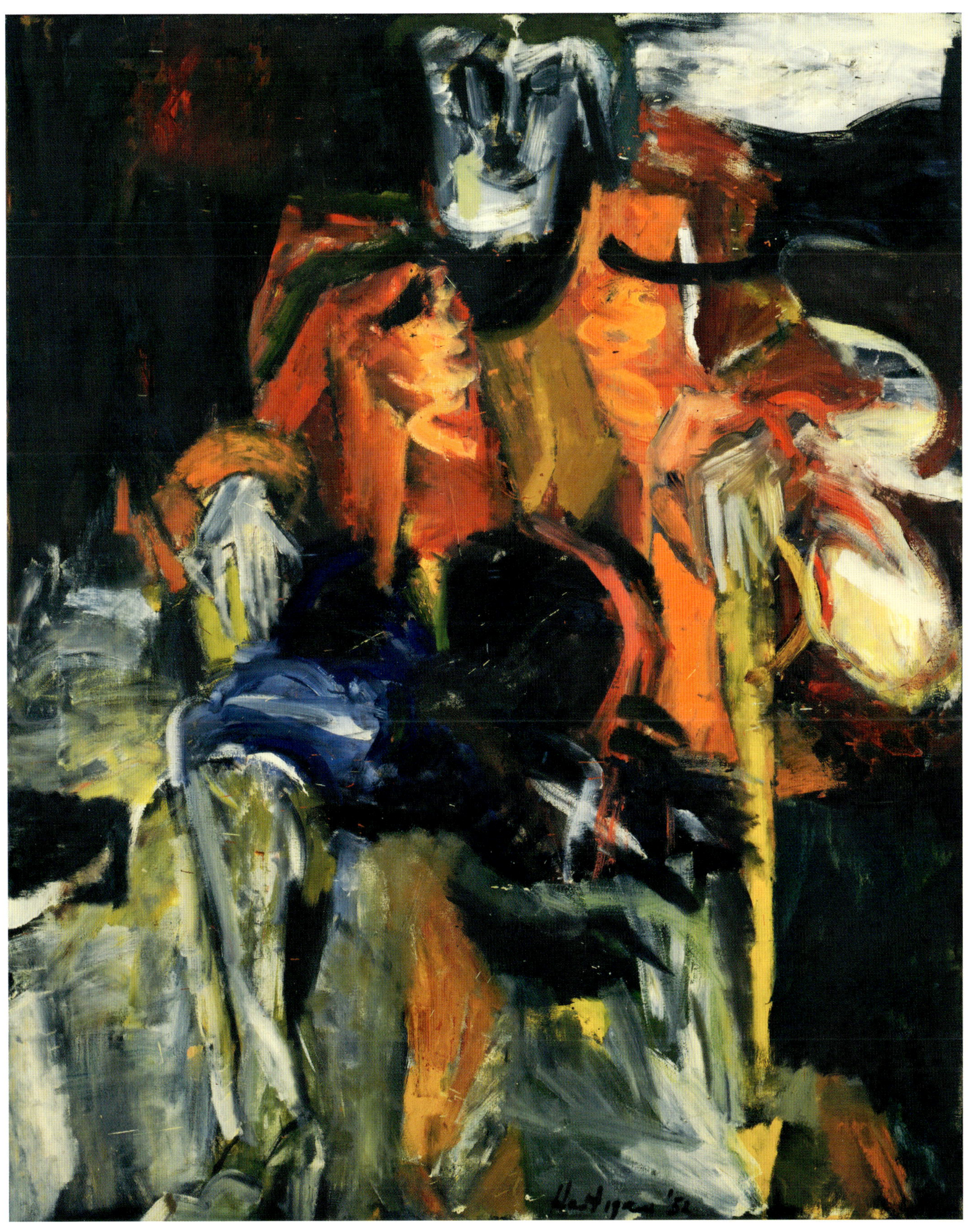

1 *The Persian Jacket* 1952

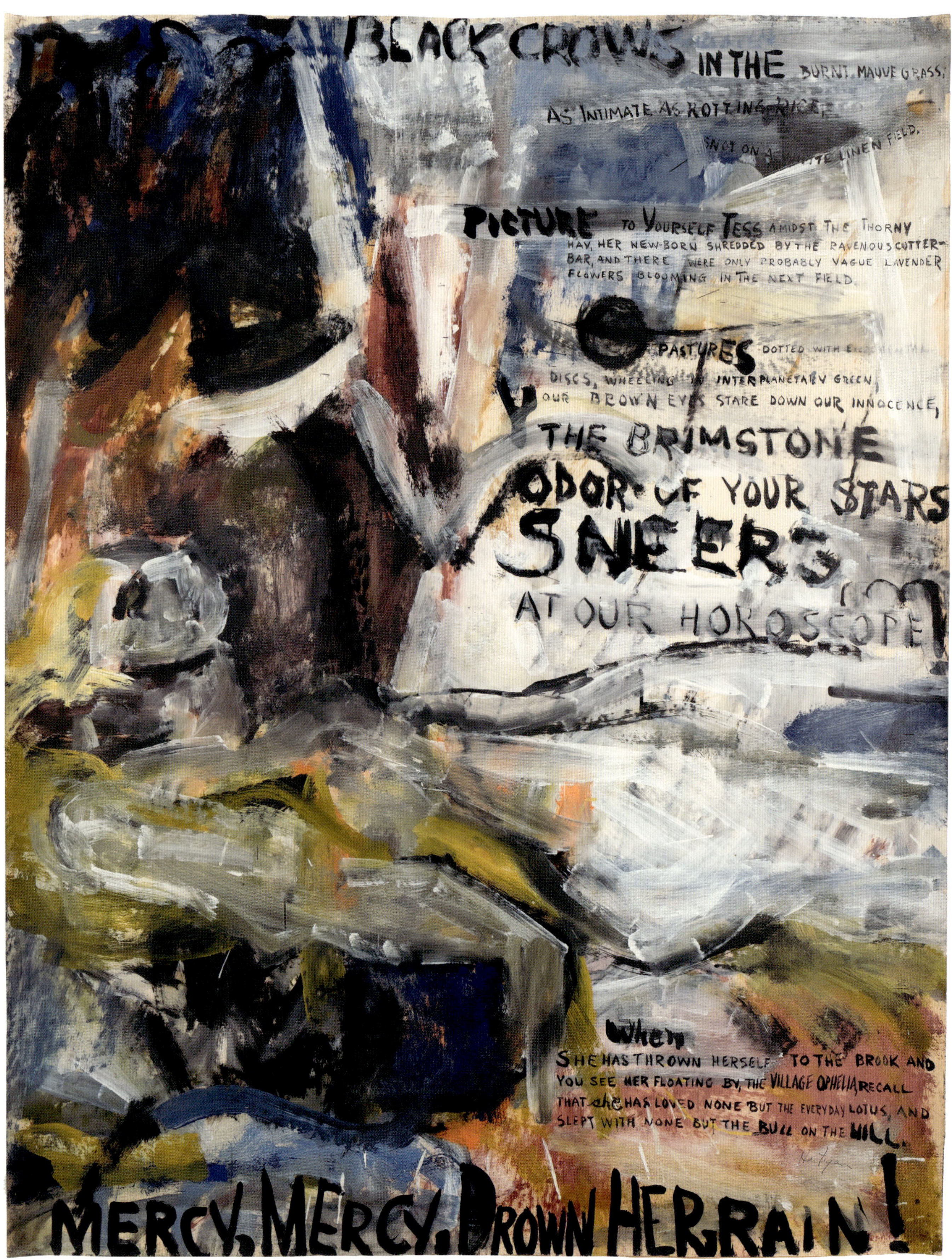

2 Black Crows (Oranges No. 1) 1952

Frank O'Hara
ORANGES I
from *Oranges: 12 Pastorals*

I

Black crows in the burnt mauve grass, as intimate as rotting rice, snot on a white linen field.

Picture to yourselves Tess amidst the thorny hay, her new-born shredded by the ravenous cutter-bar, and there were only probably vague lavender flowers blooming in the next field.

O pastures dotted with excremental discs, wheeling in interplanetary green, your brown eyes stare down our innocence, the brimstone odor of your stars sneers at our horoscope!

When she has thrown herself to the brook and you see her floating by, the village Ophelia, recall that she loved none but the everyday lotus, and slept with none but the bull on the hill.

Mercy, mercy, drown her, rain!

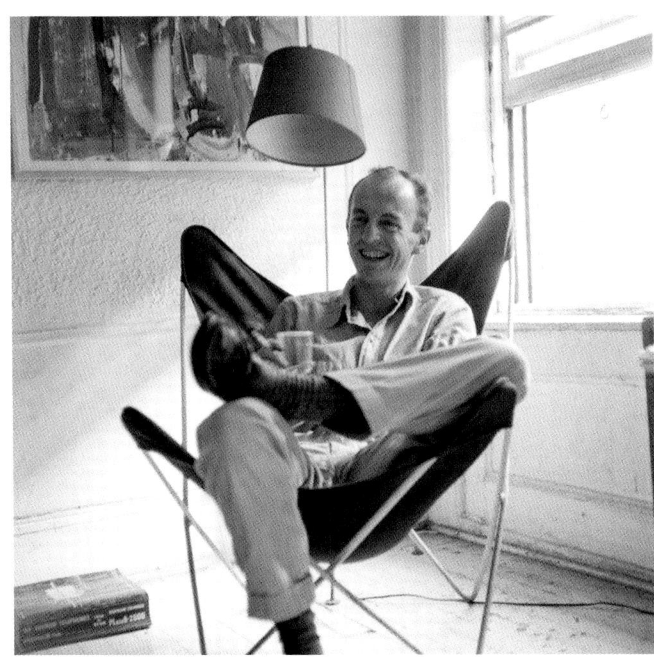

Fig. 30 Fred W. McDarrah, Frank O'Hara at his apartment at 441 East 9th Street, New York, September 26, 1959

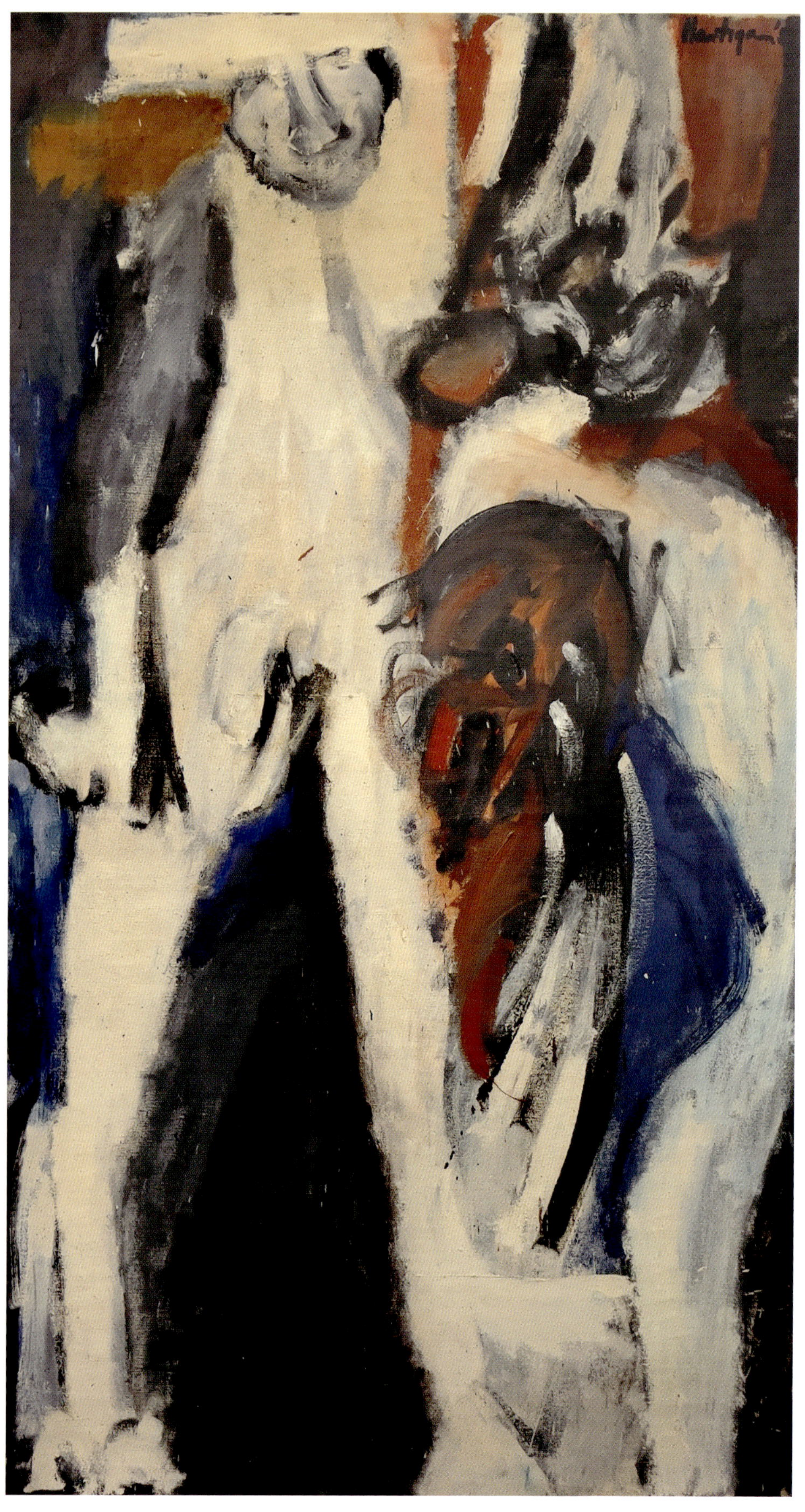

  3 *Frank O'Hara and the Demons* 1952

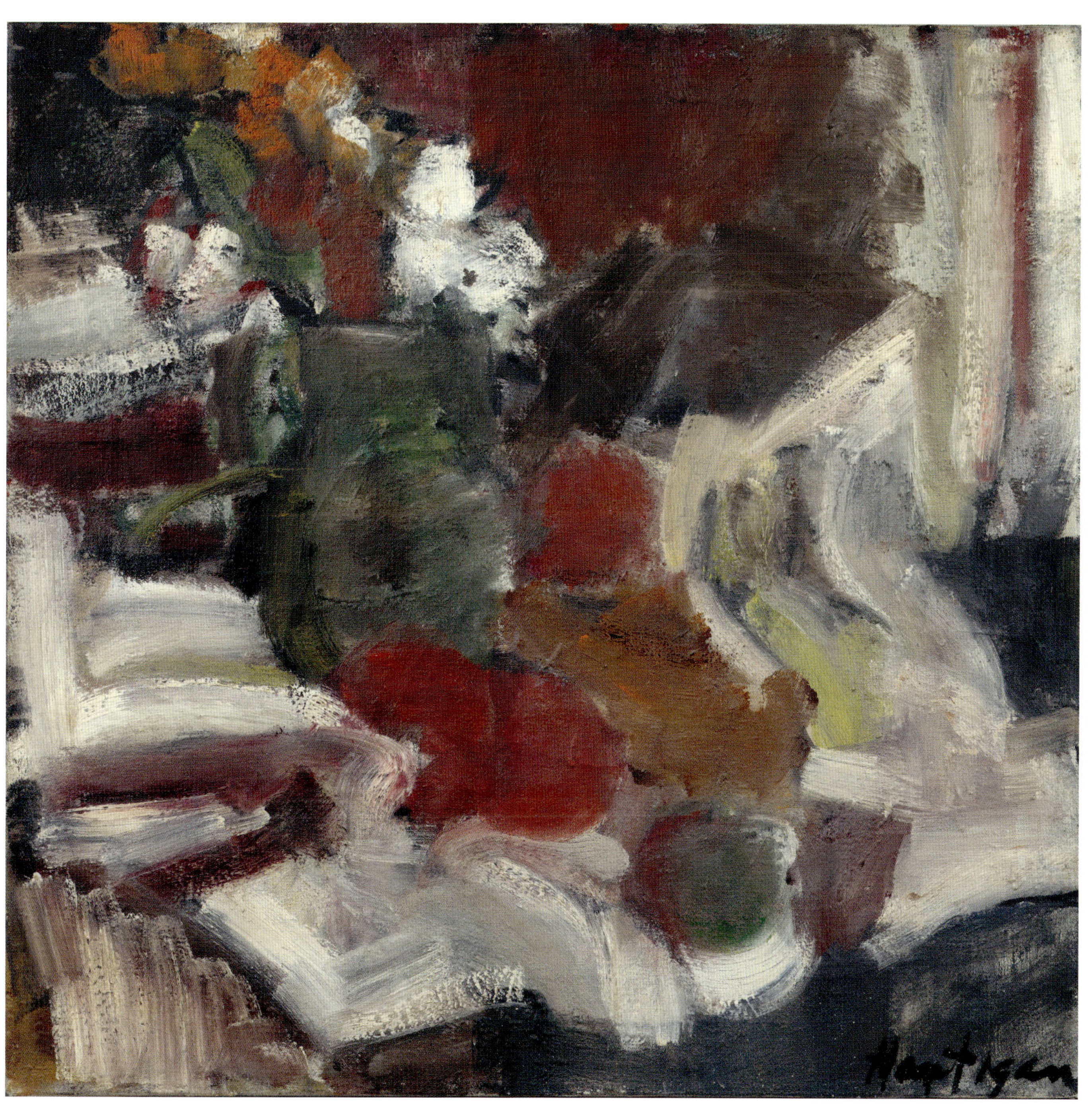

4 *Artificial Flowers and Apples* 1952

Frank O'Hara, "Reviews: George Hartigan,"
ARTnews, February 1954, 45.

George Hartigan [De Nagy; to Feb. 20], in these new paintings, brings dramatic intensity to traditional subjects—still-life, self-portrait with flowers, matador—while retaining compositional openness and handling which is emphatically abstract: the values of the picture's organization are always asserted above those of subject, observation or sentiment. The largest pictures, *River Bathers* (cool and languorous) and *Ocean Bathers* (feverish and active), show free use of the inspiration Matisse's *River* and *Moroccans* afford us all, while developing images of activity and conflict with nature quite unlike Matisse's. Her paintings seem to be a means of dealing with experience on her own terms and insisting on her own meanings. The degree of abstraction serves this purpose, it has nothing to do with objectivity; sometimes the subject is used merely as a natural organization and image for emotion of an entirely different kind—viewed in this way *Black Still-life* might as well be called *Dark Night of the Soul*, for the painting is invested with as strong an emotion as the structure can bear. The freedom of emphasis has given this work a variety which is often willful but never arbitrary, and in some pictures, notably the *Coffee Pot and Cucumber* and *River Bathers*, there is a richness of performance which includes the pleasures of virtuosity without verging on display. $50–$1,000. F. o'H.

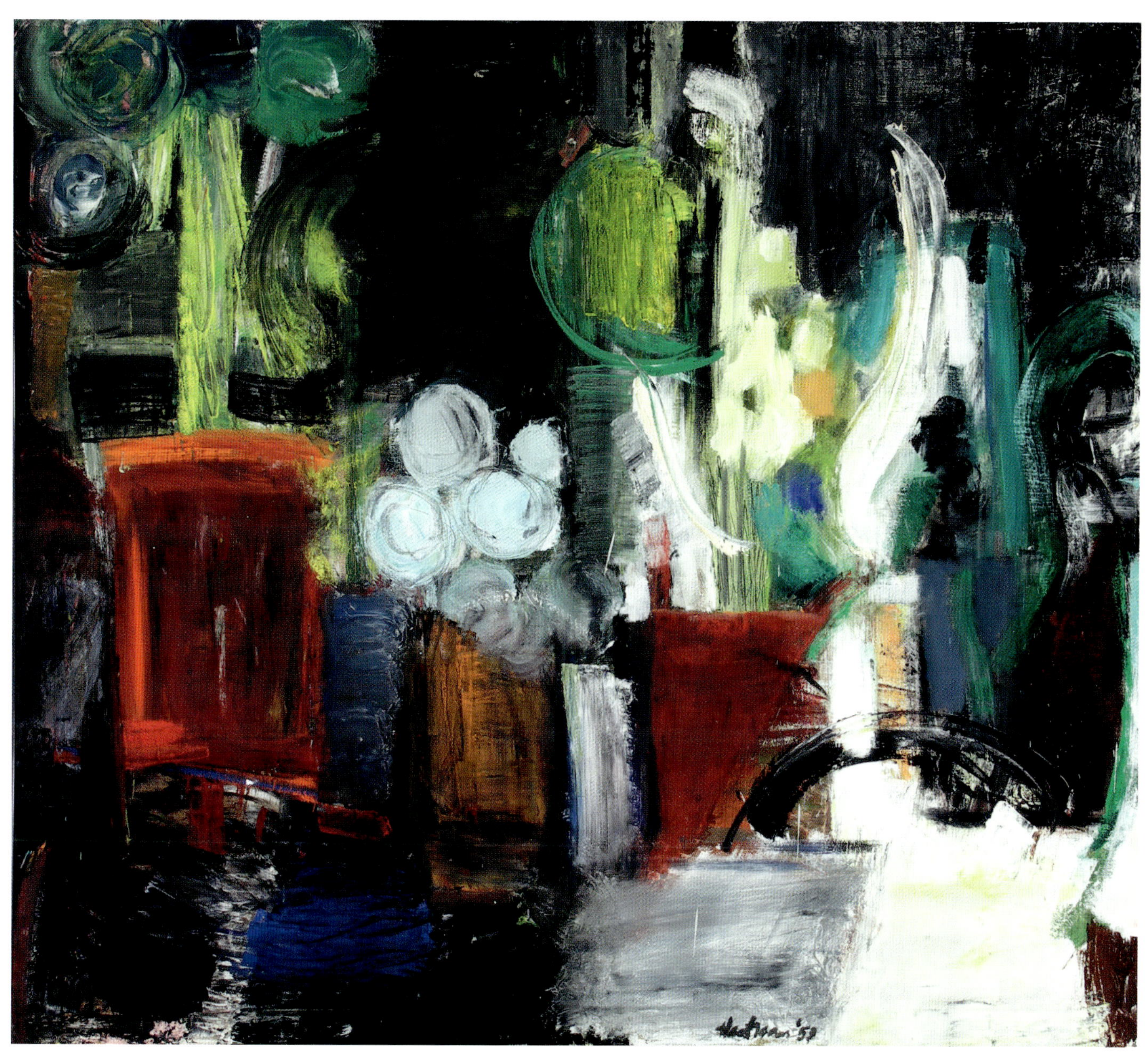

5 *Black Still Life* 1953

FOLDER

1

POEMS

JOHN ASHBERY
DAISY ALDAN
GIORGIO CAPRONI
JEAN GARRIGUE
LEON HECHT
KENNETH KOCH
JAMES MERRILL
FRANK O'HARA
ALEXANDER RANDOLPH
JAMES SCHUYLER
EDWIN TREITLER
SANDRA WOOL

A PLAYLET

JAMES SCHUYLER

SHORT STORIES

FREDERICK ENGLISH
GIUSEPPE PATRONI GRIFFI
ROBERT HELLMAN
WILLIAM FENSE WEAVER

THREE ORIGINAL SILK SCREEN PRINTS
GEORGE HARTIGAN

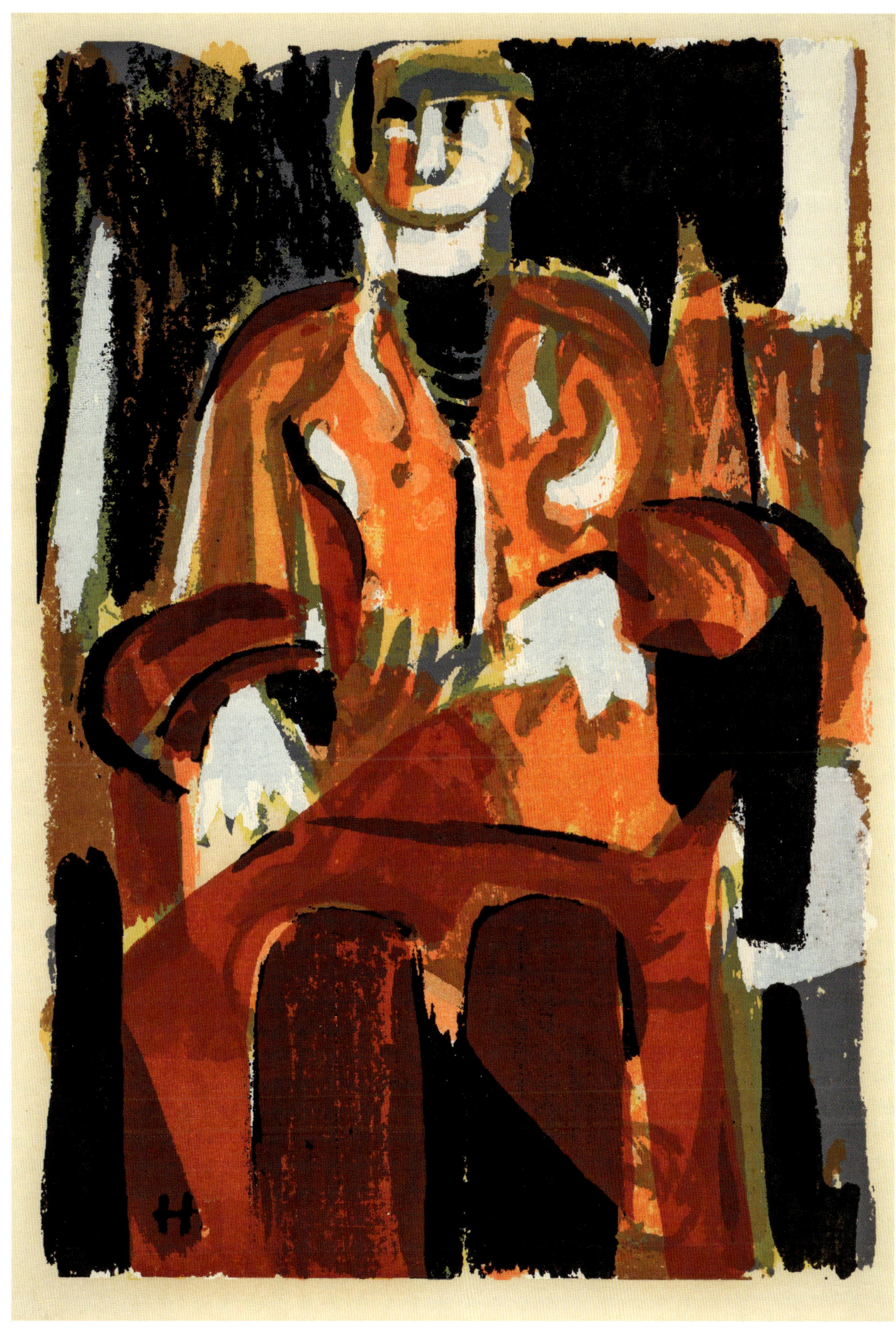

7 *The Persian Robe from Folder, no. 1 1953*

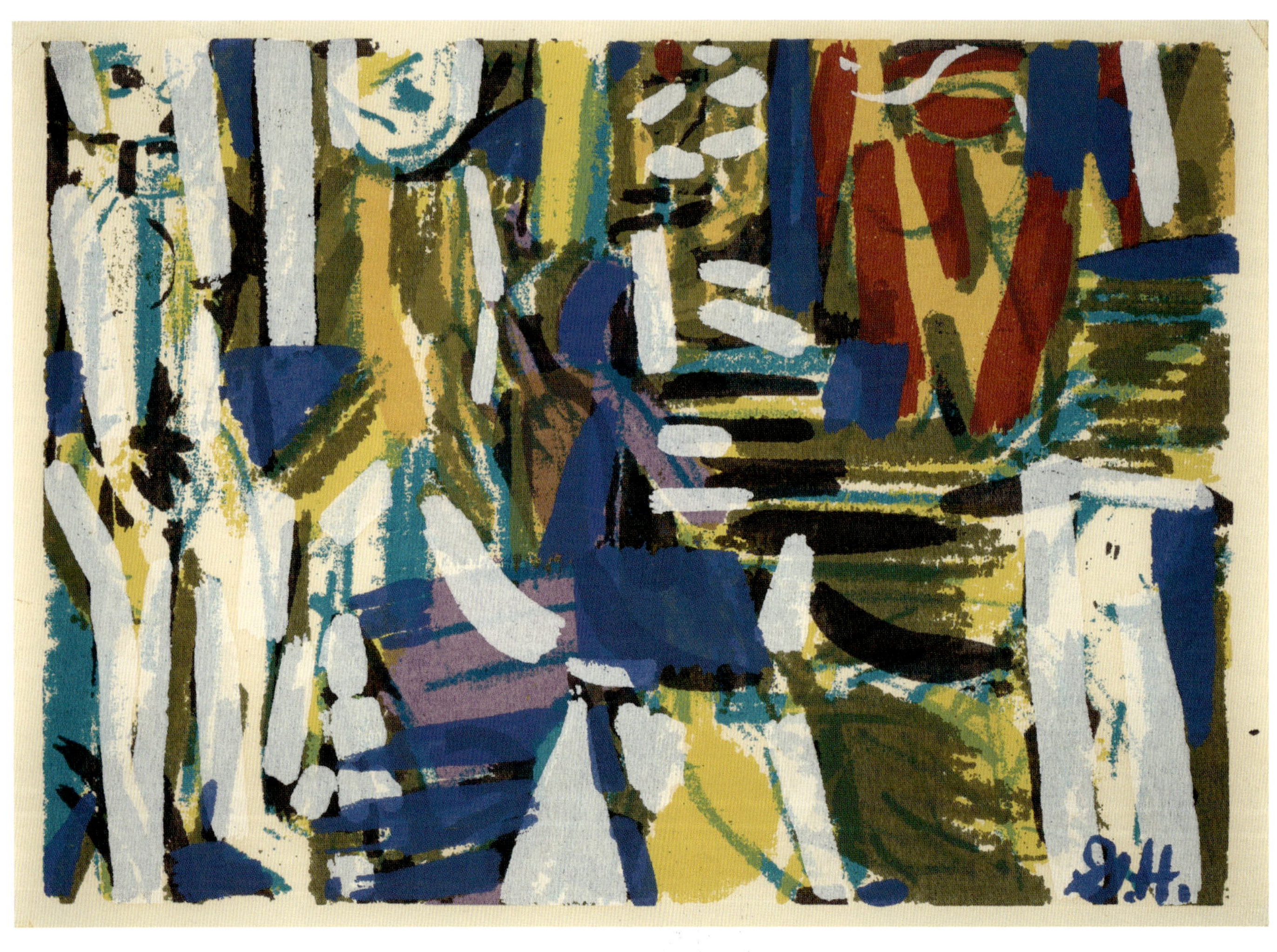

  8 *Pastorale from Folder, no.* 1 1953

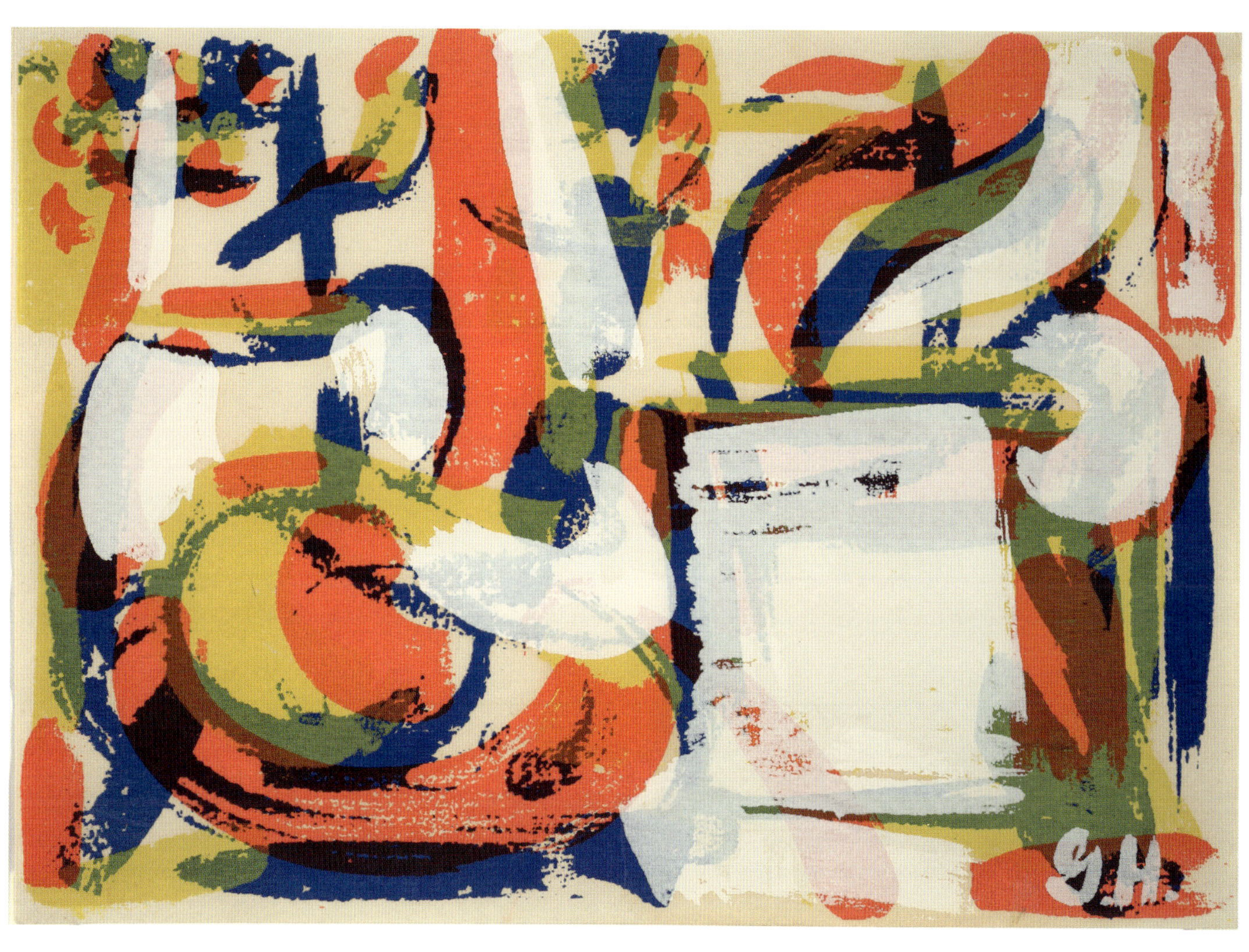

9 *Still Life in Primary Colors from Folder, no. 1* 1953

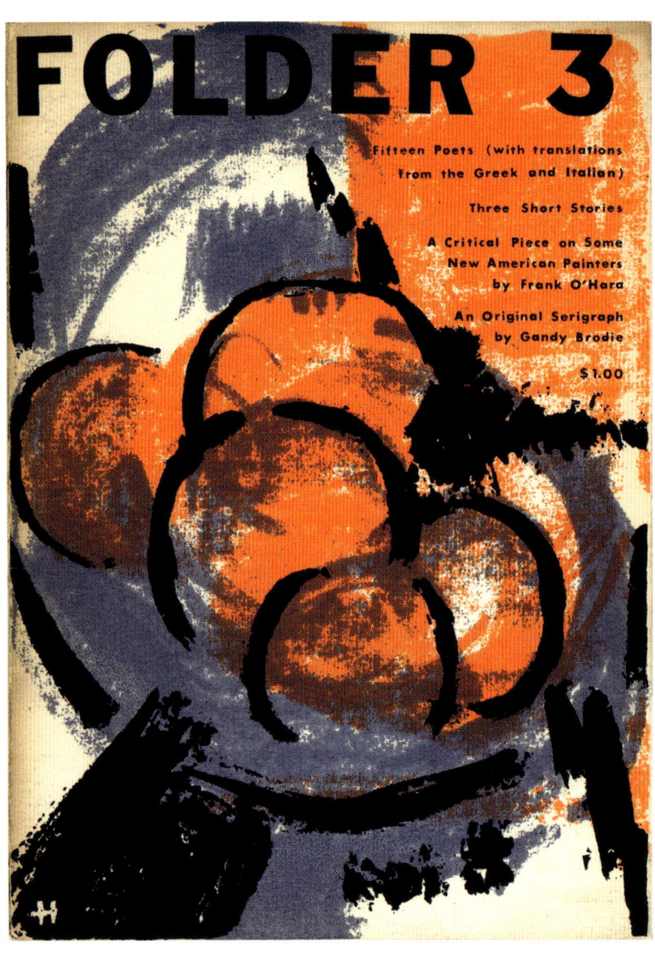

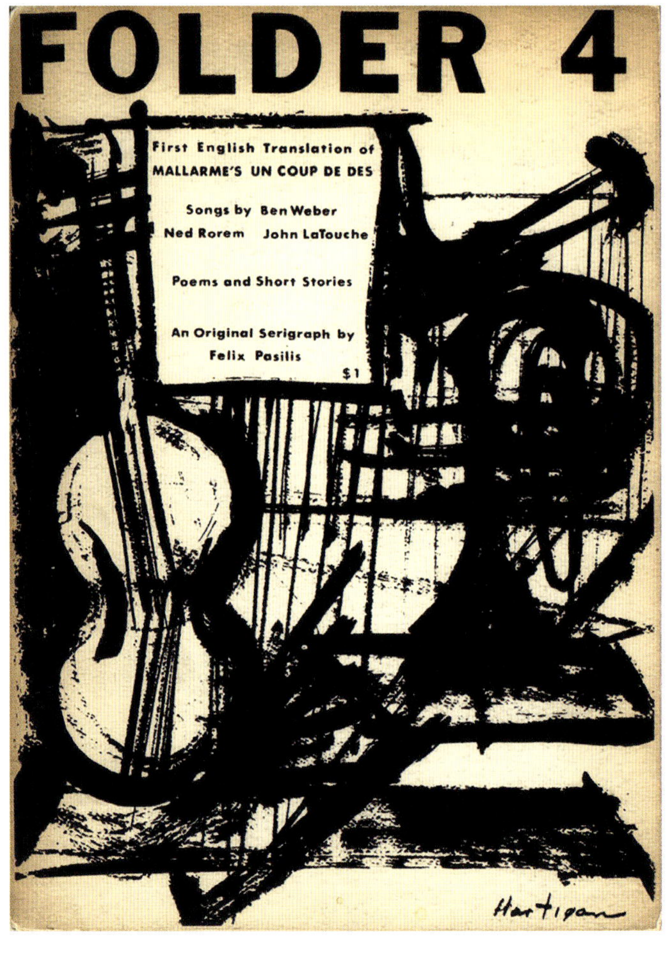

10 *Folder*, nos. 3 and 4 1955–1956, with covers designed by Hartigan

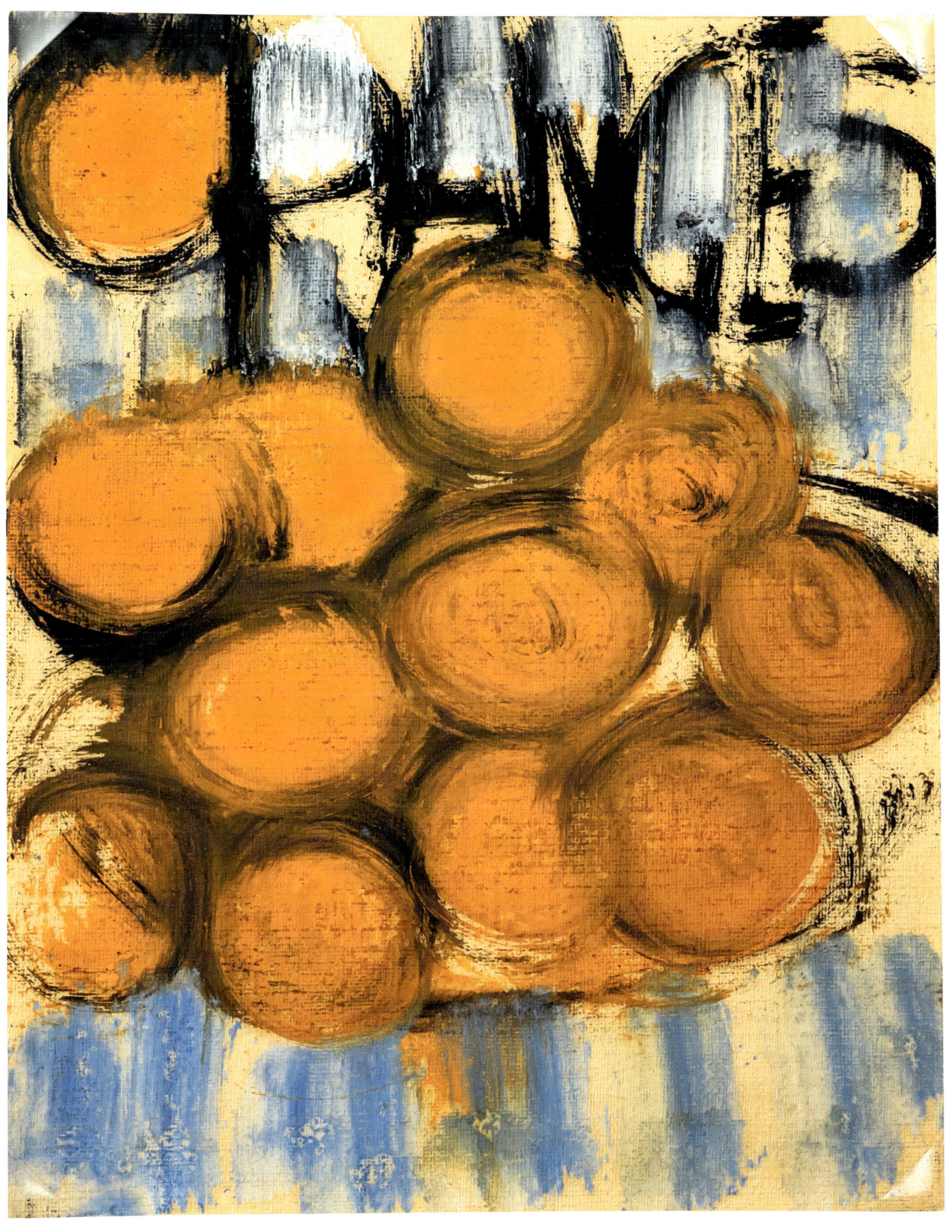

11 Frank O'Hara and Grace Hartigan, *Oranges: 12 Pastorals* 1953

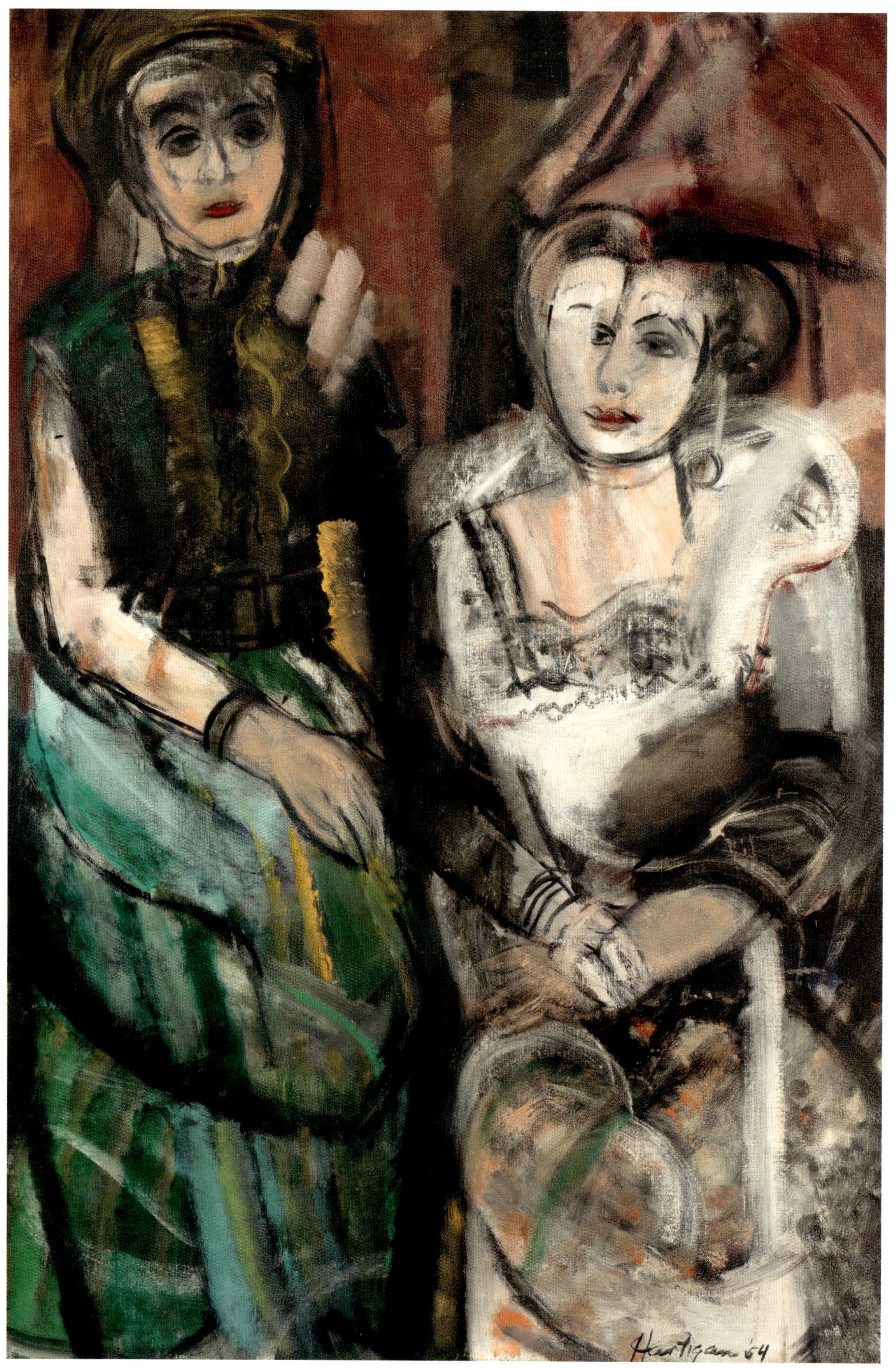

   12 *Two Women* 1954

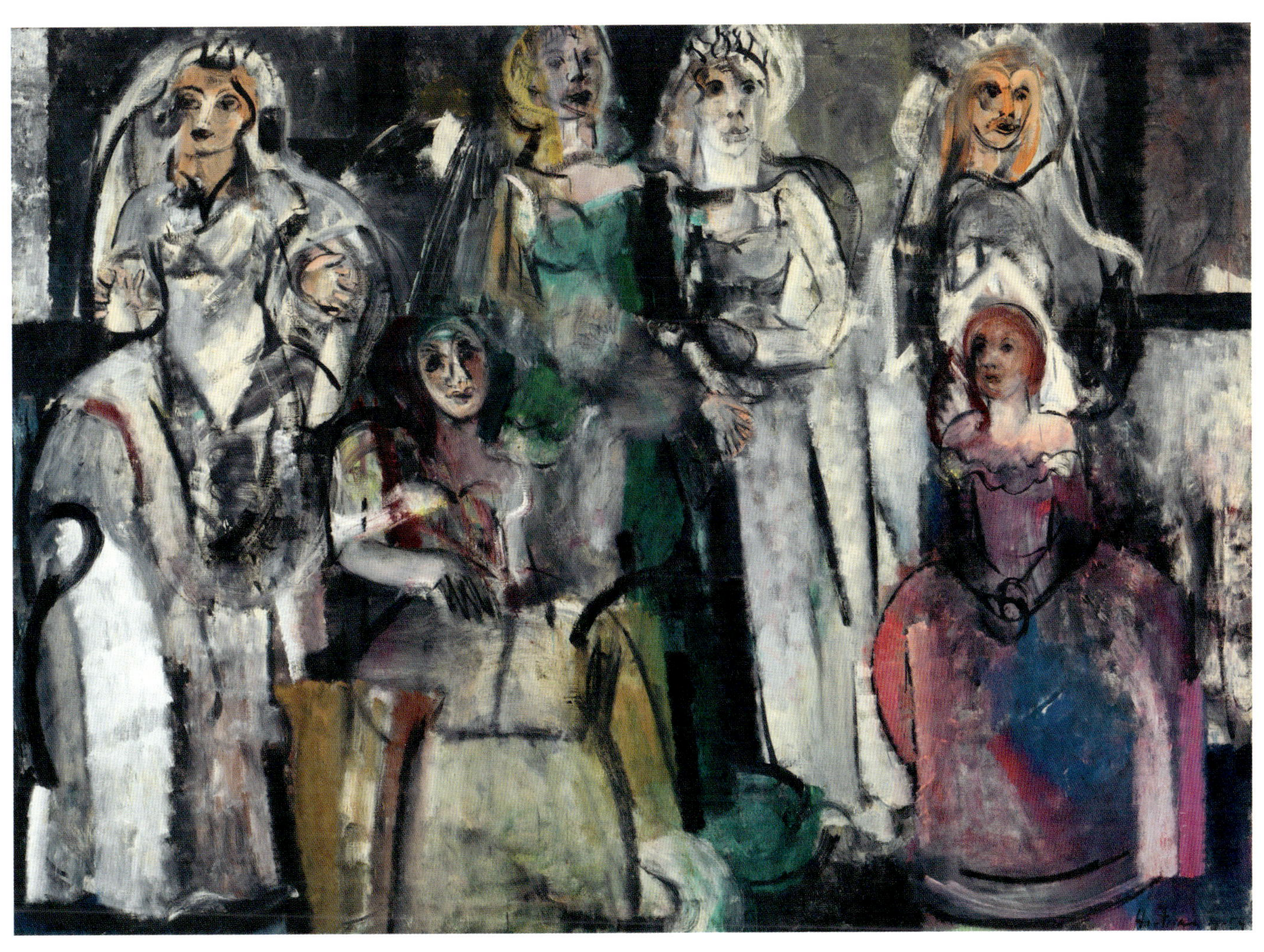

13 *Grand Street Brides* 1954

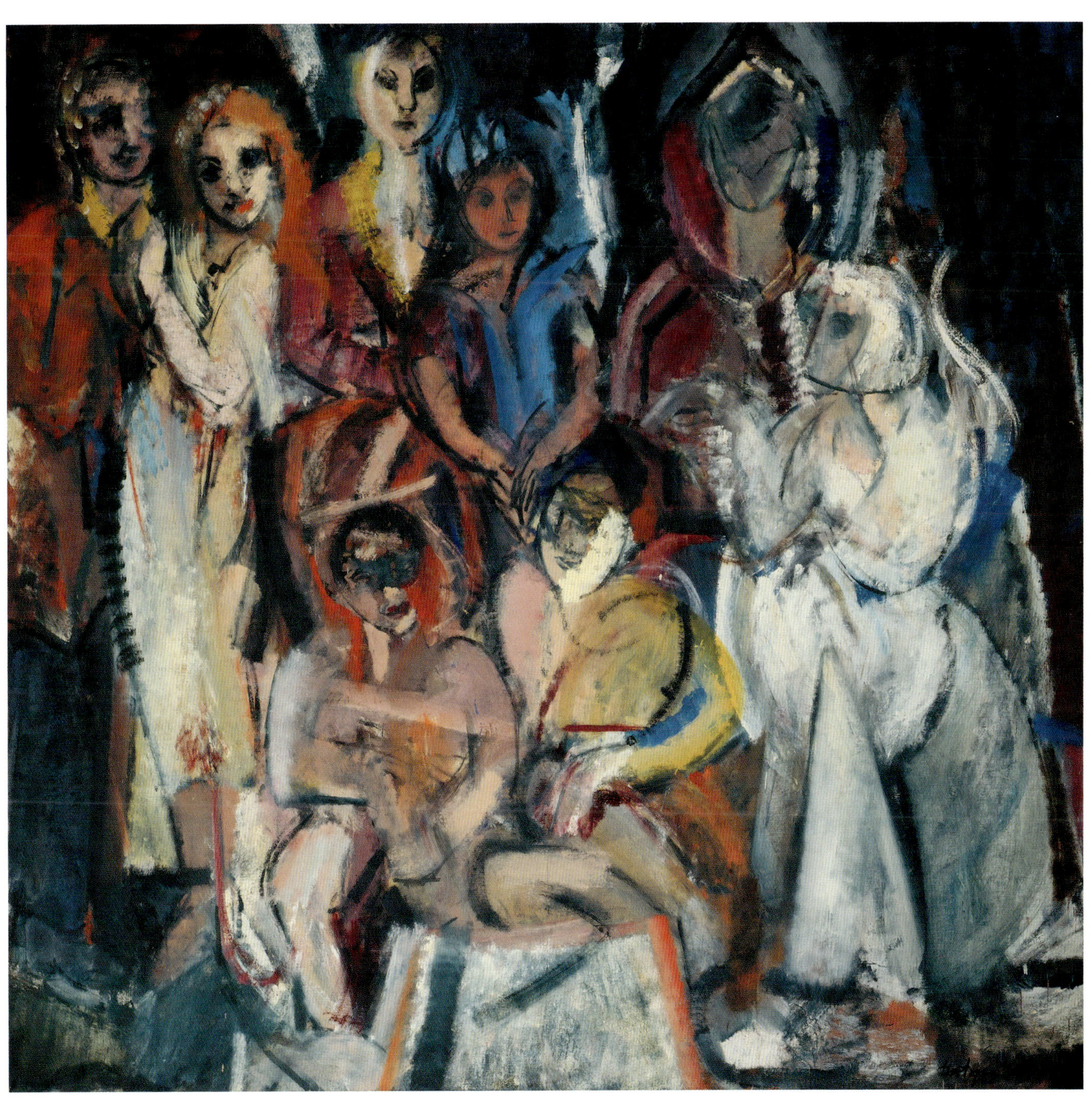

14 Masquerade 1954

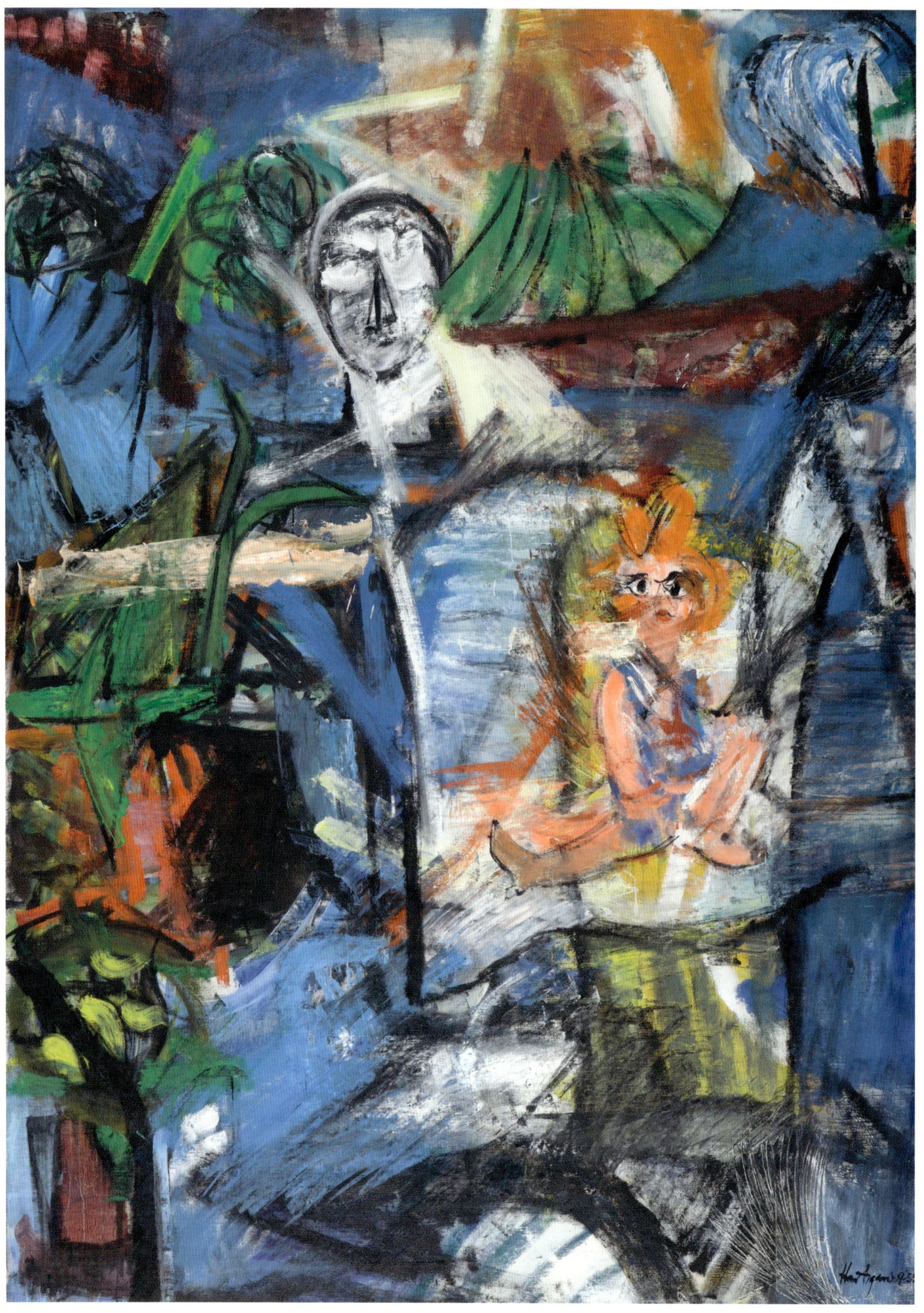

  15 *Interior with Mexican Doll* 1955

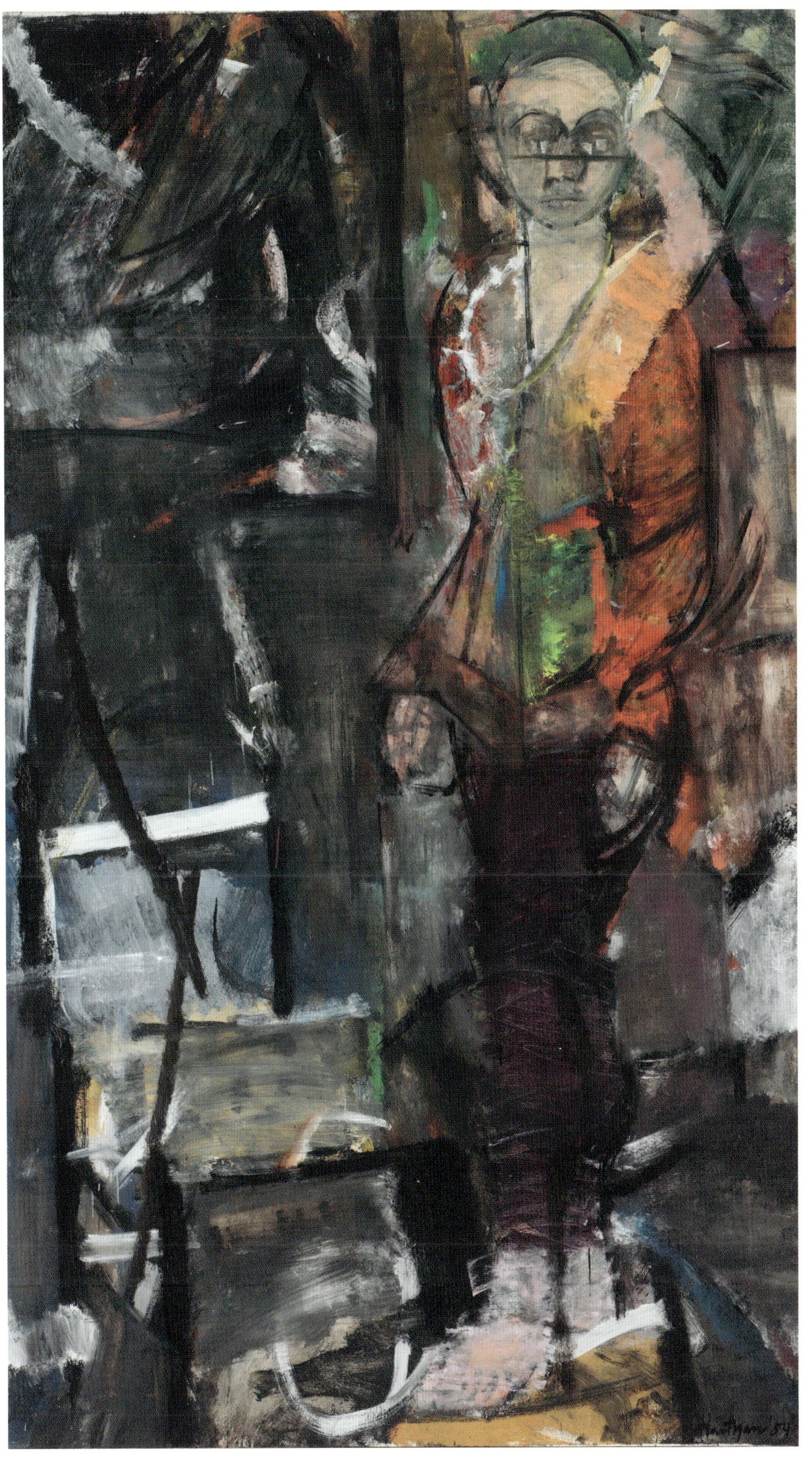

16 *The Masker* 1954

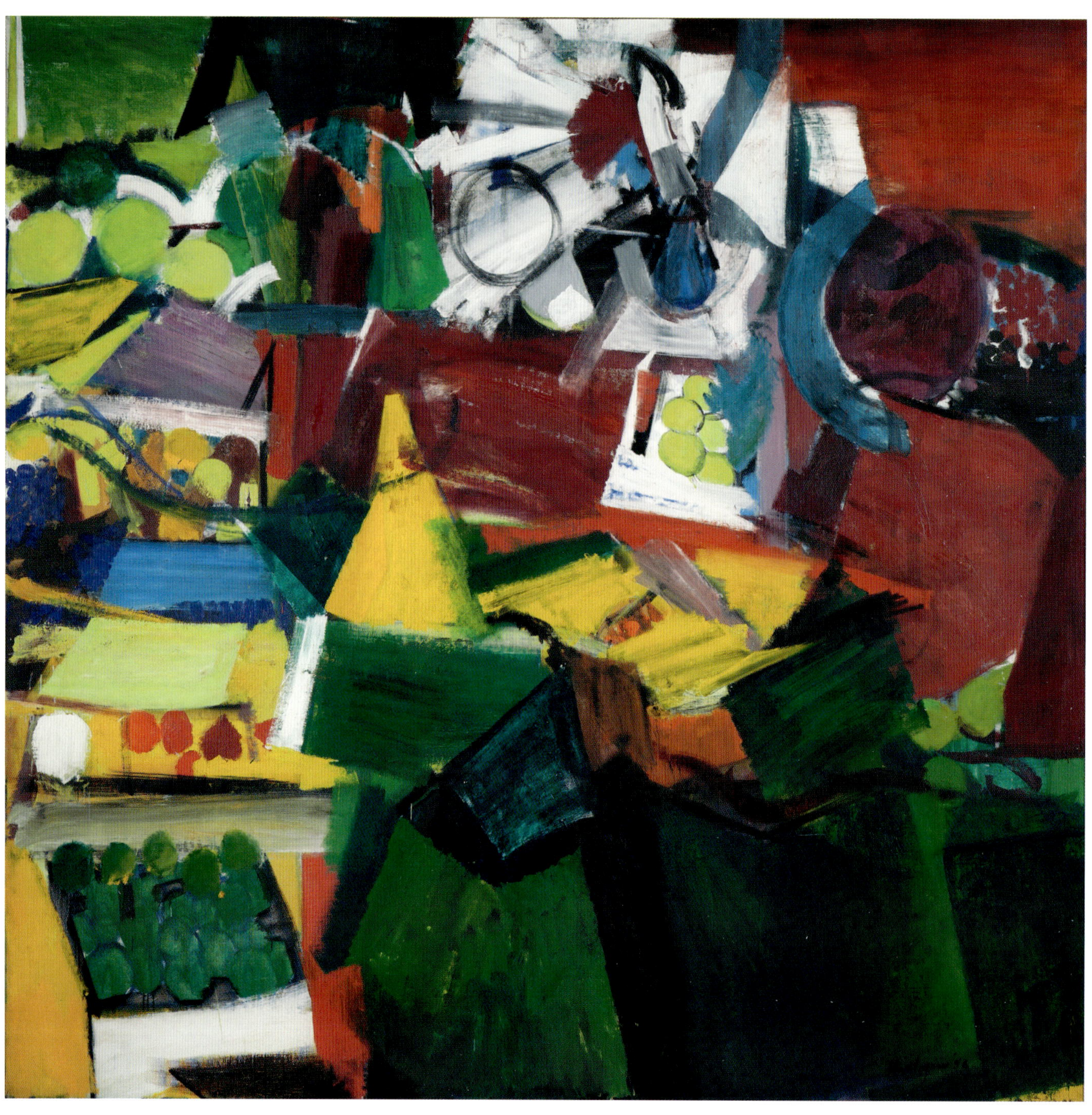

17 *East Side Sunday* 1956

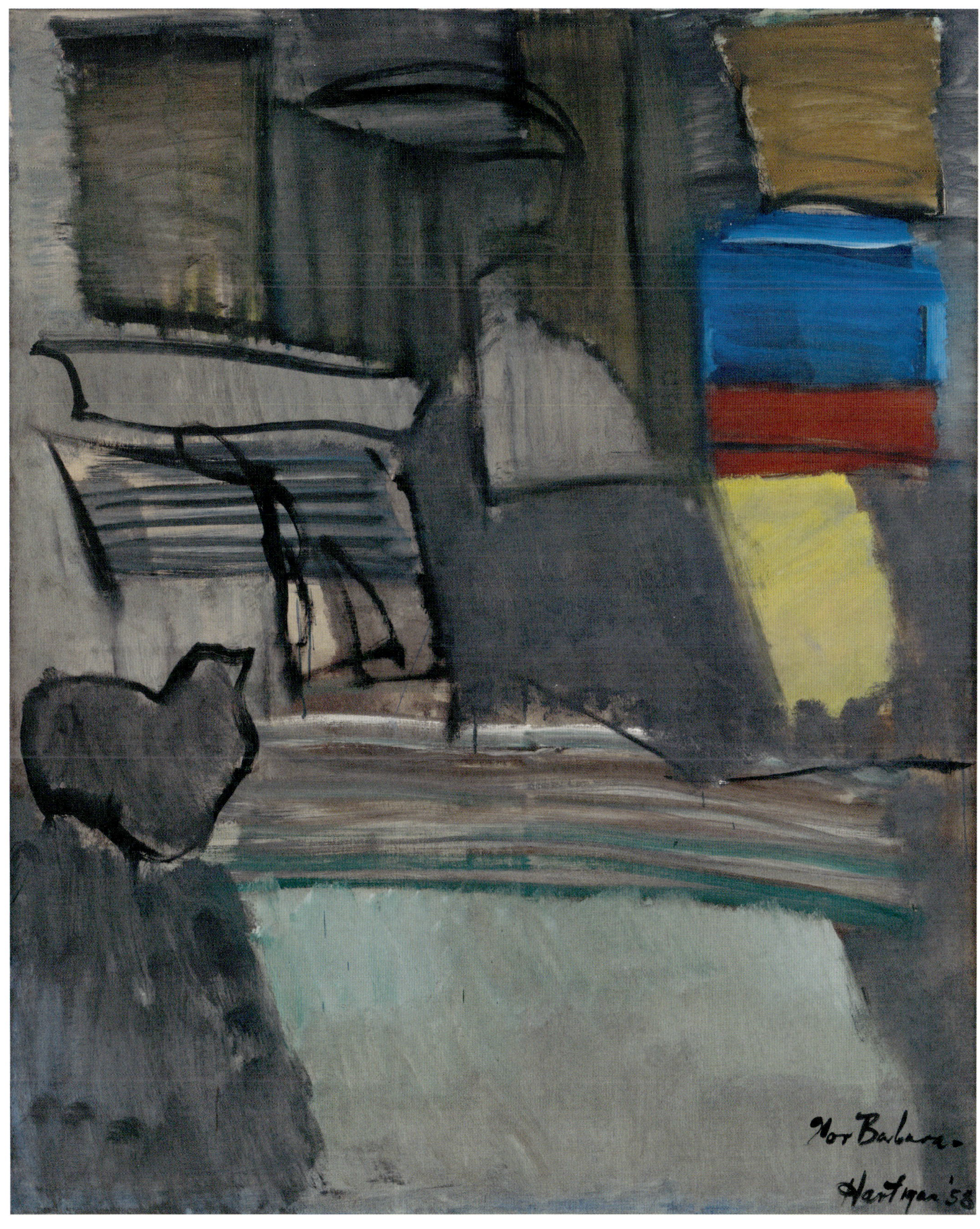

18 *Untitled [or New York]* 1958

James Schuyler, "Reviews and Previews: Grace Hartigan,"
ARTnews, May 1959, 13.

Grace Hartigan [de Nagy; to May 30] last showed in 1957, when the turn her work was taking seemed toward a painstaking and original strength of structure, not mere "tightness," or the exposure of scaffolding, but to retain the generous amplitude that is first nature to her work, and yet make color, edge, line or stroke, enforce their role in free abstract paintings by further significances in relation to each other—and it is not a buckeye matter of "this plus this equals that." The big try was worth it, and these pictures prove it. On Miss Hartigan's first trip to Europe her imagination, and sense of identity, were stirred by Eire: the "Irish" in her, always taken for granted, became conscious and palpable; Dublin was not a city documented to death (perhaps the *Mona Lisa* is invisible). But *Ireland* is called that simply to commemorate what jogged her inspiration. Its color acidities (urban colors, like weathered and brutal boardings, more kinds of brick than there are roses, cheap ready-to-wear drying and fading on clothes-lines) devour an unhidden horizon: it goes left to right, the picture goes complexly all over. *Dublin* forces apart its sooted elements with a rich absorbent blue whose shape is as idiosyncratic as a wharf-divided river. *Bray* (a seedy watering place outside Dublin) achieves its poise between speed and speed: not weight or repose against speed or against themselves—both means are used in other pictures—the speed shown in brush drawing that sometimes counts as line or enclosure and just as often not; it is not unrelated to [Mark] Tobey's "writing" and the alphabet [Bradley Walker] Tomlin invented. Blue flows all through it, unwatery but changeable and bold as a deep clear sky reflected in a harbor surface shattered by traffic and a light wind. The force of Miss Hartigan's newest pictures is not a simple boldness: in *Bray* a chunky stroke of orange, a dash of pink almost lost in the process of creating, are necessities, not decorative stuck-ons. Then there is *Sweden* (which she is not about to visit), probably the strongest picture in the show; *Dun Laoghaire, Guiness,* and about a dozen drawing-collages that make the new spareness explicit: a deceptive spareness, charged with implication—the opposite of [miserliness]. ... Prices unquoted. J. S.

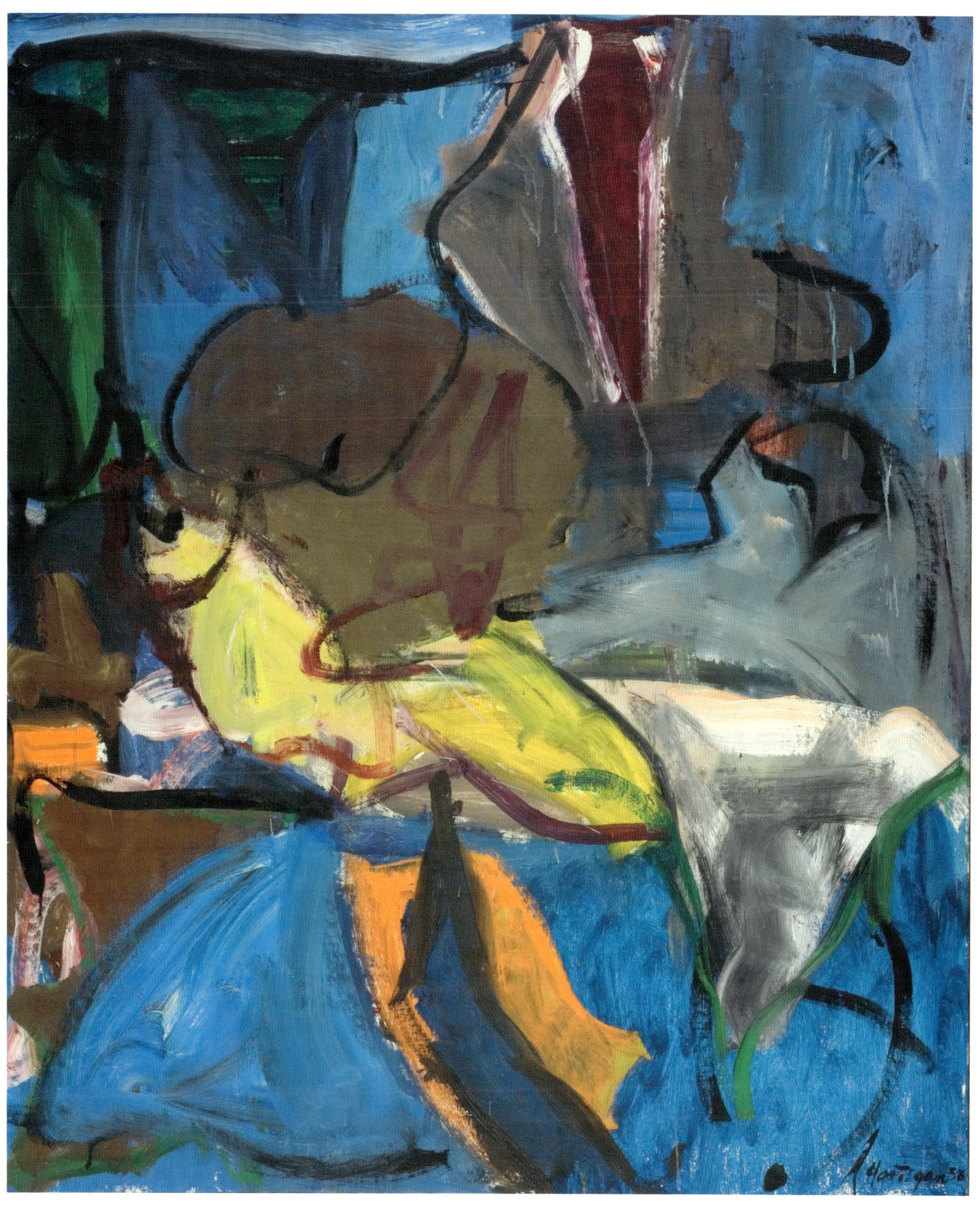

19 Bray 1958   65

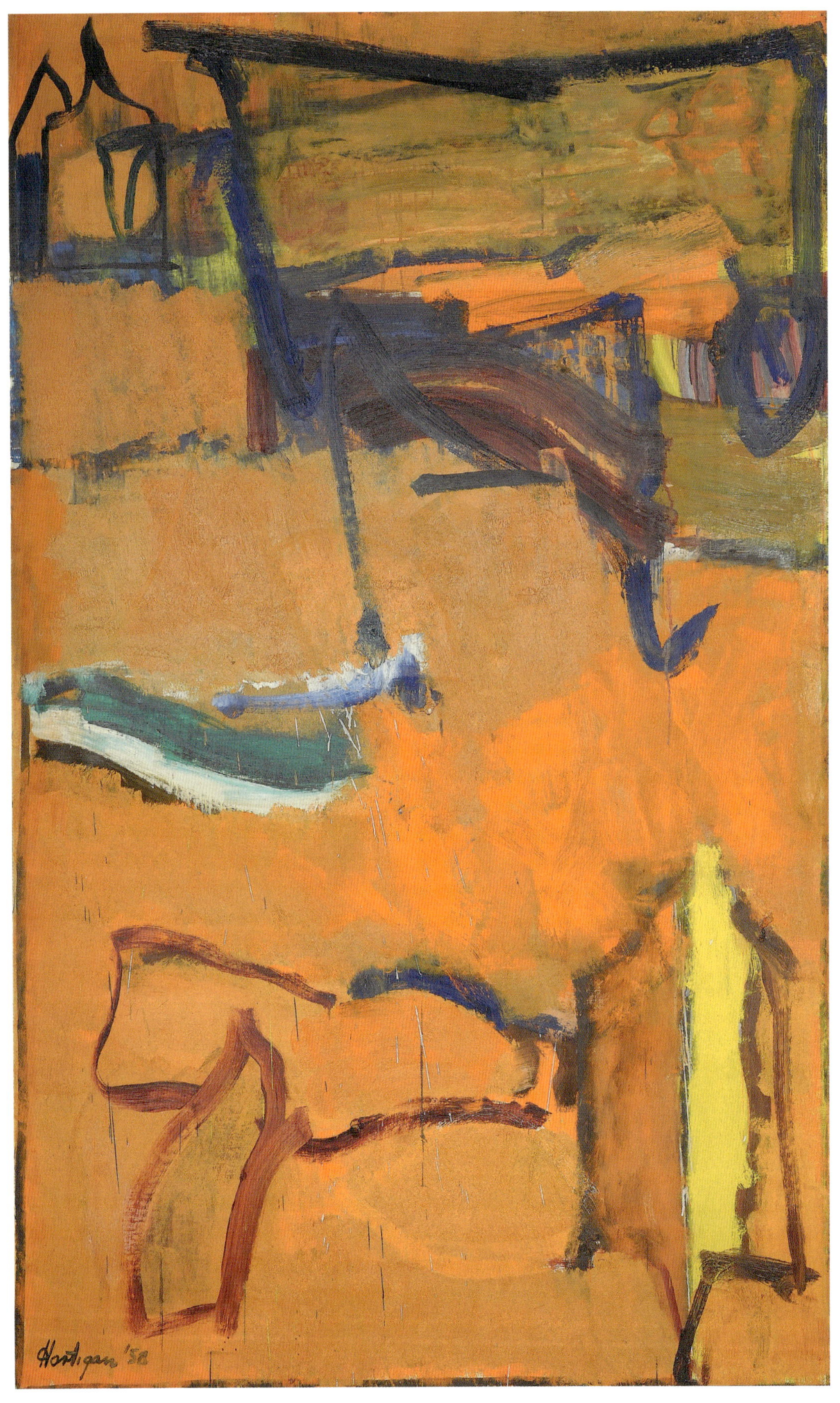

  20 *Orange Field* 1958

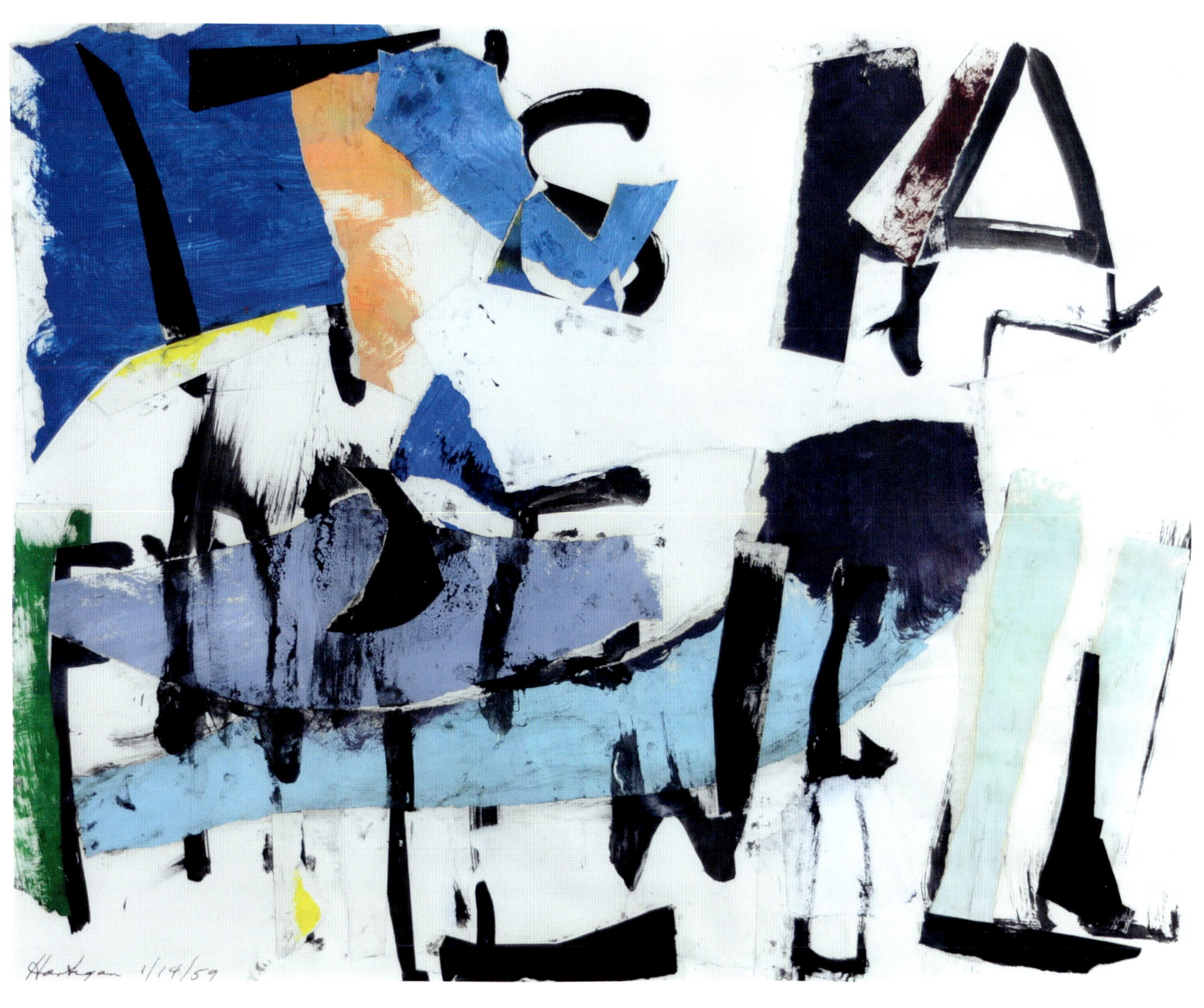

21 *It's a Farewell* 1959

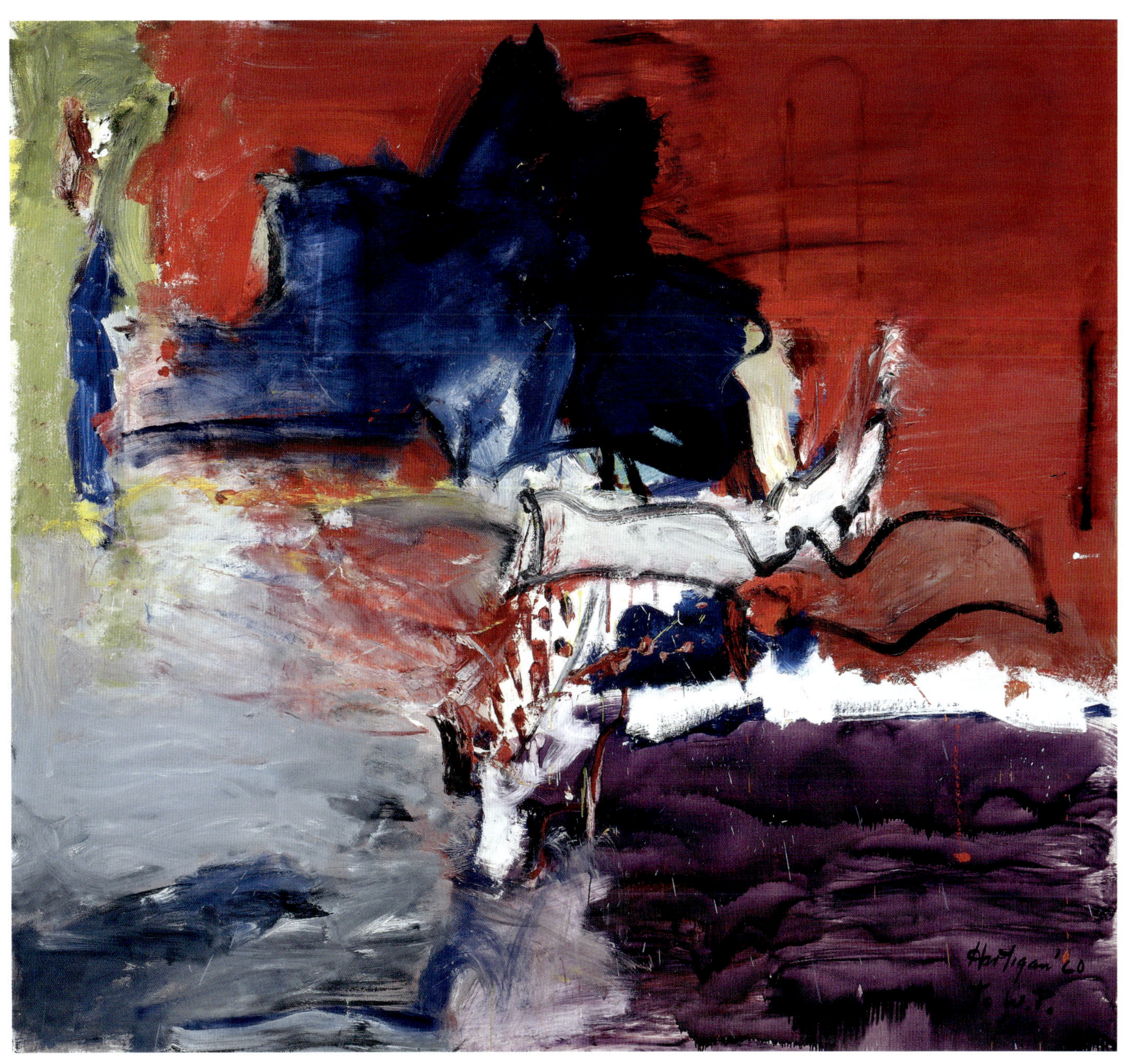

22 *Dido* 1960

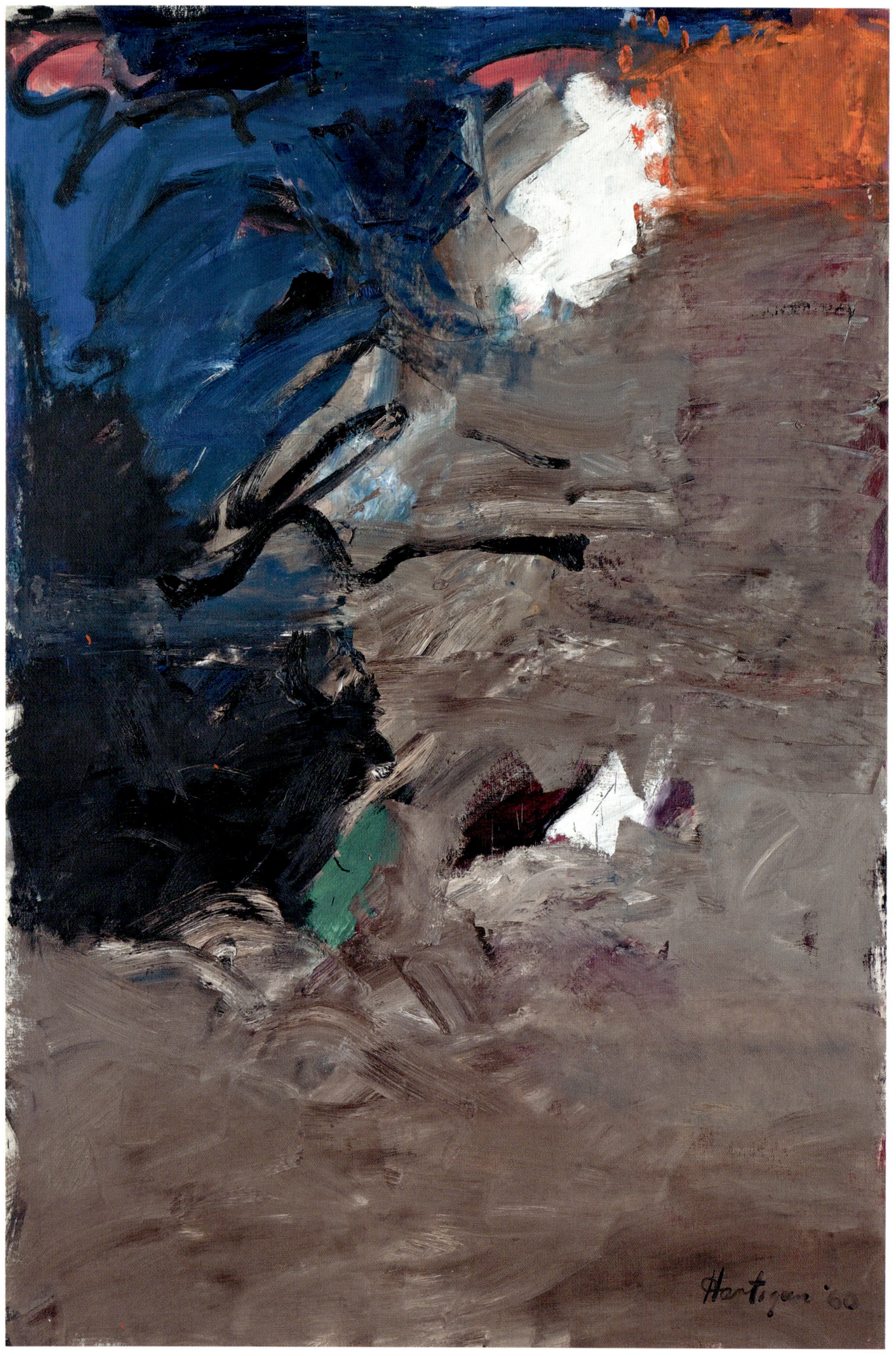

70   **23** *The Hero* 1960

Barbara Guest
THE HERO LEAVES HIS SHIP
from *The Location of Things* (1960)

I wonder if this new reality is going to destroy me.
There under the leaves a loaf
The brick wall on it someone has put bananas
The bricks have come loose under the weight,
What a precarious architecture these apartments,
As giants once in a garden. Dear roots
Your slivers repair my throat when anguish
commences to heat and glow.

    From the water
A roar. The sea has its own strong wrist
The green turf is made of shells
        it is new.

    I am about to use my voice
Why am I afraid that salty wing
Flying over a real hearth will stop me?

    Yesterday the yellow
Tokening clouds. I said "no" to my burden,
The shrub planted on my shoulders. When snow
Falls or in rain, birds gather there
In the short evergreen. They repeat their disastrous
Beckoning songs as if the earth
Were rich and many warriors coming out of it,
As if the calm was blue, one sky over
A shore and the tide welcoming a fleet
Bronzed and strong as breakers,

    Their limbs in this light
Fused of sand and wave are lifted once
Then sunk under aquamarine, the phosphorous.
Afterwards this soundless bay,
Gulls fly over it. The dark is mixed
With wings. I ask if that house is real,
If geese drink at the pond, if the goatherd takes
To the mountain, if the couple love and sup,

    I cross the elemental stations
from windy field to still close. Good night I go to my bed.
This roof will hold me. Outside the gods survive.

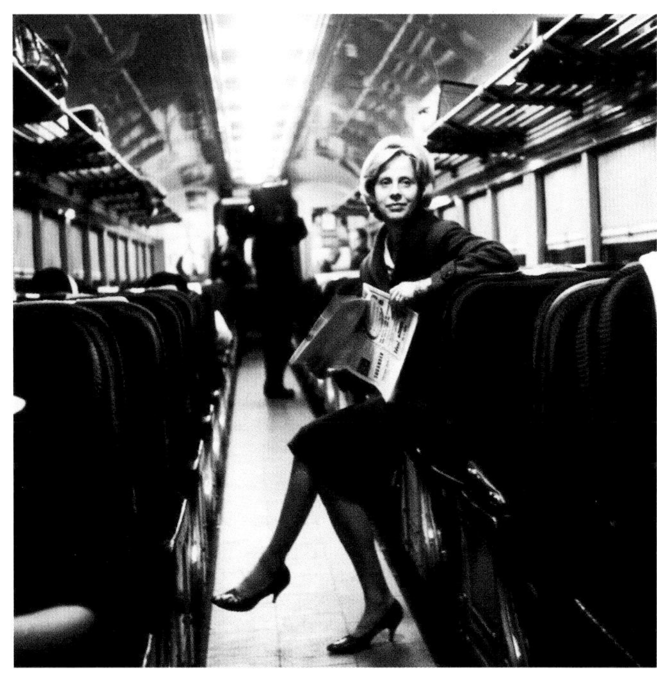

Fig. 31 Fred W. McDarrah, Barbara Guest on a train in Pennsylvania Station, New York, October 16, 1959

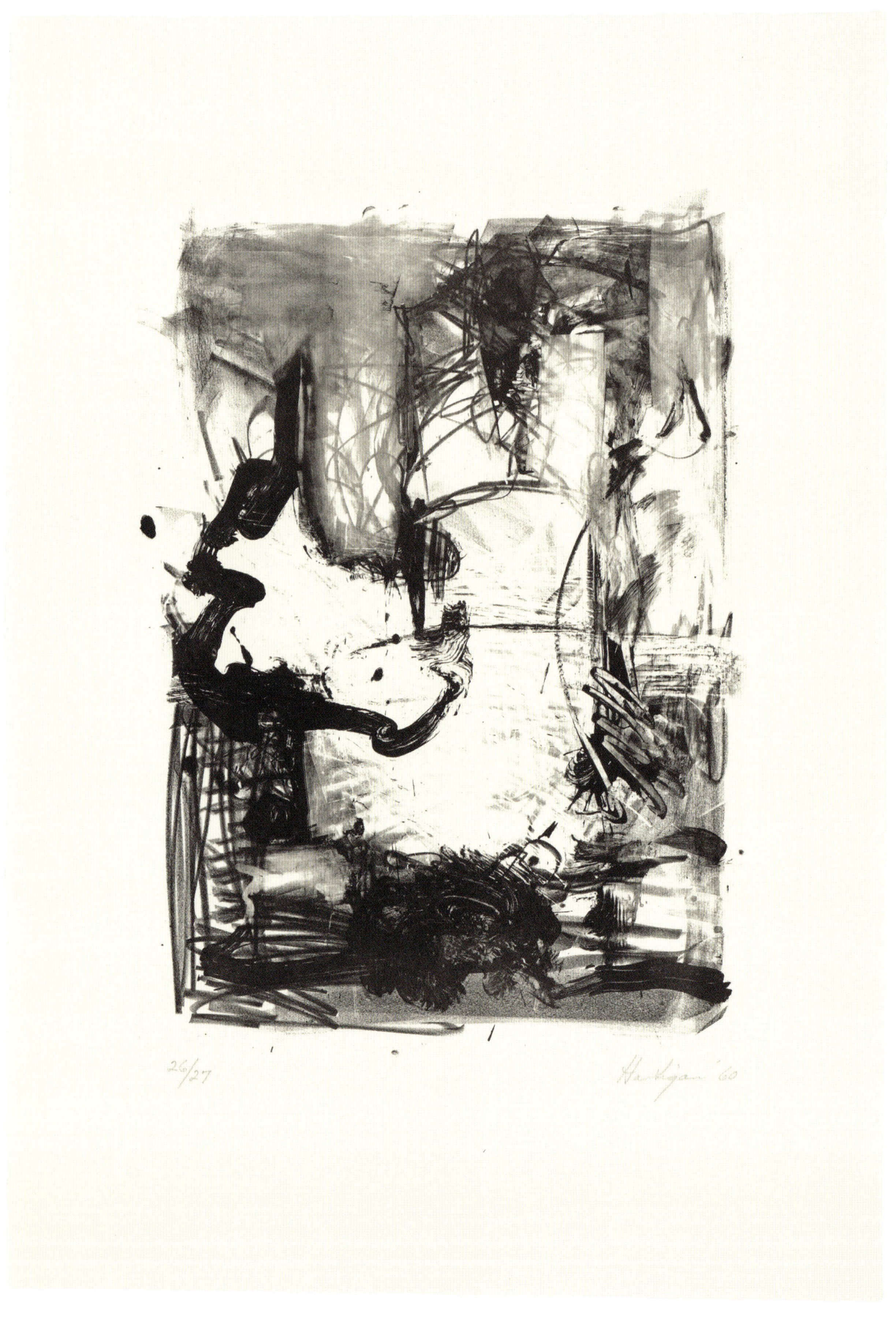

24 *Untitled* from *The Hero Leaves His Ship* 1960

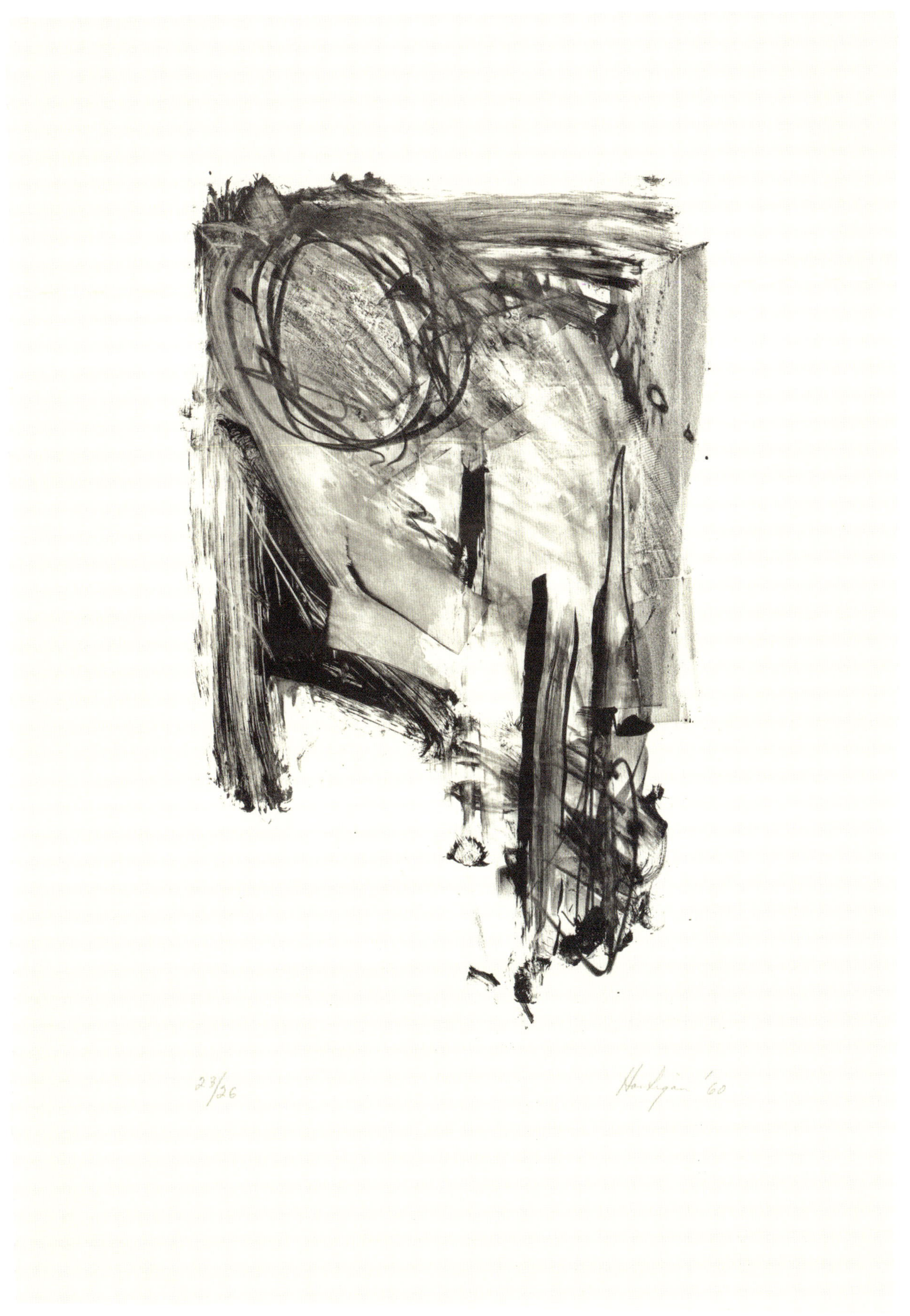

25 *Untitled* from *The Hero Leaves His Ship* 1960

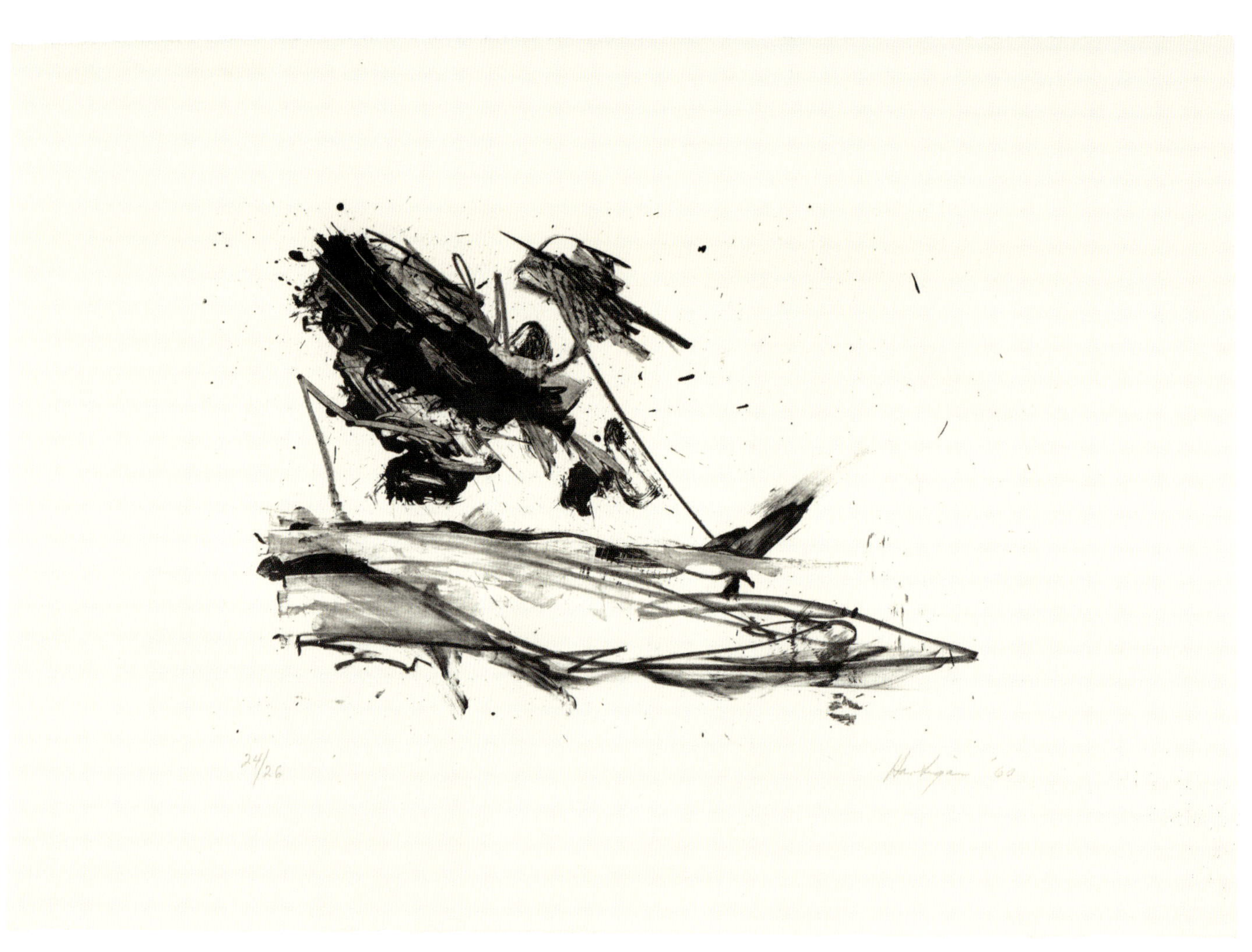

  26 *Untitled from* The Hero Leaves His Ship *1960*

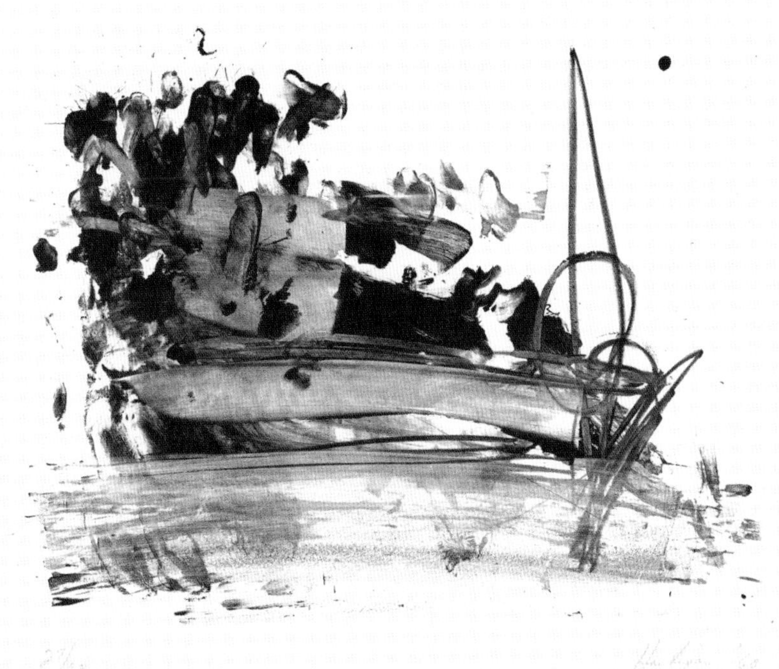

27 *Untitled* from *The Hero Leaves His Ship* 1960

Barbara Guest
SNOW ANGEL
from *The Open Skies* (1962)

                  The storm's threat and ache
Angels are in peril there on the rooftops
Angels are grey
                  Sticks the prancing
sticks to give them shelter it rained and webs
broke wings shrank the branch–bearing river
shook
                  bewildered as a sun
                  Magister who brings
thunder the firs are ready for their burden
underground fires are lit
                  in the dark sits
the first Angel of snow
                  tomorrow in the outraged
sky
                  his form

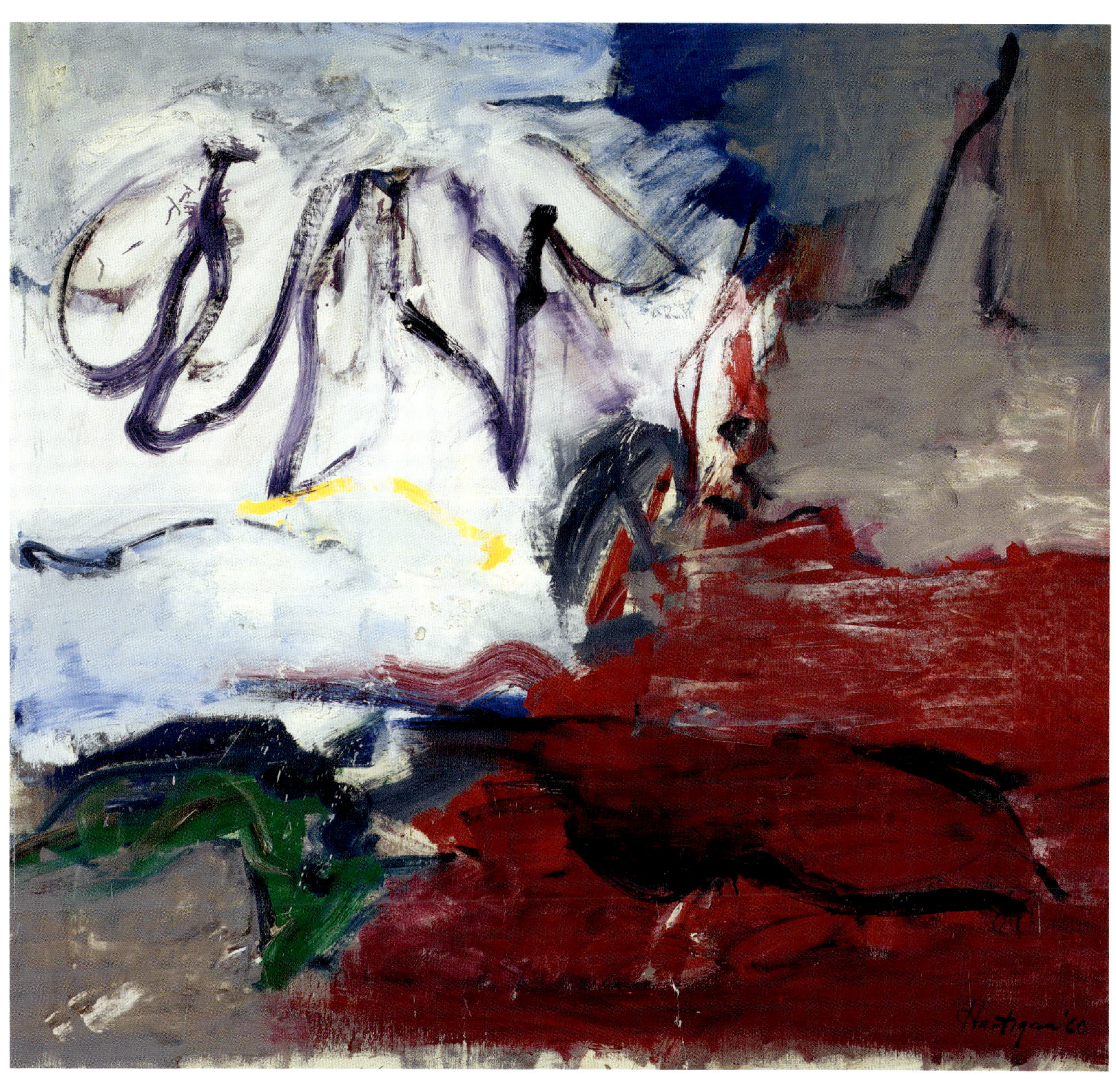

28 *Snow Angel* 1960

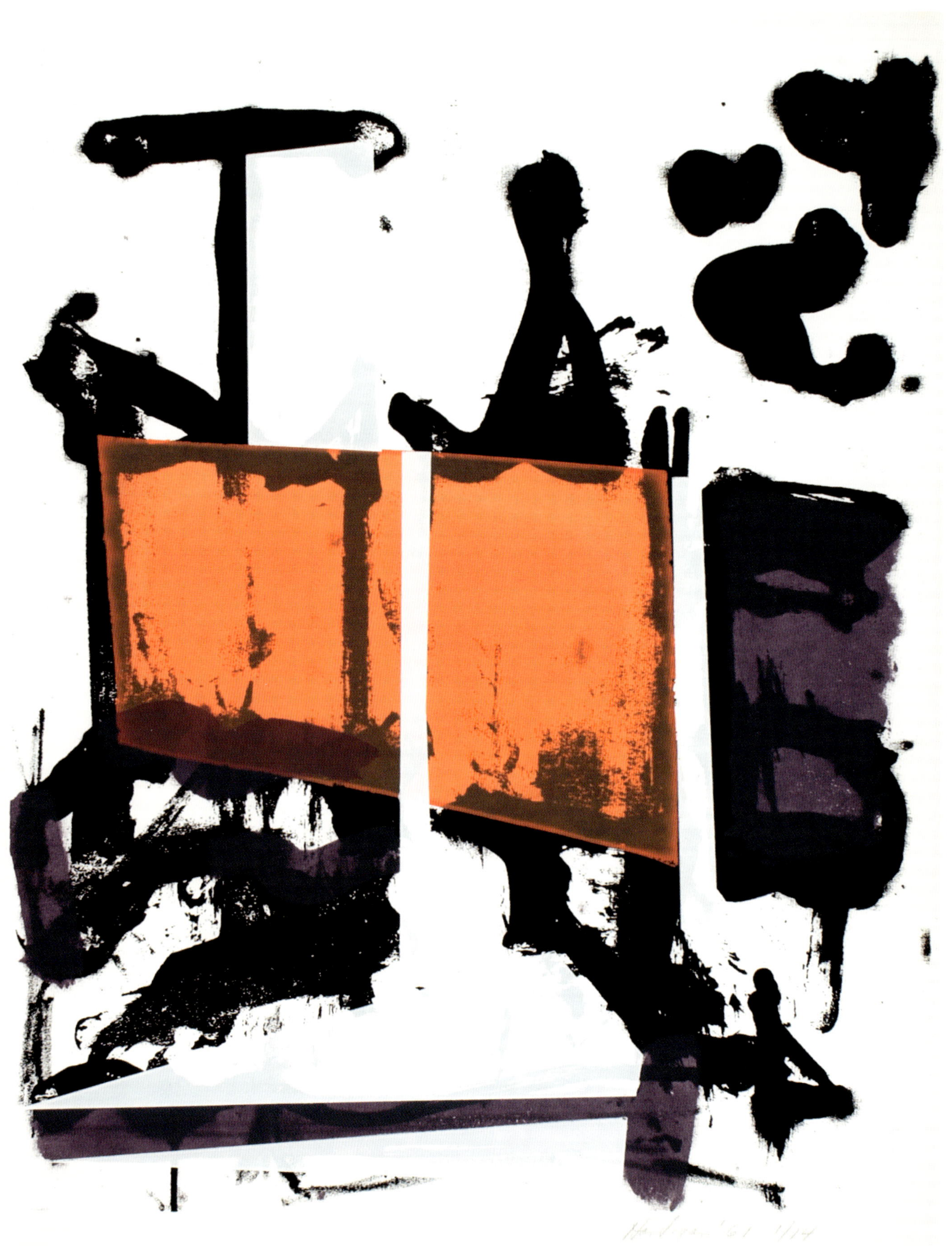

  29 *The Canal to the Sky* 1960, printed 1961

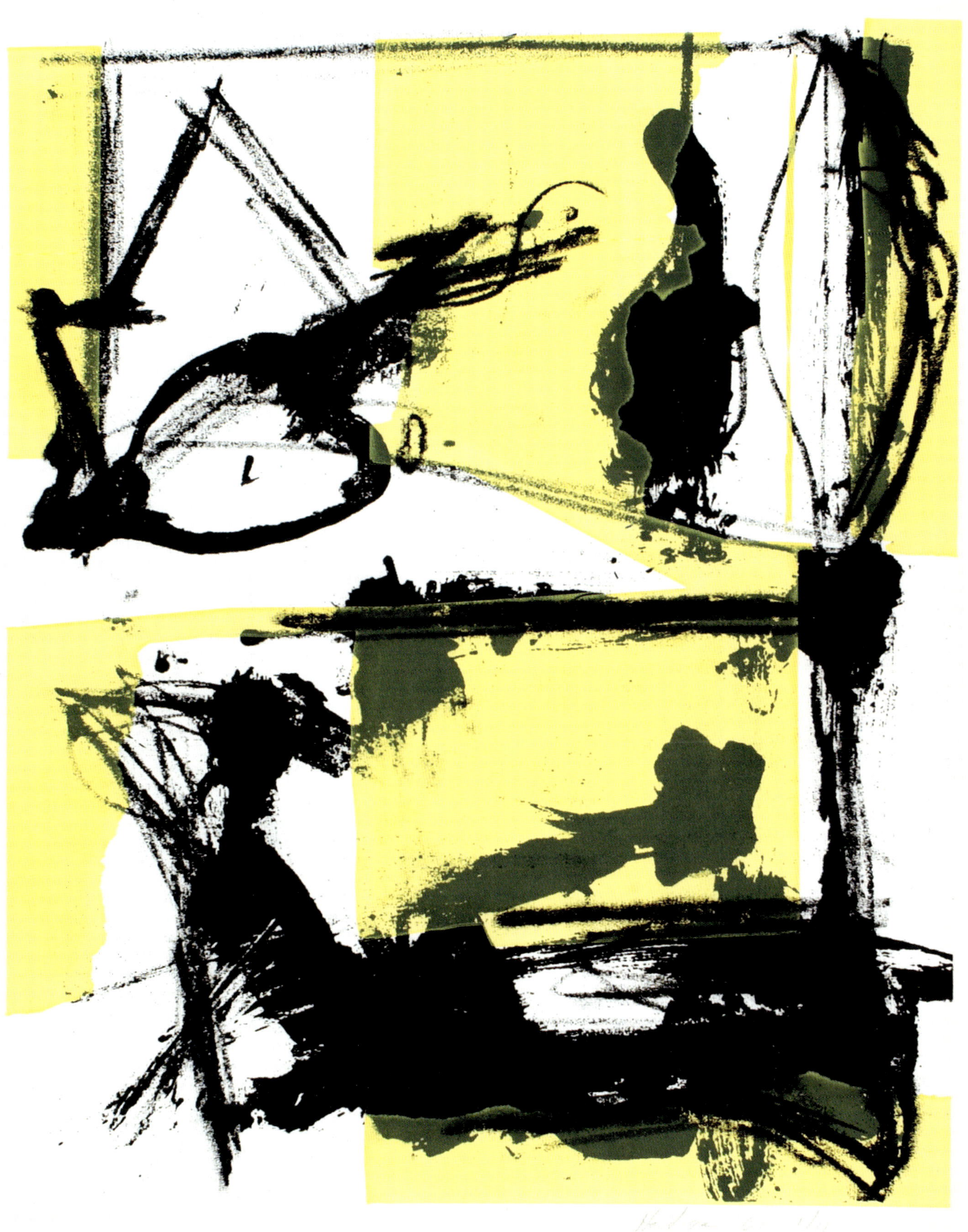

30 *This So-Called Angel* 1960, printed 1961

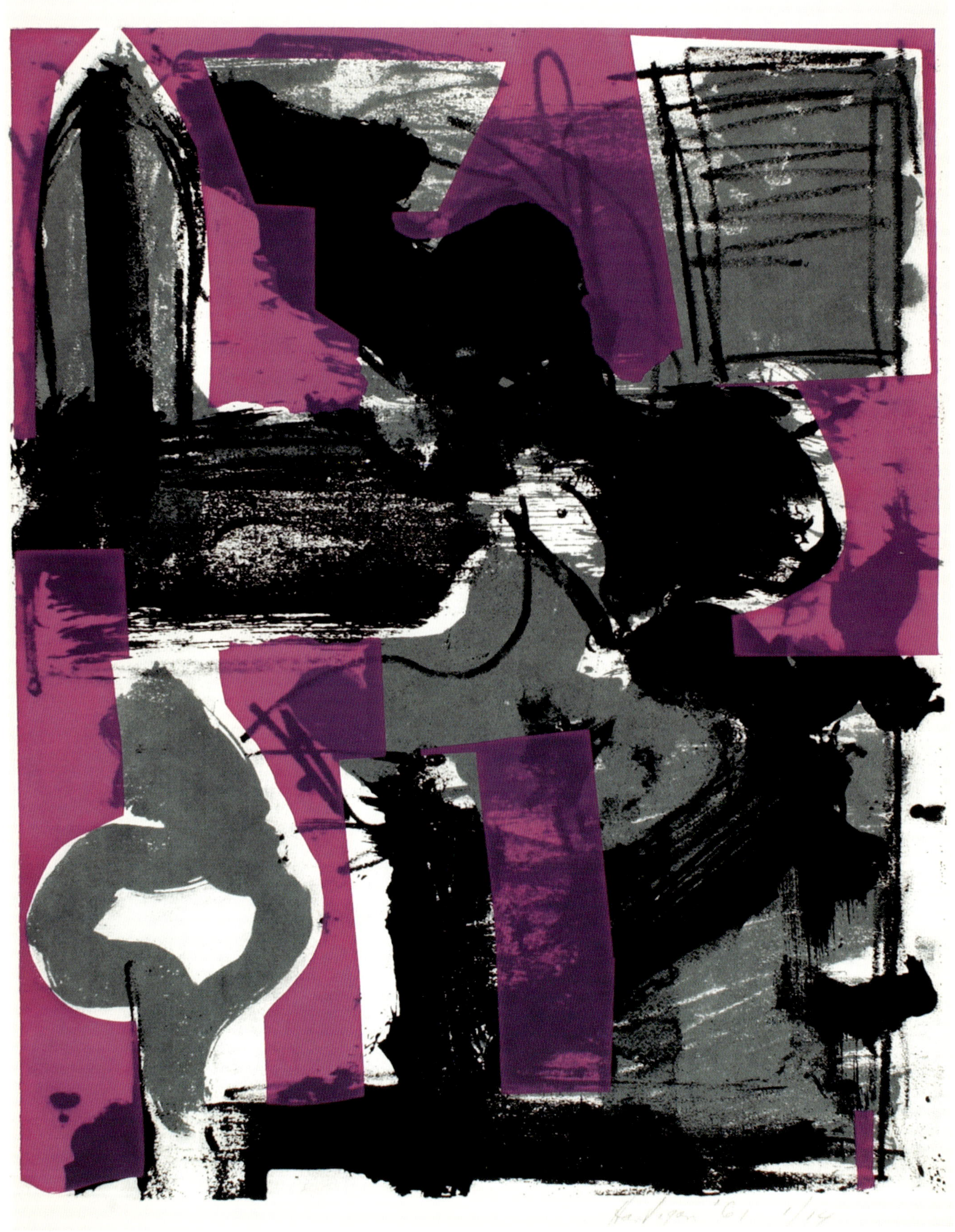

 31 *On a Tar Roof* 1960, printed 1961

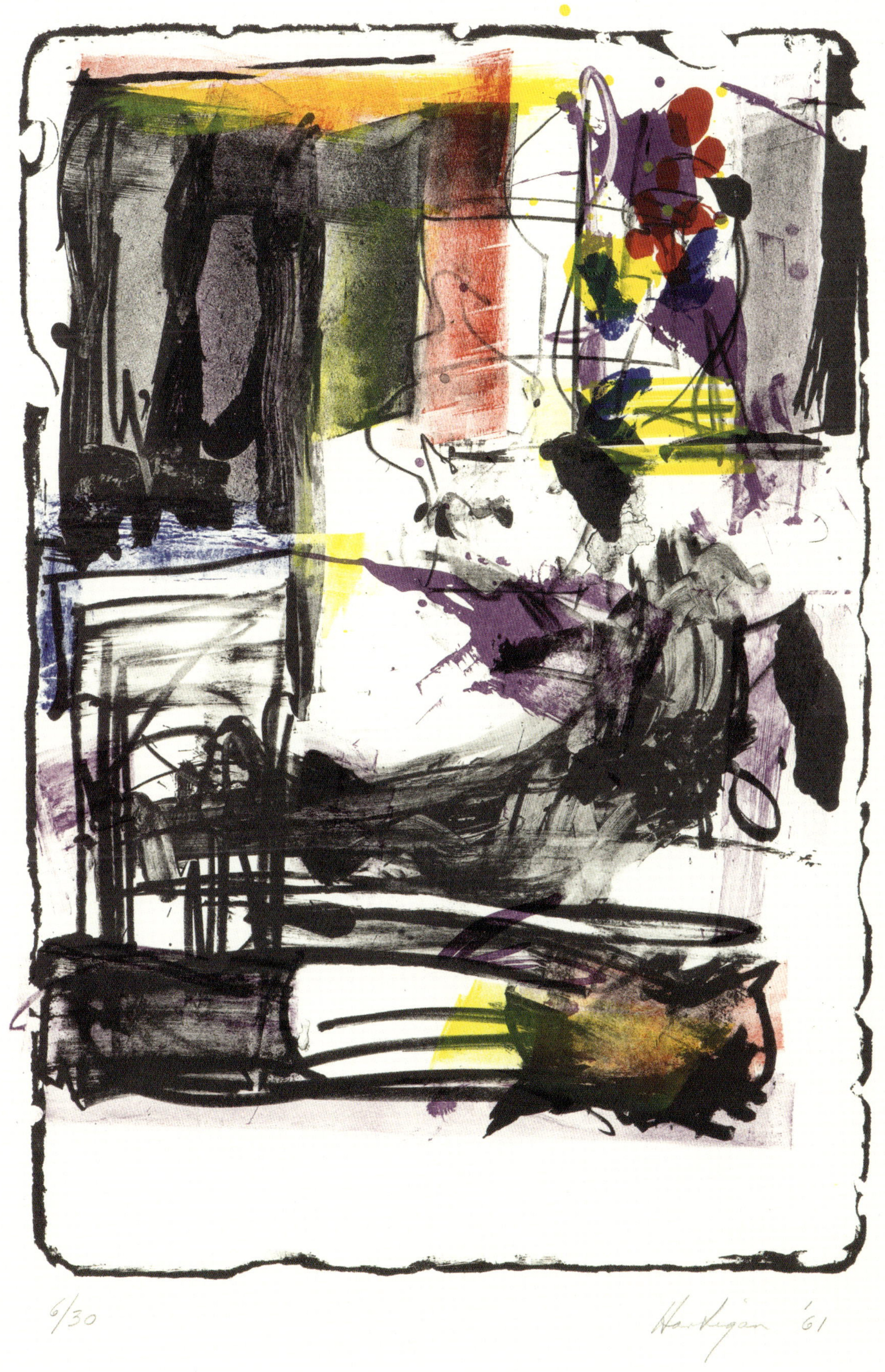

32 *Untitled (Pallas-Athene)* 1961

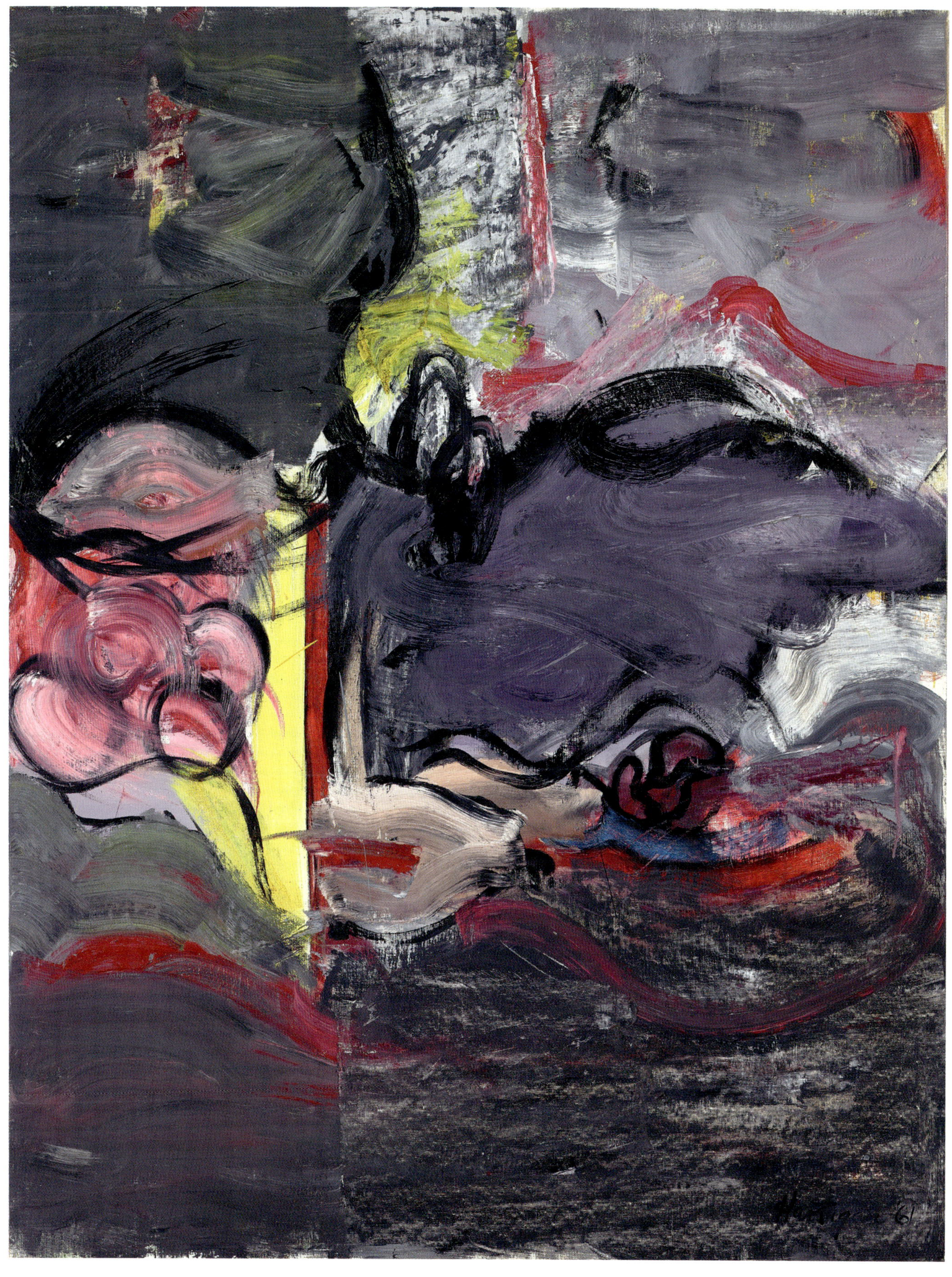

33 *Grey-Eyed Athena* 1961

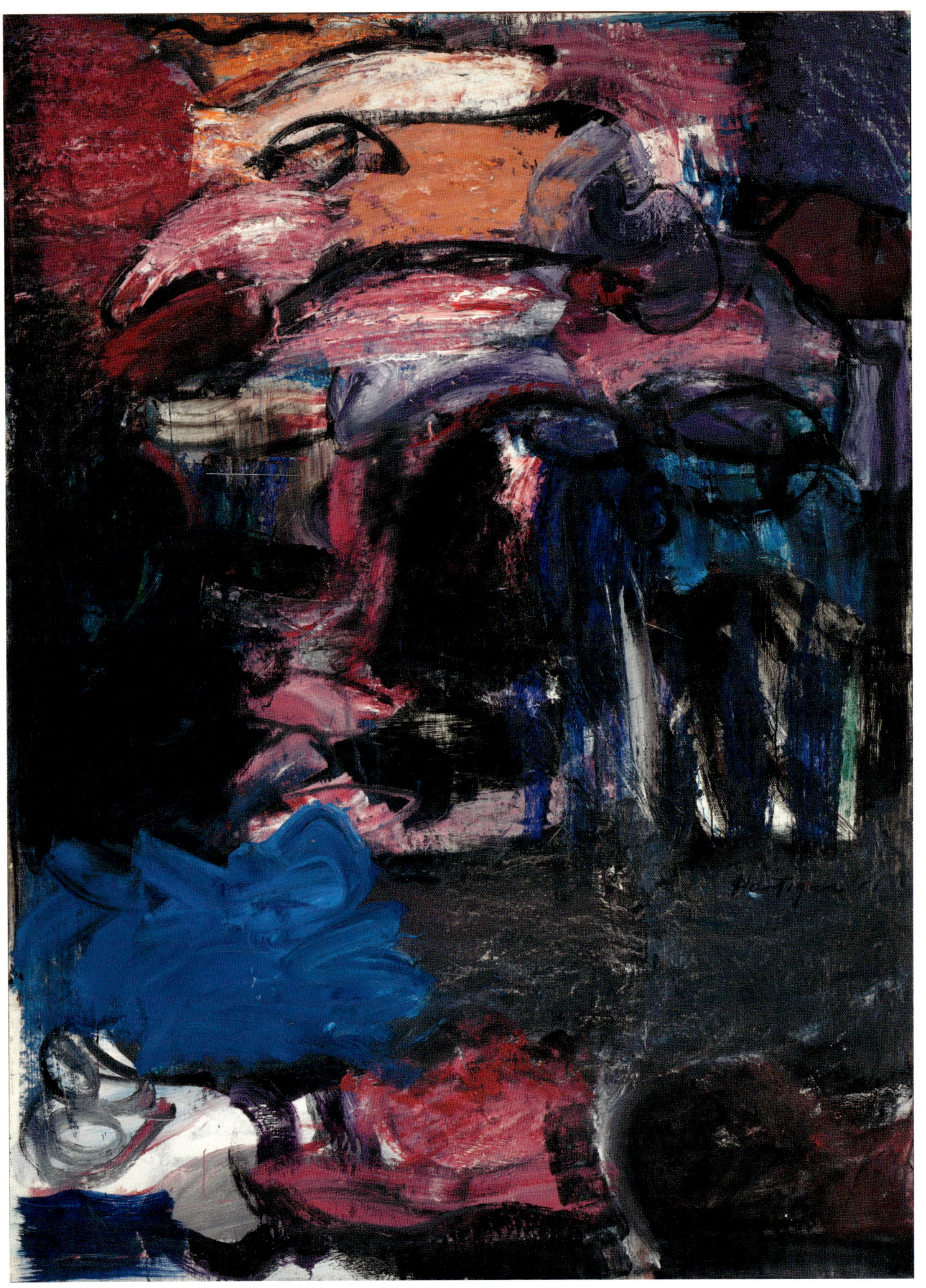

   34 *Pallas Athena—Fire* 1961

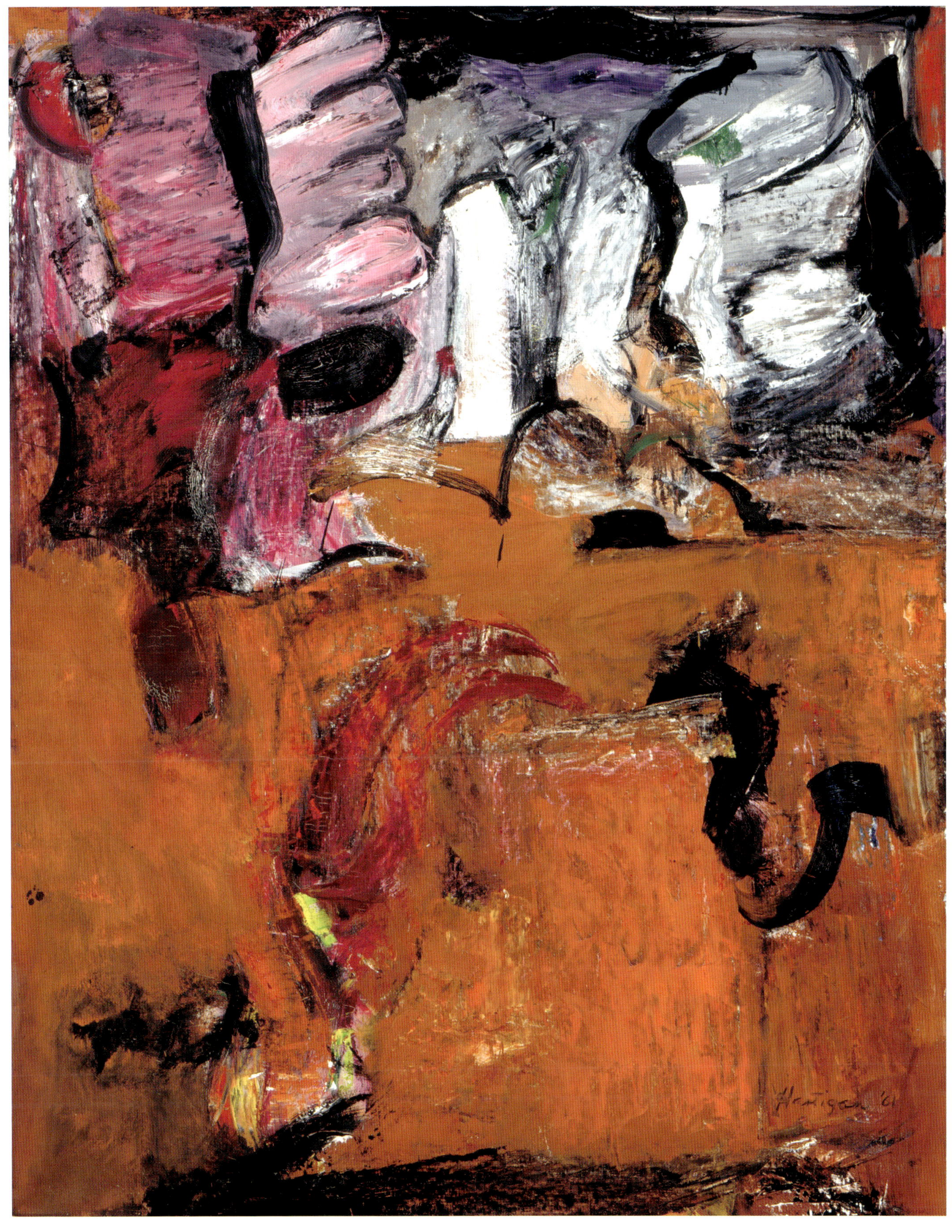

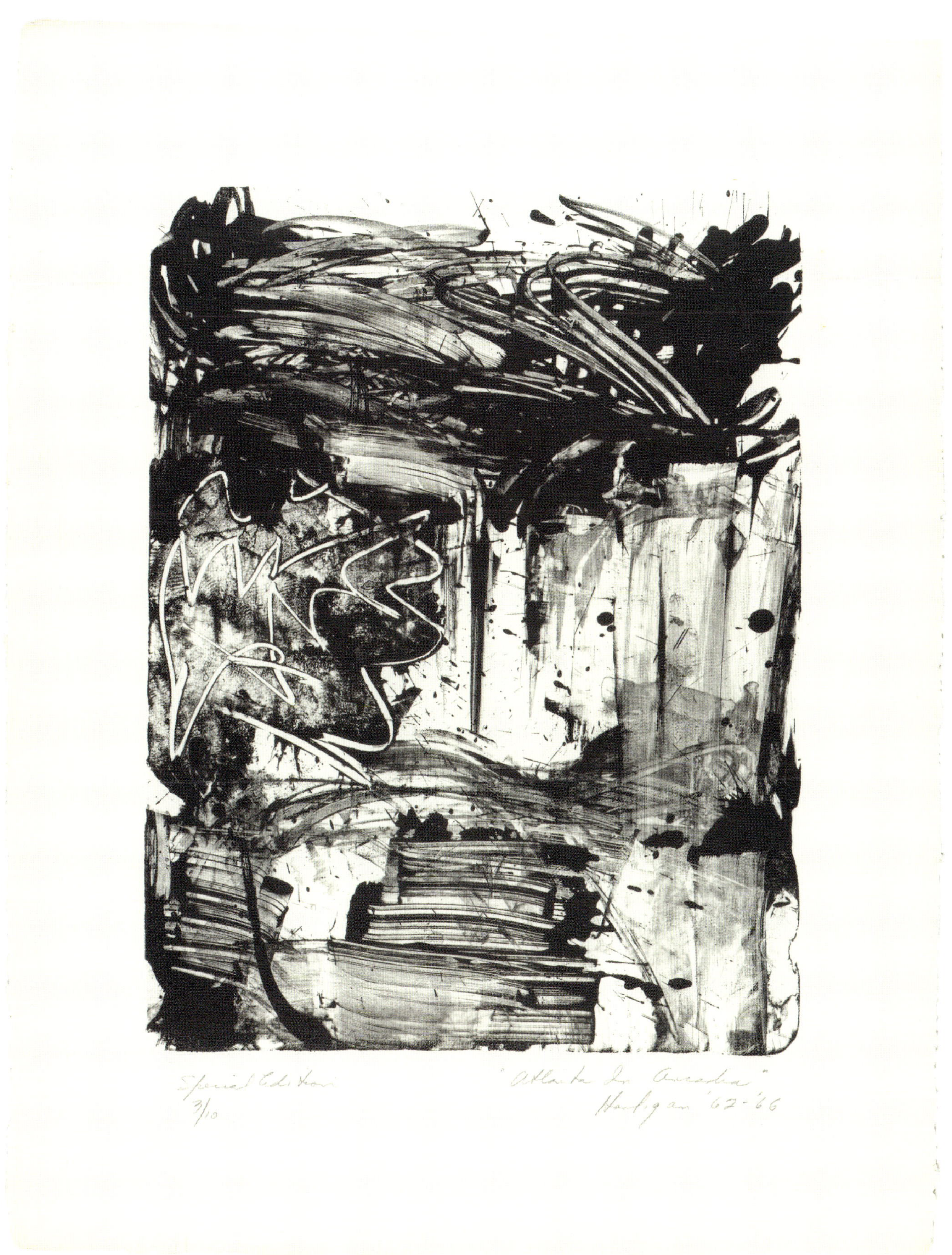

36 *Atlanta in Arcadia* from *The Archaics* 1962–1966

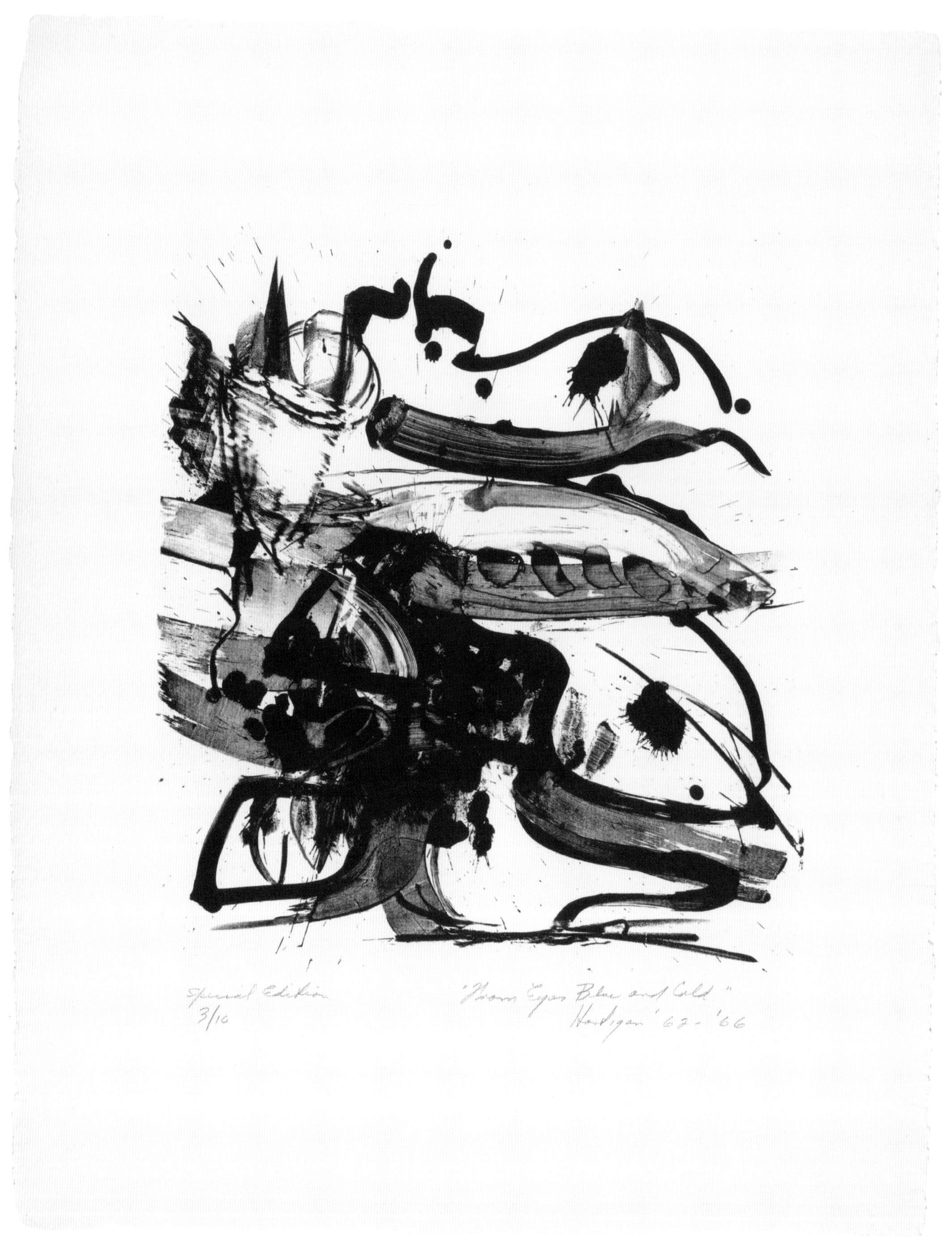

  37 From Eyes Blue and Cold from *The Archaics* 1962–1966

From eyes blue and cold
the nymphs drink
           your snow

Olympus

          There on watchful
heights dawn prepares her lesson
as the groves thicken with
one's first song

          See now its wing arch
over the valley and the brisk foot
of the satyr no longer limping

From eyes blue and cold
out of the abandoning water
          another goddess

Again Olympus
from your delicate forgeries
          a naïve daybreak

Hoof, reed, horn
will bring to the sandy river
a far-off coastal lithesomeness
          when she awakes
with seaweed in her arms
from eyes blue and cold
          shares that beauty

Barbara Guest
DIDO TO AENEAS
from *Archaics* (1962)

        I love you
I have permitted myself to say choirs
(as if the late birds sang in branches) when for them
in the dusk at wind set
the garage eave yields its water cup.

            Not for us the paling light
the white urn at the driveway,
nor for us the palmettos and the squeak
of tiles. The fountain at noonday cries,
"You are not here" and the sea at its distance
calls to a single path flanked by hibiscus,
the sea reminds itself each day
that it is solitary and the bather gambles
in its waves as a suicide who says "tomorrow is
another" an hour in the wrecker foam.

        I love you
I am writing your name as if I were a Trojan
who expected someone else to smooth the shore
                of souls who said
to the great reaches of wave and salt,
"I am replenishing as a light falling on a single tree"
and it is wonderful like ice on a floe,

        I love you
miracle, mirror, word, all the same
                you come, you go
        I love you
(on my rioting lawns the plaster flamingos
endure your wonder)

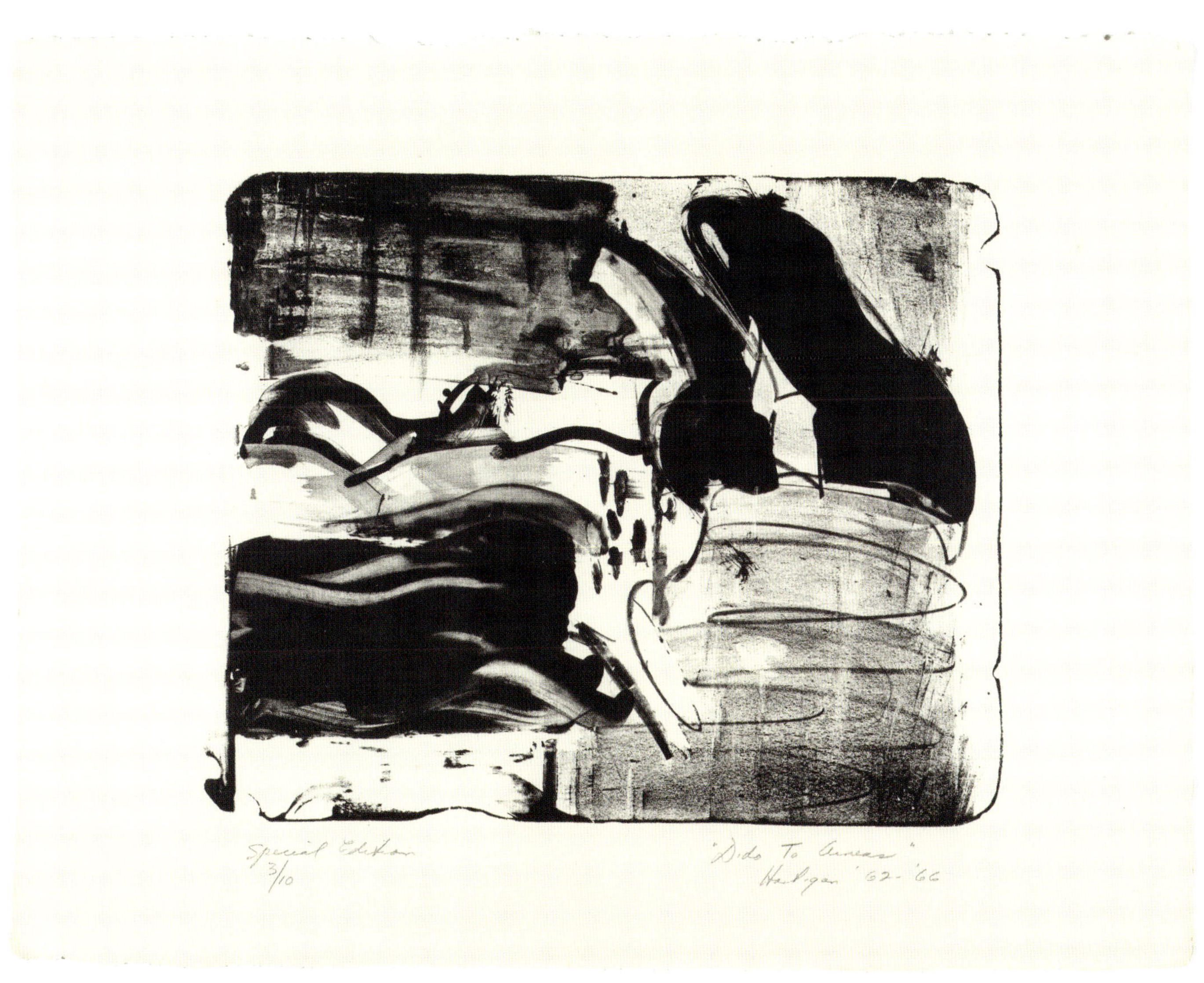

38 *Dido to Aeneas* from *The Archaics* 1962–1966

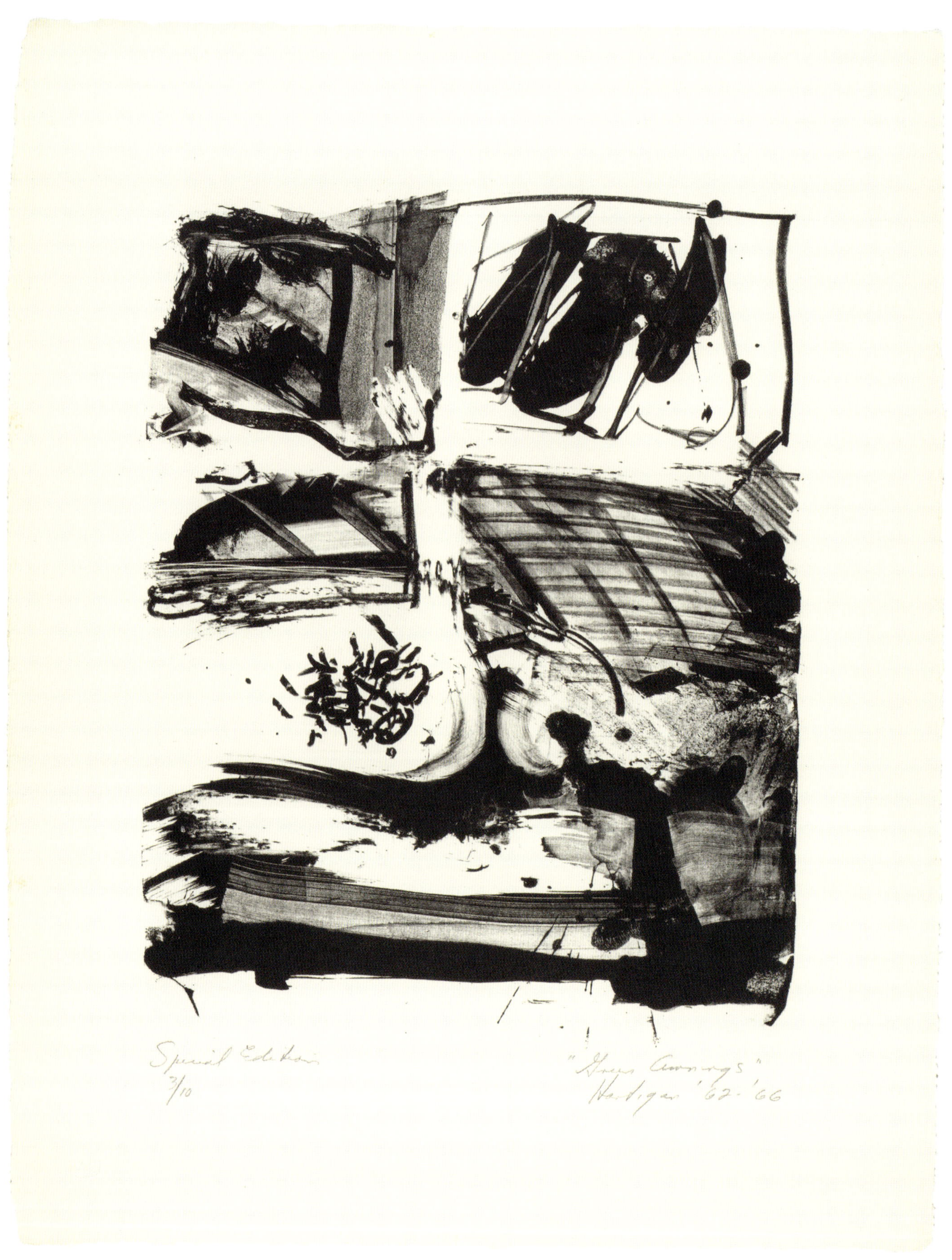

 39 Green Awnings from *The Archaics* 1962–1966

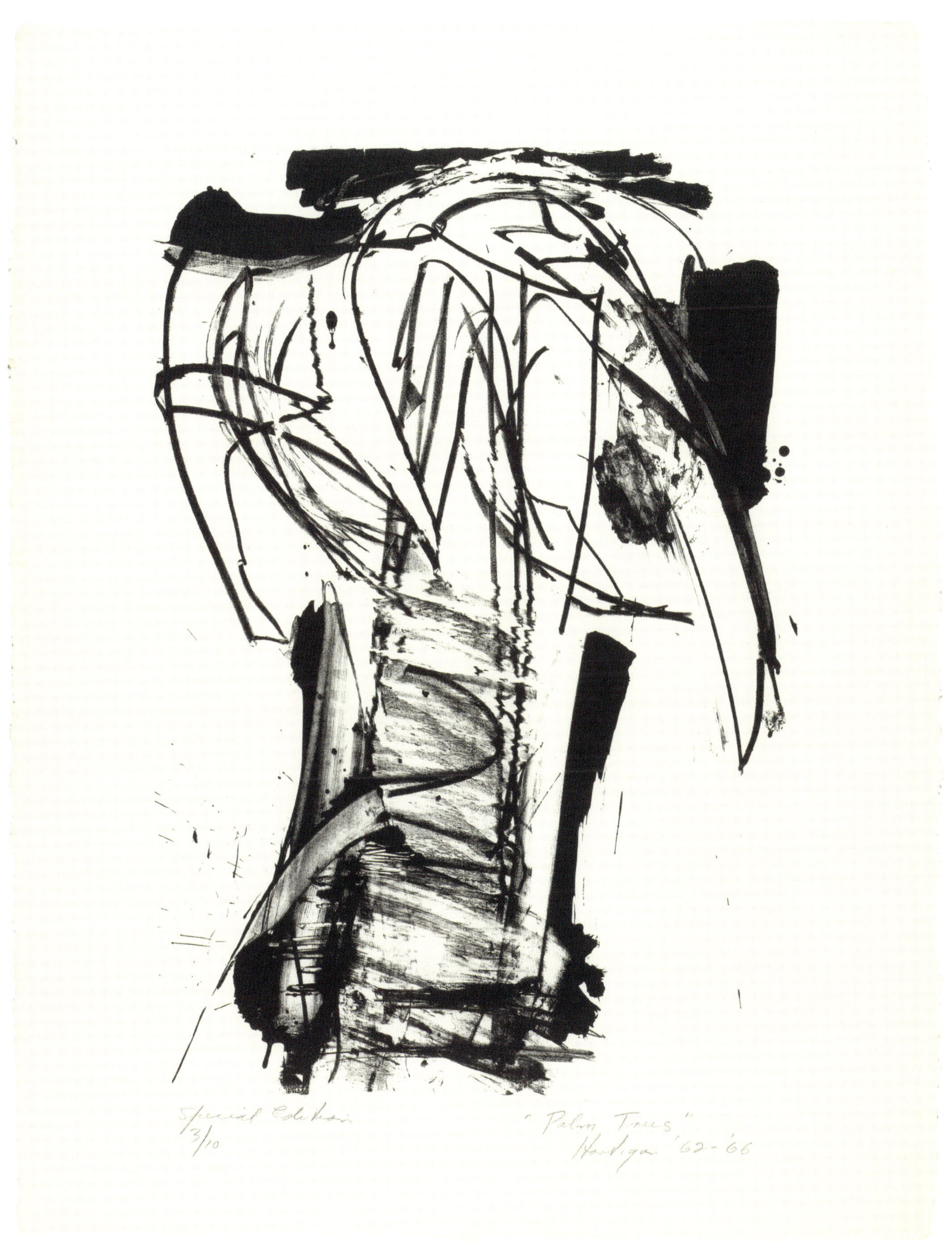

40 Palm Trees from *The Archaics* 1962–1966

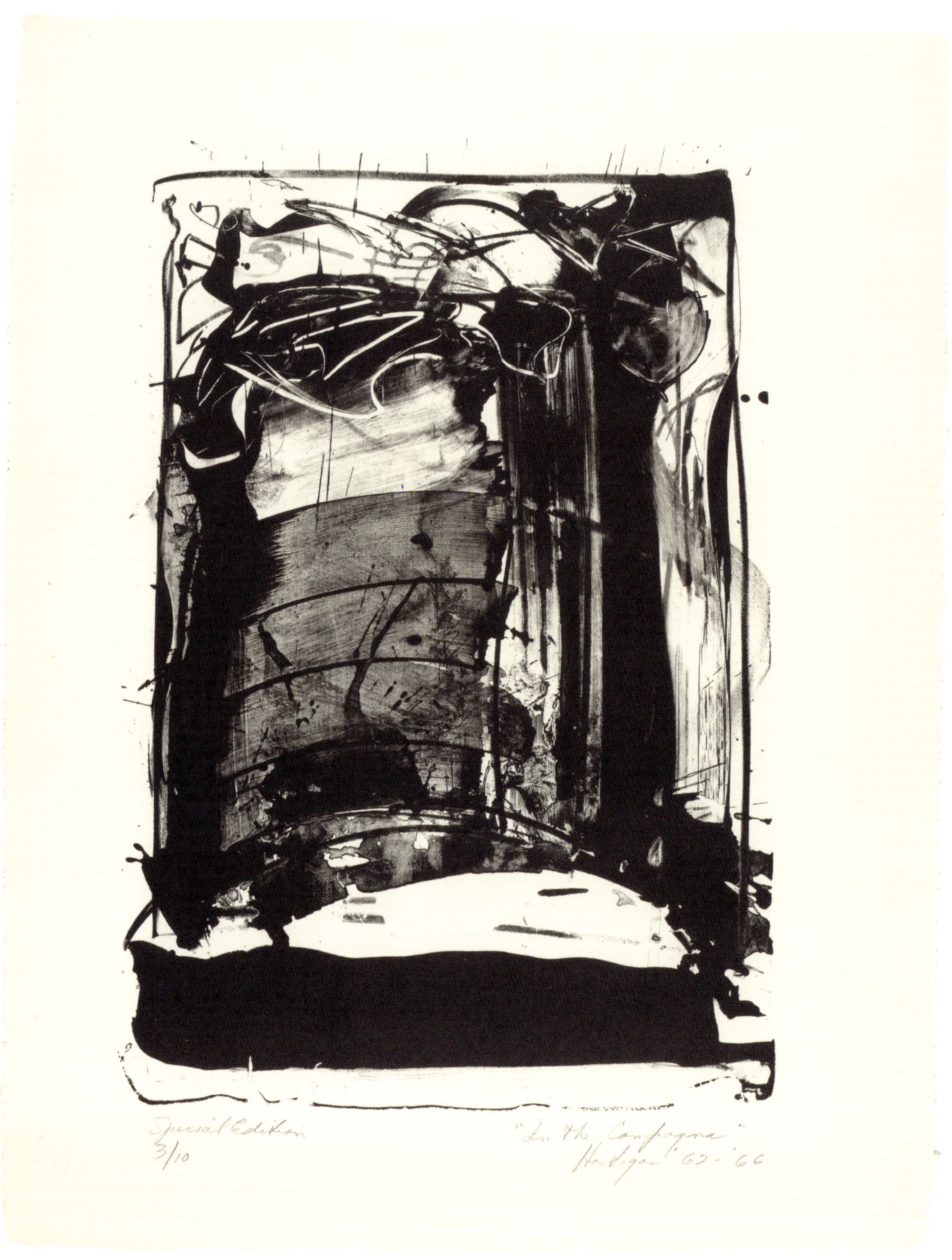

 41 *In the Campagna* from *The Archaics* 1962–1966

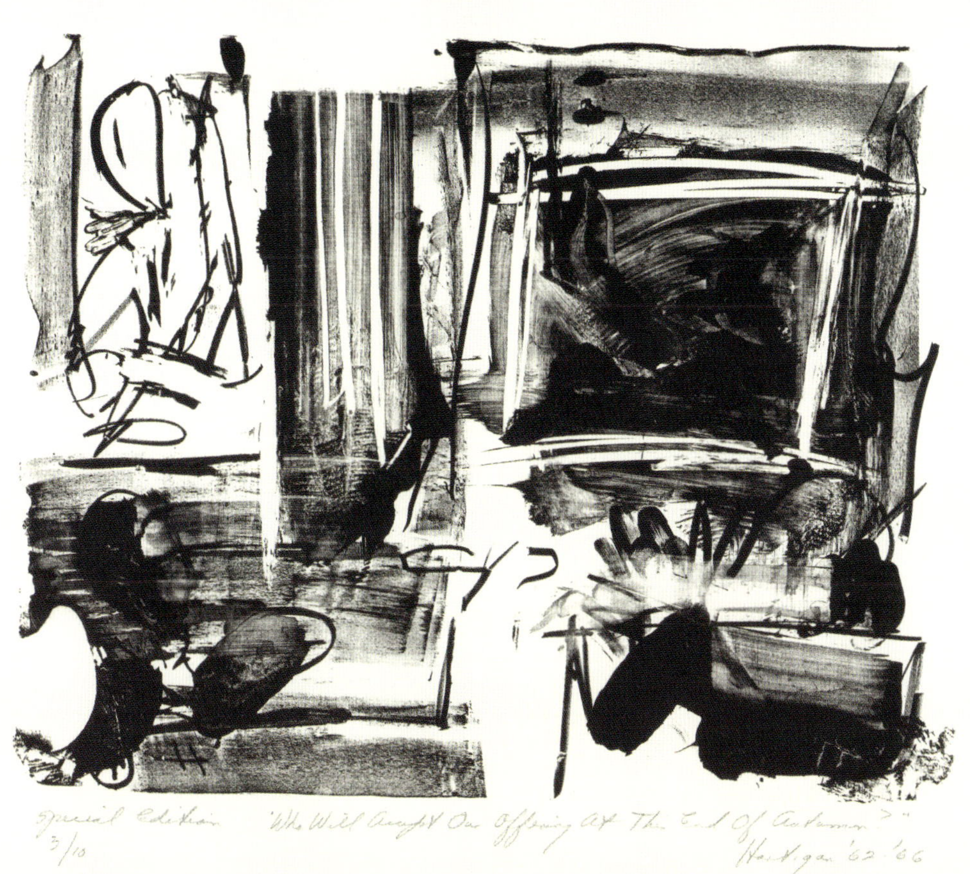

42 Who Will Accept Our Offering at the End of Autumn?
from *The Archaics* 1962–1966

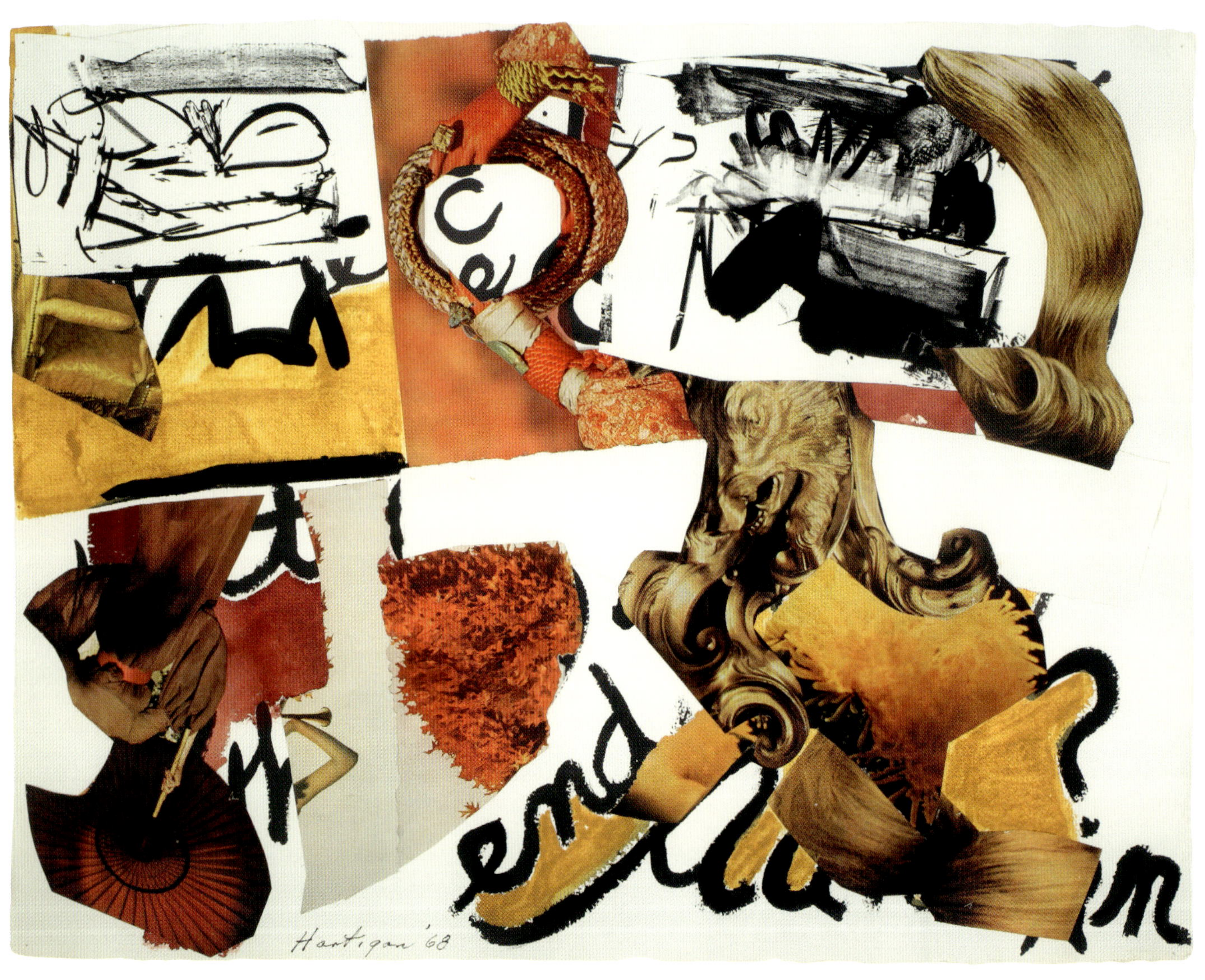

43 Barbara Guest Archaics 1968

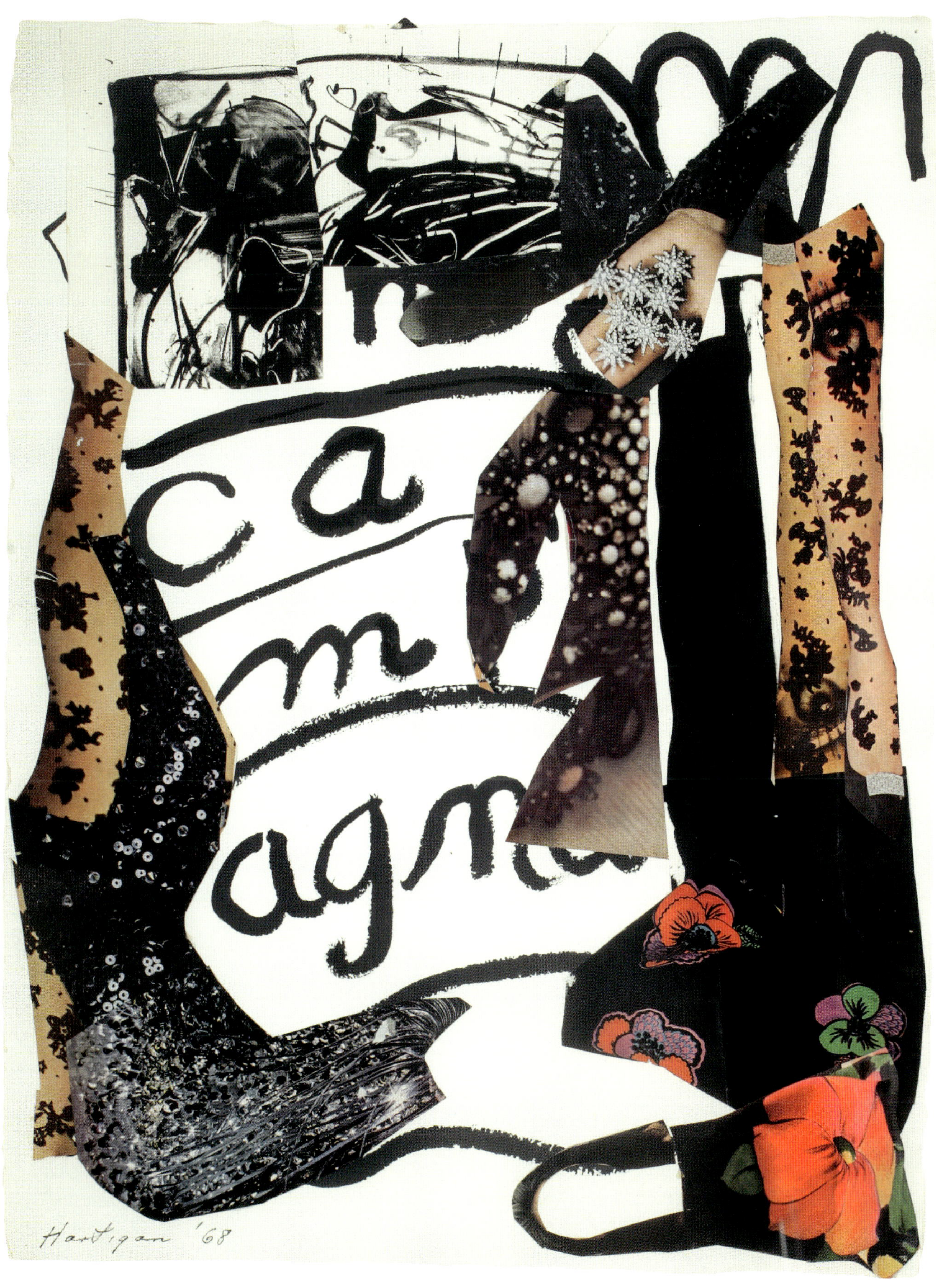

44 *Barbara Guest Archaics 1968*

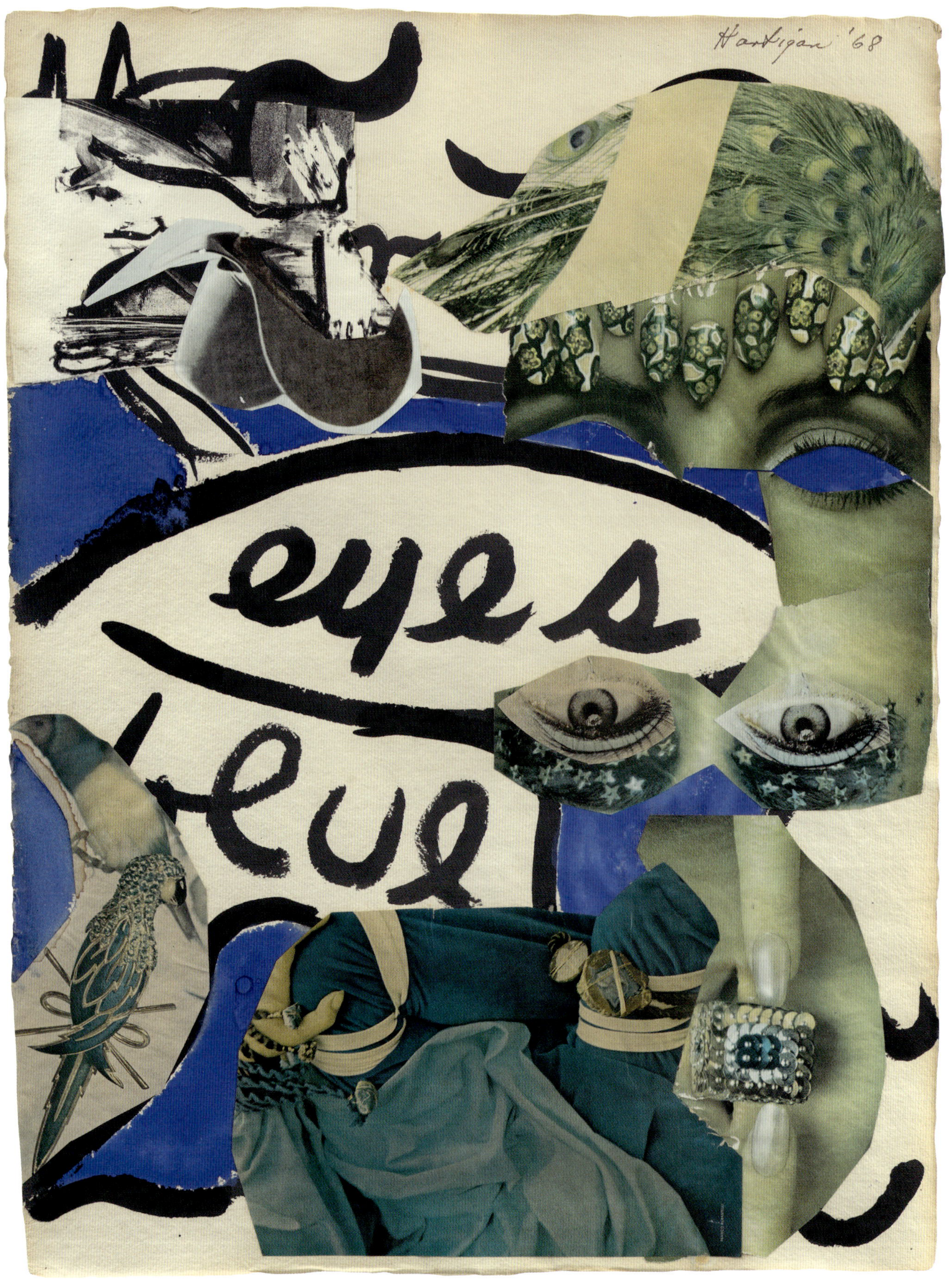

      45 Eyes Blue 1968

Works List

1

The Persian Jacket
1952
Oil on canvas
57½ × 48 in.
The Museum of Modern Art, New York, Gift of George Poindexter, 413.1953

2

Black Crows (Oranges No. 1)
1952
Oil on paper
44¼ × 33½ in.
University at Buffalo Art Galleries: Gift of the David K. Anderson Family, 2000

3

Frank O'Hara and the Demons
1952
Oil on canvas
72 × 36 in.
Rex R. Stevens and the Grace Hartigan Estate
Not in exhibition

4

Artificial Flowers and Apples
1952
Oil on canvas
24¼ × 25 in.
Collection of Steven and Beverly Newborn

5

Black Still Life
1953
Oil on canvas
42³⁄₈ × 48¼ in.
The University of Arizona Museum of Art, Gift of Edward Joseph Gallagher Jr., 1961.005.005

6

Daisy Aldan and Richard Miller, editors
Folder, no. 1
1953
Screen print
10⅝ × 7⅝ in.
Publisher: Tiber Press
Albert and Shirley Small Special Collections Library, University of Virginia

7

The Persian Robe from *Folder, no. 1*
1953
Screen print
Image: 10³⁄₁₆ × 6⅞ in.,
sheet: 10⅝ × 7⅝ in.
Publisher: Tiber Press
Special Collections Research Center, Syracuse University Libraries (Raleigh)
Albert and Shirley Small Special Collections Library, University of Virginia (Portland and Lincoln)

8

Pastorale from *Folder, no. 1*
1953
Screen print
Image and sheet: 7⅝ × 10⅝ in.
Publisher: Tiber Press
Special Collections Research Center, Syracuse University Libraries (Raleigh)
Albert and Shirley Small Special Collections Library, University of Virginia (Portland and Lincoln)

9

Still Life in Primary Colors from *Folder, no. 1*
1953
Screen print
Image: 6¹⁵⁄₁₆ × 10¹⁄₁₆ in.,
sheet: 7½ × 10⅝ in.
Publisher: Tiber Press
Special Collections Research Center, Syracuse University Libraries (Raleigh)
Albert and Shirley Small Special Collections Library, University of Virginia (Portland and Lincoln)

10

Daisy Aldan and Richard Miller, editors
Folder, nos. 3 and 4
1955–1956
Screen print
10⅝ × 7⅝ in.
Publisher: Tiber Press
Albert and Shirley Small Special Collections Library, University of Virginia

11

Frank O'Hara and Grace Hartigan
Oranges: 12 Pastorals
1953
9 unnumbered leaves, paperbound, original painting by Hartigan pasted on front cover
11³⁄₈ in. (height)
The Raymond Danowski Poetry Library, Emory University

12

Two Women
1954
Oil on canvas
54 × 36 in.
The Levett Collection

13
Grand Street Brides
1954
Oil on canvas
72⁹⁄₁₆ × 102³⁄₈ in.
Whitney Museum of American Art,
New York; purchase, with funds from
an anonymous donor

14
Masquerade
1954
Oil on canvas
81¾ × 86¼ in.
Collection of Lizbeth and
George Krupp

15
Interior with Mexican Doll
1955
Oil on canvas
80½ × 58½ in.
North Carolina Museum of Art,
Gift of James I. Merrill, 1957 (G.57.3.3)

16
The Masker
1954
Oil on canvas
72 × 42 in.
Collection of The Frances Lehman
Loeb Art Center, Vassar College,
Museum Purchase, 1954.9

17
East Side Sunday
1956
Oil on canvas
80 × 82 in.
Brooklyn Museum, Gift of James I.
Merrill, 1957, 56.180

18
Untitled [or New York]
1958
Oil on canvas
59¾ × 50 in. (framed)
Private collection

19
Bray
1958
Oil on canvas
60 × 50 in.
The Nelson-Atkins Musuem of Art,
Kansas City, Missouri, Gift of William
Inge, 61-76

20
Orange Field
1958
Oil on canvas
83¼ × 51½ in.
Carnegie Museum of Art, Patrons Art
Fund and gift of James Merrill, by
exchange

21
It's a Farewell
1959
Mixed media
29¹⁄₁₆ × 34⁷⁄₈ in.
Collection of the James Merrill House
& Writer-In-Residence Program
(Stonington, CT)

22
Dido
1960
Oil on canvas
82 × 91 in.
Collection of The McNay Art Museum,
Gift of Jane and Arthur Stieren, 1988.3

23
The Hero
1960
Oil on canvas
81 × 55 in.
Collection of Paul Fingersh and
Brenda Althouse, Courtesy of Neal
Meltzer Fine Art

24
Untitled from *The Hero Leaves
His Ship*
1960
Lithograph
Image: 20½ × 14¾ in.,
sheet: 29¹³⁄₁₆ × 21¼ in.
Publisher: Universal Limited
Art Editions
The Museum of Modern Art, New
York, Gift of the artist, 425.1961.1

25
Untitled from *The Hero Leaves
His Ship*
1960
Lithograph
Image: 19¹¹⁄₁₆ × 12¾ in.,
sheet: 29¹³⁄₁₆ × 21¹⁄₁₆ in.
Publisher: Universal Limited
Art Editions
The Museum of Modern Art, New
York, Gift of the artist, 425.1961.2

26
Untitled from *The Hero Leaves
His Ship*
1960
Lithograph
Image: 12⁷⁄₈ × 16³⁄₈ in.,
sheet: 21¹⁄₁₆ × 29¹³⁄₁₆ in.
Publisher: Universal Limited
Art Editions
The Museum of Modern Art, New
York, Gift of the artist, 425.1961.4

27
Untitled from *The Hero Leaves His Ship*
1960
Lithograph
Image: 12¹³⁄₁₆ × 20⁷⁄₁₆ in.,
sheet: 21¼ × 29¹⁵⁄₁₆ in.
Publisher: Universal Limited
Art Editions
The Museum of Modern Art, New York, Gift of the artist, 425.1961.3

28
Snow Angel
1960
Oil on canvas
69 × 75¼ in.
Private collection

29
The Canal to the Sky
1960, printed 1961
Screen print
Image: 17³⁄₁₆ × 14⅛ in.,
sheet: 18¹⁄₁₆ × 14³⁄₈ in.
Publisher: Tiber Press
Special Collections Research Center, Syracuse University Libraries (Raleigh)
National Gallery of Art (Portland and Lincoln)

30
This So-Called Angel
1960, printed 1961
Screen print
Image: 18¹⁄₁₆ × 14⁵⁄₁₆ in.,
sheet: 17³⁄₁₆ × 14 in.
Special Collections Research Center, Syracuse University Libraries (Raleigh)
National Gallery of Art (Portland and Lincoln)

31
On a Tar Roof
1960, printed 1961
Screen print
Image: 18¹⁄₁₆ × 14³⁄₈ in.,
sheet: 17³⁄₁₆ × 14¹⁄₁₆ in.
Publisher: Tiber Press
Special Collections Research Center, Syracuse University Libraries (Raleigh)
National Gallery of Art (Portland and Lincoln)

32
Untitled (Pallas-Athene)
1961
Lithograph on Arches paper
Image: 20¼ × 14 in.,
sheet: 30¹⁄₁₆ × 22½ in.
Publisher: Universal Limited
Art Editions
North Carolina Museum of Art, Gift of Mr. and Mrs. Robert B. Herbert Jr., 1982 (LC.82.10)

33
Grey-Eyed Athena
1961
Oil on canvas
69 × 64 in.
Collection of Hart Perry

34
Pallas Athena—Fire
1961
Oil on canvas
82½ × 61 in.
Baltimore Museum of Art, Gift of Valerie B. and J. Woodford Howard Jr., Baltimore, 2013.290

35
Pallas Athena—Earth
1961
Oil on canvas
64⅛ × 52⅛ in.
Smithsonian American Art Museum, Gift of S. C. Johnson & Son, Inc., 1969.47.17

36
Atlanta in Arcadia from *The Archaics*
1962–1966
Lithograph
Image: 18³⁄₁₆ × 14 in.,
sheet: 27½ × 19⅞ in.
Publisher: Universal Limited
Art Editions
The Museum of Modern Art, New York, Gift of the Celeste and Armand Bartos Foundation, 656.1966

37
From Eyes Blue and Cold from *The Archaics*
1962–1966
Lithograph
Image: 16 × 14³⁄₁₆ in.,
sheet: 27½ × 19⅞ in.
Publisher: Universal Limited
Art Editions
The Museum of Modern Art, New York, Gift of the Celeste and Armand Bartos Foundation, 655.1966

38
Dido to Aeneas from *The Archaics*
1962–1966
Lithograph
Image: 13¹⁵⁄₁₆ × 17³⁄₄ in.,
sheet: 19⅞ × 27⁹⁄₁₆ in.
Publisher: Universal Limited
Art Editions
The Museum of Modern Art, New York, Gift of the Celeste and Armand Bartos Foundation, 652.1966

39
Green Awnings from *The Archaics*
1962–1966
Lithograph
Image: 17$\frac{15}{16}$ × 14$\frac{3}{16}$ in.,
sheet: 27$\frac{1}{2}$ × 19$\frac{7}{8}$ in.
Publisher: Universal Limited
Art Editions
The Museum of Modern Art, New
York, Gift of the Celeste and Armand
Bartos Foundation, 651.1966

40
Palm Trees from *The Archaics*
1962–1966
Lithograph
Image: 19$\frac{7}{8}$ × 14 in.,
sheet: 27$\frac{1}{2}$ × 19$\frac{15}{16}$ in.
Publisher: Universal Limited
Art Editions
The Museum of Modern Art, New
York, Gift of the Celeste and Armand
Bartos Foundation, 654.1966

41
In the Campagna from *The Archaics*
1962–1966
Lithograph
Image: 20$\frac{5}{16}$ × 13$\frac{11}{16}$ in.,
sheet: 27$\frac{1}{2}$ × 19$\frac{13}{16}$ in.
Publisher: Universal Limited
Art Editions
The Museum of Modern Art, New
York, Gift of the Celeste and Armand
Bartos Foundation, 653.1966

42
*Who Will Accept Our Offering
at the End of Autumn?*
from *The Archaics*
1962–1966
Lithograph
Image: 14 × 18 in.,
sheet: 18$\frac{3}{8}$ × 27$\frac{3}{8}$ in.
Publisher: Universal Limited
Art Editions
The Museum of Modern Art, New
York, Gift of the Celeste and Armand
Bartos Foundation, 657.1966

43
Barbara Guest Archaics
1968
Ink and collage on paper
24 × 30 in.
Rex R. Stevens and the Grace
Hartigan Estate

44
Barbara Guest Archaics
1968
Ink and collage on paper
30 × 24 in.
Rex R. Stevens and the Grace
Hartigan Estate

45
Eyes Blue
1968
Collage
26 × 20 in.
Collection of Steven and
Beverly Newborn

Notes

GRACE HARTIGAN: IMAGE MAKER

1   Donald Allen, preface to *The New American Poetry 1945–1960*, ed. Donald Allen (1960; repr., Berkeley: University of California Press, 1999), xi.

2   Ezra Pound, *ABC of Reading* (1934; repr., New York: New Directions, 1960), 29.

3   Terence Diggory, introduction to *The Journals of Grace Hartigan 1951–1955*, by Grace Hartigan, ed. William T. La Moye and Joseph P. McCaffrey (Syracuse, NY: Syracuse University Press, 2009), xvii–xviii.

4   Clement Greenberg, "Towards a Newer Laocoon" (1940), in *The Collected Essays and Criticism 1: Perceptions and Judgments 1939–1944*, ed. John O'Brian (Chicago: University of Chicago Press, 1986), 23.

5   Hartigan, *Journals*, 29, 67.

6   Hartigan quoted in Brad Gooch, *City Poet: The Life and Times of Frank O'Hara* (New York: Knopf, 1993), 236.

7   Gooch, 216.

8   Frank O'Hara, "Notes on Second Avenue" (1957), in *Standing Still and Walking in New York*, ed. Donald Allen (San Francisco: Grey Fox, 1983), 40.

9   Grace Hartigan, artist's statement in *12 Americans*, ed. Dorothy Miller (New York: Museum of Modern Art, 1956), 53.

10   Susan Sontag, "Notes on 'Camp'" (1964), in *Against Interpretation and Other Essays* (New York: Dell, 1966), 281.

11   O'Hara, "Nature and New Painting" (1954), in *Standing Still*, 45.

12   Sontag, "Notes on 'Camp,'" 292. Hartigan was presented as a pop precursor in the exhibition *Hand-Painted Pop: American Art in Transition 1955–1962*, organized by Paul Schimmel and Donna De Salvo for the Museum of Contemporary Art, Los Angeles, 1993.

13   On "permission," Grace Hartigan, "Artists Talk on Art," interview by Irving Sandler, Fulcrum Gallery, New York, November 11, 1994. On "emotional state," Grace Hartigan, letter to author, December 12, 1994.

14   Hartigan quoted in Jo Page, "Artist Hartigan Answers Big Questions," *Times Union* (Albany, NY), March 21, 1993, H5.

15   For the translation see Cathy Curtis, *Restless Ambition: Grace Hartigan, Painter* (New York: Oxford University Press, 2015), 53. For Hartigan's reference to witchcraft in mid-career, see Barbara Flanagan, "Lively Artist Rebels at Labeling and Doesn't Like to Be Lionized," *Minneapolis Tribune*, September 24, 1963, clipping in Grace Hartigan Papers, Special Collections Research Center, Syracuse University Libraries.

16   R. G. [Robert Goodnough], "George Hartigan," *ARTnews*, April 1952, 44; and B. H. [Betty Holiday], "George Hartigan," *ARTnews*, April 1953, 39.

17   Grace Hartigan, interview by Cindy Nemser, *Art Talk: Conversations with Twelve Women Artists* (New York: Scribner's, 1975), 159.

"THE BASIS OF MY OWN CREATION"

1   Grace Hartigan to Barbara Guest, March 26, 1960, box 17, folder 342, Barbara Guest Papers, Yale Collection of American Literature, Beinecke Rare Book and Manuscript Library, Yale University.

2   Grace Hartigan, interview by Julia Link Haifley, May 10, 1979, Archives of American Art, Smithsonian Institution.

3   Robert Saltonstall Mattison, *Grace Hartigan: A Painter's World* (New York: Hudson Hills, 1990), 11.

4   Mattison, 12.

5   Mattison, 13.

6   On the division between "first-" and "second-generation" abstract expressionists, Hartigan said in 1979, "It wasn't that clear as the historians are making it now. We were just younger friends, that was all. I don't think they went around saying, 'I'm first generation and you're second.'" Grace Hartigan, interview.

7   John Ashbery, "The Invisible Avant-Garde," in *The Avant-Garde*, ed. John Ashbery, Art News Annual 34 (New York: Macmillan, 1968), 125.

8   Ashbery, 128.

9   Grace Glueck, "John Bernard Myers, Dealer in Artworks and Literature," *New York Times*, July 28, 1987, sec. B.

10   Edited by writers Charles Henri Ford and Parker Tyler, who had previously co-authored *The Young and Evil* (1933), a milestone in gay literature, *View* magazine had overtly queer oversight.

11   John Bernard Myers, *Tracking the Marvelous: A Life in the New York Art World* (New York: Random House, 1983), 111.

12   Myers, 126.

13   Grace Hartigan to Terence Diggory, April 30, 1992, Courtesy of Terence Diggory.

14   Terence Diggory has noted that Hartigan's switch between gender roles paralleled O'Hara's ambivalence toward sexuality. Although it's unclear if Hartigan knew O'Hara at the time she adopted the pseudonym George, Diggory's argument is valid and one that will be built on later in this essay. "Questions of Identity in *Oranges* by Frank O'Hara and Grace Hartigan," *Art Journal* 52, no. 4 (1993): 49.

15   In her brilliant study *Ninth Street Women*, Mary Gabriel highlighted the sexist pressures women artists endured during this time: "The decision of whether to have children confronted almost every woman artist … and the choice for most was wrenching. It was difficult enough to be taken seriously as a woman

who painted or sculpted amid the increasingly powerful forces that had begun to assemble under the banner 'art business' in the late 1940s. Adding the word 'mother' to that already damning description would almost surely condemn her to a life of artistic isolation and indifference." "Separate Trouble," in *Ninth Street Women, Lee Krasner, Elaine de Kooning, Grace Hartigan, Joan Mitchell, and Helen Frankenthaler: Five Painters and the Movement That Changed Modern Art* (New York: Back Bay Books, 2019), 187.

16 Grace Hartigan to Terence Diggory, April 30, 1992.

17 Myers, *Tracking the Marvelous*, 147.

18 Grace Hartigan, *The Journals of Grace Hartigan 1951–1955*, ed. William T. La Moy and Joseph P. McCaffrey (Syracuse, NY: Syracuse University Press, 2009), 28.

19 Brad Gooch, *City Poet: The Life and Times of Frank O'Hara* (New York: Alfred and Knopf, 1993), 212.

20 Gabriel, *Ninth Street Women*, 436; Gooch, *City Poet*, 212; and Mattison, *Grace Hartigan*, 28.

21 Hartigan, *Journals*, 25.

22 Hartigan, 28.

23 Gooch, *City Poet*, 213.

24 Gabriel, *Ninth Street Women*, 629.

25 Hartigan, *Journals*, 40.

26 Hartigan, 69.

27 In her master's thesis, Marjorie Rawle also argued that *Demons* is indebted to "Portrait of Grace." However, Rawle's argument emphasizes that the painting expands Hartigan's "openness to discontinuity and accrual," which she noted is rooted in the artist and O'Hara's complex relationship and the slippery construction of subjectivity. See "Grace Hartigan and Frank O'Hara: Partnership, Painting, and Camp in the New York School" (master's thesis, Tulane University, 2019), 43–45.

28 Hartigan originally referred to the work as *Poet (The Masker)* in her journals. Hartigan, *Journals*, 149.

29 Frank O'Hara, "Nature and New Painting," *Folder*, no. 3 (1954–55).

30 According to her journals, Hartigan embarked on painting a portrait of Ashbery around July 1952. Although she worked on the picture for several months and it was displayed in her April 1953 exhibition at Tibor de Nagy, Hartigan either destroyed or painted over the work, or it remains to be found. Hartigan, *Journals*, 39.

31 "The 1950s are generally considered the most politically conservative and expressly homophobic decade of the twentieth century," art historian Richard Meyer has argued. Because of this, queer artists in the United States in particular employed code in their work to indicate homosexuality. Considering this, *Two Women* is all the more significant, especially since lesbian imagery of the 1950s is often found only through lesbian pulp novels and snapshots that have been rediscovered. See Catherine Lord and Richard Meyer, *Art & Queer Culture* (London: Phaidon, 2019), 22–23, 95–96.

32 Hartigan, *Journals*, 138.

33 Tibor de Nagy Gallery Records, 1941–2016, box 34, folder 6, Archives of American Art, Smithsonian Institution.

34 Hartigan, *Journals*, 137.

35 In 1949 Pollock's persona in photographs accompanying the *Life* magazine article "Is He the Greatest Living Painter in the United States?" greatly promoted a rugged American man and heterosexual lifestyle. "One of the main reasons" for Pollock's crowning, argued art historian Ann Eden Gibson, was that Pollock "fit the most popular model for an American hero: the anti-intellectual man of action." As Gibson has noted, abstract expressionism came to represent American ideals such as "frontier heroism" due to several of its heterosexual, white male practitioners applying overt physicality as a technique, which was broadly interpreted as a measure of masculinity. See *Abstract Expressionism: Other Politics* (New Haven, CT: Yale University Press, 1997), 2–3.

36 Cathy Curtis, *Restless Ambition: Grace Hartigan, Painter* (New York: Oxford University Press, 2015), 96.

37 Grace Hartigan, artist's statement in *12 Americans*, ed. Dorothy Miller (New York: Museum of Modern Art, 1956), 53.

38 Joe LeSueur, *Digressions on Some Poems by Frank O'Hara: A Memoir* (New York: Farrar, Straus and Giroux, 2003), 178.

39 Marjorie Perloff, "Frank O'Hara and the Aesthetics of Attention," *boundary 2*, 4, no. 3 (Spring 1976): 796.

40 Maggie Nelson, *Women, the New York School, and Other True Abstractions* (Iowa City: University of Iowa Press, 2007), 55.

41 Several queer visual artists of the period were also working between abstraction and figuration. For instance, Jasper Johns's apt painting *In Memory of My Feelings—Frank O'Hara* (1961; Museum of Contemporary Art Chicago) features two abstract canvases hinged at the side, while a fork and knife have been affixed to the surface.

42 Diggory's "Questions of Identity" provides an excellent analysis of the works in relation to subjectivity, sexuality, and the self. Mattison, *Grace Hartigan*, 28–31, delivers a thorough overview of the works. See also Curtis, *Restless Ambition*, 108–9; Karen Ware, "Frank O'Hara's *Oranges*: Poetry, Painters, and Painting" (master's thesis, University of Louisville, 1994); and Thomas Lavazzi, "Lucky Pierre Gets into Finger Paint: Grace Hartigan and Frank O'Hara's *Oranges*," *Aurora, The Journal of the History of Art* 1 (2000): 122–37.

43 Mattison, *Grace Hartigan*, 28.

44 Grace Hartigan, transcript of lecture at North Carolina Museum of Art, January 30, 1986, Grace Hartigan artist file, Art Reference Library, North Carolina Museum of Art.

45 Hartigan, *Journals*, 56. Hartigan's twelve paintings after O'Hara's poems were included in a 1953 exhibition at Tibor de Nagy Gallery, where Myers had one hundred mimeographed copies of the *Oranges* poems made to accompany the show. They sold for $1 apiece. On twenty of these copies is an original illustration by Hartigan depicting a bowl brimming with oranges (plate 11).

46 Aldan and Miller were married, but it was a marriage of convenience, since Miller was also gay. See Frances Lazare's essay in this publication for a further analysis of the queer environment surrounding *Folder*.

47 Hartigan's screen prints for *Folder* magazine generally lack official titles, even though she titles *The Persian Robe* and *Still Life in Primary Colors* in her journals. That these prints exist with various titles is very much in the casual spirit of *Folder*.

48 Hartigan, *Journals*, 89. Hartigan's former father-in-law and her son's grandfather had just passed away from lung cancer, which meant her son, Jeffrey, was staying with her in New York City during this period. This may have contributed to the intensity of which she speaks.

49 John Ashbery, "The Way They Took," *Folder*, no. 1 (1953).

50 Barbara Guest, interview by Charles Bernstein, *LINEbreak*, 1995, https://writing.upenn.edu/pennsound/x/Guest.php.

51 Grace Hartigan to Barbara Guest, March 26, 1960, Barbara Guest Papers.

52 Grace Hartigan to Barbara Guest, March 30, 1960, Barbara Guest Papers.

53 For a further analysis of these bodies of work, see Rachel Blau DuPlessis's lyrical study in this publication.

54 Barbara Guest to Grace Hartigan, March 28, 1960, Grace Hartigan Papers, Special Collections Research Center, Syracuse University Libraries.

55 Hartigan to Guest, March 26, 1960. *Snow Angel* appears in the background of a photograph featuring Guest and Hartigan accompanying the article by Amelia Young, "Poet, Painter Have Artist's Exchange," *Washington, DC Star*, September 29, 1961.

56 Grace Hartigan, transcript of lecture at NCMA.

57 Hartigan biographer Cathy Curtis noted that the artist's choice of colors may have been influenced by the last stanza of "Pallas," a poem written by queer poet H. D. (Hilda Doolittle) and a favorite of Barbara Guest. The last stanza reads: "Ah, could they know / how violets throw strange fire, / red and purple and gold, / how they glow / gold and purple and red / where her feet tread." *Restless Ambition*, 354n16.

58 Grace Hartigan to Cleve Gray, June 25, 1961, box 2, folder 22, Cleve Gray Papers, 1933–2005, Archives of American Art, Smithsonian Institution, cited in Curtis, *Restless Ambition*, 354n21; and "Meet Grace Hartigan," January 16, 2009, video, 4:17, https://www.youtube.com/watch?v=e-mzSLQL1nk&t=3s.

59 Frank O'Hara to Grace Hartigan, December 20, 1957, Grace Hartigan Papers.

60 Frank O'Hara, "Reviews: George Hartigan," *ARTnews*, February 1954, 45.

61 James Schuyler, "Reviews and Previews: Grace Hartigan," *ARTnews*, May 1959, 13.

62 John Bernard Myers to Grace Hartigan, June 2, [circa 1962], Grace Hartigan Papers.

63 Merrill established the Ingram Merrill Foundation in 1956, which awarded monetary grants to artists, institutions, and writers, among other recipients. Merrill sat on its jurying committee.

64 Although the Whitney credits the acquisition of *Grand Street Brides* as anonymous, a bill of sale records Merrill as funder of the acquisition. Series 1, box 3: Clients and Colleagues, Tibor de Nagy Gallery Records, 1941–2016, Archives of American Art, Smithsonian Institution. The acquisition was also mentioned in Gabriel, *Ninth Street Women*, 552.

65 Myers to Hartigan, June 2, [ca. 1962].

66 Hartigan, *Journals*, 132.

67 John Myers to James Merrill, April [1955], James Merrill Papers, Department of Special Collections, Washington University Libraries, St. Louis.

68 Myers to Merrill, April [1955].

69 Hartigan was most likely invited by the NCMA's then assistant director, James Byrnes, who was connected to Myers. In fact, through written correspondence Myers updated Merrill that Hartigan was "off to North Carolina" and that the NCMA "is a brand new museum that I am most enthusiastic about, since Mr. Byrnes, the assistant director—is quite a live wire and completely sympathetic to contemporary art." John Myers to James Merrill, undated [circa 1957], James Merrill Papers.

70 James Byrnes, *Panel's Choice: 1957* (Raleigh: North Carolina Museum of Art, 1957). I am grateful to my NCMA colleague Lyle Humphrey, associate curator of European art and collections history, for first bringing this to my attention.

71 In 1985 the Nasher Museum of Art at Duke University received five watercolors by Hartigan from that period of her career. In 2013 the Mint Museum in Charlotte acquired Hartigan's painting *Scotland* (1960).

72 *Interior with Mexican Doll* curatorial object file, North Carolina Museum of Art.

73 Grace Hartigan, interview.

74 Grace Hartigan, interview.

75 Grace Hartigan quoted in Young, "Poet, Painter."

"BEING TOGETHER IN THE WORLD"

1 Frank O'Hara, "Nature and New Painting," *Folder*, no. 3 (1954–55): n.p. O'Hara's essay explores the relationship between the human realm and natural realm, specifically as it is thematized in 1950s painting, and identifies a new style that blends elements of abstract expressionism—which he sees as a method rather than a style or as a "cult of mechanics"—and representational subject matter.

2 O'Hara, n.p.

3 This thinking is indebted to Lytle Shaw's theorization of the role of "heterogeneity" in O'Hara's poetry. See *Frank O'Hara: The Poetics of Coterie* (Iowa City: University of Iowa Press, 2006), 1–7.

4 Grace Hartigan, *The Journals of Grace Hartigan 1951–1955*, ed. William T. La Moy and Joseph P. McCaffrey (Syracuse, NY: Syracuse University Press, 2009), August 30, 1953, 94–95.

5 Riva Castleman, "Floriano Vecchi and the Tiber Press," *Print Quarterly* 21, no. 2 (2004): 127–45. The Tiber Press is best documented in this article by Castleman, print scholar and MoMA curator of prints and illustrated books, whose impressively detailed history of the press comes out of a series of interviews conducted with the project's participants.

6 See Valerie Ward, ed., "Interview with Daisy Aldan," in *Celebration with Anaïs Nin* (Riverside, CT: Magic Circle Press, 1973), 66.

7 Daisy Aldan, "Poetry & a One-Woman Press," in *The Publish-It-Yourself Handbook: Literary Tradition & How-To*, ed. Bill Henderson (New York: Pushcart Book Press, 1973), 230. Here, Aldan was likely addressing the bias of university-based magazines associated with the rise of the critical method known as New Criticism in the 1940s.

8 Note, n.d., MS-00056, box 1, folder 8, Daisy Aldan Papers, Harry Ransom Center, University of Texas at Austin. Traditional printmaking processes used in the production of artists' books—including lithography and etching—were out of reach because of their high costs. Vecchi, Aldan, and Miller covered their overhead by printing greeting cards and other paper goods on a homemade screen Aldan fashioned from prefabricated wooden frames. Aldan, "Poetry & a One-Woman Press," 101.

9 Castleman, "Floriano Vecchi," 127.

10 David Leddick, *Intimate Companions: A Triography of George Platt Lynes, Paul Cadmus, Lincoln Kirstein, and Their Circle* (New York: St. Martin's Press, 2000), 73.

11 Leddick, 73.

12 Aldan, "Poetry & a One-Woman Press," 101.

13 Ian Patterson, "New York Poets: *Folder* (1953–6); *Neon* (1954–60); and *Yugen* (1958–62)," in *The Oxford Critical and Cultural History of Modernist Magazines*, vol. 2, *North America 1894–1960*, ed. Peter Brooker and Andrew Thacker (Oxford: Oxford University Press, 2012; online edition, Oxford Academic, March 3, 2015), n.p., https://doi.org/10.1093/acprof:osobl/9780199545810.003.0057.

14 The term *print renaissance* is sometimes used to describe an upsurge of interest in printmaking among American artists from the late 1950s. It was characterized by the opening of several workshops specializing in the creation of high-quality artists' prints. See Trudy V. Hansen, et al., *Printmaking in America: Collaborative Prints and Presses, 1960–1990* (New York: Harry N. Abrams, 1995), 1.

15 For an example, see Jared Ledesma's discussion of Hartigan's painting *Months and Moons* (fig. 6) in "'The Basis of My Own Creation': Grace Hartigan and Poetic Exchange," 7, in this publication.

16 Hartigan, *Journals*, October 30, 1952, 16.

17 Leo Steinberg, *The New York School: Second Generation* (New York: Jewish Museum, 1957), 4–7.

18 Hartigan, *Journals*, October 30, 1952, 16.

19 Hartigan, *Journals*, October 17, 1953, 101.

20 Hartigan, *Journals*, December 16, 1953, 110.

21 Hartigan, *Journals*, March 6, 1953, 72.

22 Rachel Stella, "Unfolding the Collaborative Experience of *Folder*," *Entrevues: La Revue Des Revues* 43 (2010): 5. The other screen prints Hartigan made for *Folder*, no. 1 are *The Persian Robe* (plate 7) and *Still Life in Primary Colors* (plate 9). She would go on to produce the cover images for *Folder*, nos. 3 and 4 (plate 10).

23 Cathy Curtis, *Restless Ambition: Grace Hartigan, Painter* (New York: Oxford University Press, 2015), ix.

24 Hartigan, *Journals*, July 27, 1953, 118.

25 Dennis Barone, "Daisy Aldan: An Interview on Folder," in *The Little Magazine in America: A Modern Documentary History*, ed. Elliott Anderson and Mary Kinzie (Yonkers, NY: Pushcart Press, 1978), 264; and Lesdema, "'Basis of My Own Creation,'" 8–9.

26 Amelia Jones, *In Between Subjects: A Critical Genealogy of Queer Performance* (London: Routledge, 2021), 145–50.

27 Gavin Butt, *Between You and Me: Queer Disclosures in the New York Art World, 1948–1963* (Durham, NC: Duke University Press, 2005). For more on the fugitive nature of male homosexual desire, see Jonathan Katz, "The Art of Code: Jasper Johns and Robert Rauschenberg," in *Significant Others: Creativity and Intimate Partnership*, ed. Whitney Chadwick and Isabelle Courtivron (London: Thames and Hudson, 1993), 189–206. This argument is summated nicely in Jones, *In Between Subjects*, 149.

28 Castleman, "Floriano Vecchi," 133.

29   James Schuyler to Frank O'Hara,
May 5, 1956, MS 78, box 3,
folder 30, James Schuyler Papers,
University of California, San Diego.

A GESTURAL EROS OF POESIS

1   Barbara Guest to Grace Hartigan,
March 1960, Grace Hartigan Papers,
Special Collections Research Center,
Syracuse University Libraries.

2   Barbara Guest, *Forces of Imagination: Writing on Writing* (Berkeley,
CA: Kelsey St. Press, 2003), 107.

3   Guest, 51–52.

4   Guest, 102–3.

5   Robert Saltonstall Mattison, *Grace Hartigan: A Painter's World* (New
York: Hudson Hills Press, 1990), 28.

6   Cathy Curtis, *Restless Ambition: Grace Hartigan, Painter* (New York:
Oxford University Press, 2015),
186–88, 201–4.

Page numbers in *italics* refer to illustrations.

Contributors

TERENCE DIGGORY is emeritus professor of English at Skidmore College. Much of his research and teaching has focused on the relationship between poetry and painting, leading to such publications as *William Carlos Williams and the Ethics of Painting* (1991) and several works on the New York School, including *The Scene of My Selves: New Work on New York School Poets* (co-edited with Stephen Paul Miller, 2001) and *Encyclopedia of the New York School Poets* (2009). In 1993 he organized the exhibition *Grace Hartigan and the Poets: Paintings and Prints* for the Skidmore College art gallery. He has since written about Hartigan in a number of periodicals and exhibition catalogues.

RACHEL BLAU DUPLESSIS is a poet, critic, and collagist. In her career as a poet-critic, she has written extensively on gender, poetry, and poetics, including on the work of Barbara Guest, as well as on United States objectivist and modernist poets. Her recent and forthcoming books include *A Long Essay on the Long Poem* (2023) and the two-volume contemporary long poem *Drafts* (2025). DuPlessis has been awarded a Pew Fellowship and a residency at Bellagio for her poetry and collage.

FRANCES LAZARE is an art historian and curator whose research focuses on the histories of abstract painting from the nineteenth to the twenty-first century. She holds a PhD from the University of Southern California (USC), where she recently completed a dissertation on queer and feminist sociability in and around the New York School of painters. She has held curatorial positions at the Menil Collection; Museum of Fine Arts, Houston; and the Norton Simon Museum and taught postwar art history at USC, Southern California Institute of Architecture, and ArtCenter College of Design. She recently joined the Los Angeles County Museum of Art as a member of the modern art department.

JARED LEDESMA is curator of 20th-century art and contemporary art at the North Carolina Museum of Art. Since joining the NCMA in 2022, Ledesma has organized exhibitions such as *The Surrealist Impulse, Allana Clarke: Tender, David Gilbert: Flutter,* and *Luis-Rey Velasco.* He has also secured works by Ruth Asawa, Gwendolyn Knight, and Irene Rice Pereira, among others, for the Museum's collection. Ledesma held previous roles at the Akron Art Museum, where he led its curatorial department as senior curator, the Des Moines Art Center, where he organized the groundbreaking exhibition *Queer Abstraction,* and the San Francisco Museum of Modern Art, where he worked extensively with the institution's collection and contributed to projects such as *Matisse/ Diebenkorn.*

cover, 60   Brooklyn Museum, Gift of James I. Merrill, 56.180; Photo: © Estate of Grace Hartigan

frontispiece   Grace Hartigan Papers, Special Collections Research Center, Syracuse University Libraries

vi, 58   NCMA Digital Imaging

xii   Photo: Fred W. McDarrah/MUUS Collection via Getty Images

2   Grace Hartigan Papers, Special Collections Research Center, Syracuse University Libraries

4   The Miriam and Ira D. Wallach Division of Art, Prints and Photographs: Photography Collection, The New York Public Library; Photo: Walter Silver

6   The Art Institute of Chicago, Mr. and Mrs. Frank G. Logan Purchase Prize Fund; purchased with funds provided by Edgar J. Kaufmann, Jr., and Mr. and Mrs. Noah Goldowsky; Photo: The Art Institute of Chicago/Art Resource, NY

7   The Frances Lehman Loeb Art Center, Vassar College, Bequest of Agnes Rindge Claflin; Photo: Frances Lehman Loeb Art Center, Vassar College, Poughkeepsie, NY/Art Resource, NY

8   Photo: Courtesy of Sotheby's

10   Rex R. Stevens and the Grace Hartigan Estate; Photo: Rex Stevens

11 (top left), 59   Collection of The Frances Lehman Loeb Art Center, Vassar College, Museum Purchase, 1954.9; Photo: Frances Lehman Loeb Art Center, Vassar College, Poughkeepsie, NY/Art Resource, NY

11 (top right)   Grace Hartigan Papers, Special Collections Research Center, Syracuse University Libraries

11 (bottom)   Daisy Aldan Papers, Yale Collection of American Literature, Beinecke Rare Book and Manuscript Library

12   Grace Hartigan Papers, Special Collections Research Center, Syracuse University Libraries

15, 77   Private collection; Photo: © 2021 Christie's Images Limited

16, 84   Baltimore Museum of Art: Gift of Valerie B. and J. Woodford Howard, Jr., Baltimore, BMA 2013.290; Photo: Mitro Hood

18, 55   Whitney Museum of American Art, New York; purchase, with funds from an anonymous donor, 55.27; Digital image: © Whitney Museum of American Art/ Licensed by Scala/Art Resource, NY

20   Grace Hartigan Papers, Special Collections Research Center, Syracuse University Libraries

22, 57   Collection of Lizbeth and George Krupp; Photo: Courtesy of Sotheby's

23   Daisy Aldan Papers, Yale Collection of American Literature, Beinecke Rare Book and Manuscript Library

25   The Miriam and Ira D. Wallach Division of Art, Prints and Photographs: Photography Collection, The New York Public Library; Photo: Walter Silver

26   The Miriam and Ira D. Wallach Division of Art, Prints and Photographs: Photography Collection, The New York Public Library; Photo: Walter Silver

27 (left), 41   The Museum of Modern Art, New York. Gift of George Poindexter, 413.1953; Digital image: © The Museum of Modern Art/Licensed by SCALA/Art Resource, NY

27 (right), 49   Reba and Dave Williams Collection, Gift of Reba and Dave Williams, National Gallery of Art, 2008.115.2367

28 (left), 54   The Levett Collection; Photo: Frase Marr

28 (right)   Grace Hartigan Papers, Special Collections Research Center, Syracuse University Libraries

29   Harry Ransom Center, The University of Texas at Austin

30   Photo: Fred W. McDarrah/MUUS Collection via Getty Images

34, 42   University at Buffalo Art Galleries: Gift of the David K. Anderson Family, 2000; Photo: Nicholas Ostness

35, 74   Baltimore Museum of Art: Purchased as the gift of the Carolyn and Richard Susel Foundation, Baltimore, BMA 1989.18

36, 95   The Museum of Modern Art, Gift of the Celeste and Armand Bartos Foundation, 657.1966; Digital image: © The Museum of Modern Art/Licensed by SCALA/Art Resource, NY

38–39   Grace Hartigan Papers, Special Collections Research Center, Syracuse University Libraries

43   Photo: Fred W. McDarrah/MUUS Collection via Getty Images

44   Rex R. Stevens and the Grace Hartigan Estate; Photo: Rex Stevens

45   Collection of Steven and Beverly Newborn. Photo: Elisabeth Bernstein

47   University of Arizona Museum of Art, Gift of Edward Joseph Gallagher, Jr. 1961.005.005

48   Grace Hartigan Papers, Special Collections Research Center, Syracuse University Libraries

50   Reba and Dave Williams Collection, Gift of Reba and Dave Williams, National Gallery of Art, 2008.115.2366

51   Reba and Dave Williams Collection, Gift of Reba and Dave Williams, National Gallery of Art, 2008.115.2368

52   Grace Hartigan Papers, Special Collections Research Center, Syracuse University Libraries

53   The Poetry Collection of the University Libraries, University at Buffalo, The State University of New York

63   Private Collection. Photo: Elisabeth Bernstein

65   The Nelson-Atkins Museum of Art, Kansas City, Missouri. Gift of William Inge, 61-76; © Grace Hartigan, Image: Courtesy of Nelson-Atkins Digital Production & Preservation

66   Carnegie Museum of Art, Patrons Art Fund and gift of James Merrill, by exchange; Carnegie Museum of Art, Pittsburgh, PA/Art Resource, NY

67   Courtesy of the James Merrill House & Writer-In-Residence Program (Stonington, CT)

69   Collection of The McNay Art Museum, Gift of Jane and Arthur Stieren, 1988.3

70   Collection of Paul Fingersh and Brenda Althouse , Courtesy of Neal Meltzer Fine Art; Photo: Courtesy of Sotheby's

71   Photo: Fred W. McDarrah/MUUS Collection via Getty Images

72   Baltimore Museum of Art: Purchased as the gift of the Carolyn and Richard Susel Foundation, Baltimore, BMA 1989.15

73   Baltimore Museum of Art: Purchased as the gift of the Carolyn and Richard Susel Foundation, Baltimore, BMA 1989.16

75   Baltimore Museum of Art: Purchased as the gift of the Carolyn and Richard Susel Foundation, Baltimore, BMA 1989.17

78   Grace Hartigan Papers, Special Collections Research Center, Syracuse University Libraries

79   Grace Hartigan Papers, Special Collections Research Center, Syracuse University Libraries

80   Grace Hartigan Papers, Special Collections Research Center, Syracuse University Libraries

81   NCMA Digital Imaging

83   Collection of Hart Perry; Photo: © 2021 Christie's Images Limited

85   Smithsonian American Art Museum, Gift of S. C. Johnson & Son, Inc., 1969.47.17; Photo: Smithsonian American Art Museum, Washington, DC/Art Resource, NY

87   The Museum of Modern Art, Gift of the Celeste and Armand Bartos Foundation, 656.1966; Digital image: © The Museum of Modern Art/Licensed by SCALA/Art Resource, NY

88   The Museum of Modern Art, Gift of the Celeste and Armand Bartos Foundation, 655.1966; Digital image: © The Museum of Modern Art/Licensed by SCALA/Art Resource, NY

91   The Museum of Modern Art, Gift of the Celeste and Armand Bartos Foundation, 652.1966; Digital image: © The Museum of Modern Art/Licensed by SCALA/Art Resource, NY

92   The Museum of Modern Art, Gift of the Celeste and Armand Bartos Foundation, 651.1966; Digital image: © The Museum of Modern Art/Licensed by SCALA/Art Resource, NY

93   The Museum of Modern Art, Gift of the Celeste and Armand Bartos Foundation, 654.1966; Digital image: © The Museum of Modern Art/Licensed by SCALA/Art Resource, NY

94   The Museum of Modern Art, Gift of the Celeste and Armand Bartos Foundation, 653.1966; Digital image: © The Museum of Modern Art/Licensed by SCALA/Art Resource, NY

96   Rex R. Stevens and the Grace Hartigan Estate; Photo: Courtesy of the Estate of Grace Hartigan/ACA Galleries, New York

97   Rex R. Stevens and the Grace Hartigan Estate; Photo: Courtesy of the Estate of Grace Hartigan/ACA Galleries, New York

98   Collection of Steven and Beverly Newborn; Photo: Elisabeth Bernstein

115   Grace Hartigan Papers, Special Collections Research Center, Syracuse University Libraries

back   Grace Hartigan Papers, Special Collections Research Center, Syracuse University Libraries

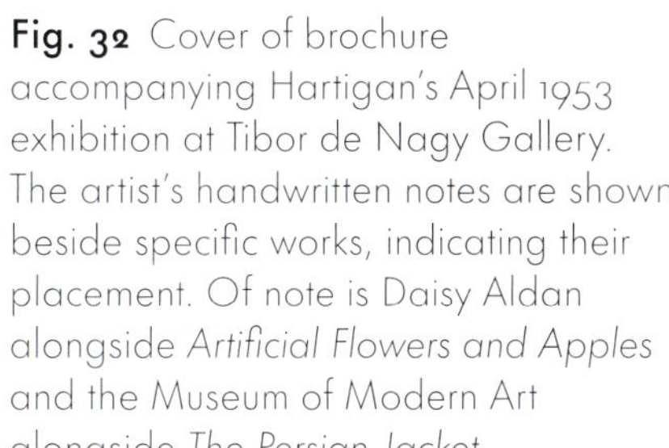

Fig. 32 Cover of brochure accompanying Hartigan's April 1953 exhibition at Tibor de Nagy Gallery. The artist's handwritten notes are shown beside specific works, indicating their placement. Of note is Daisy Aldan alongside *Artificial Flowers and Apples* and the Museum of Modern Art alongside *The Persian Jacket*.

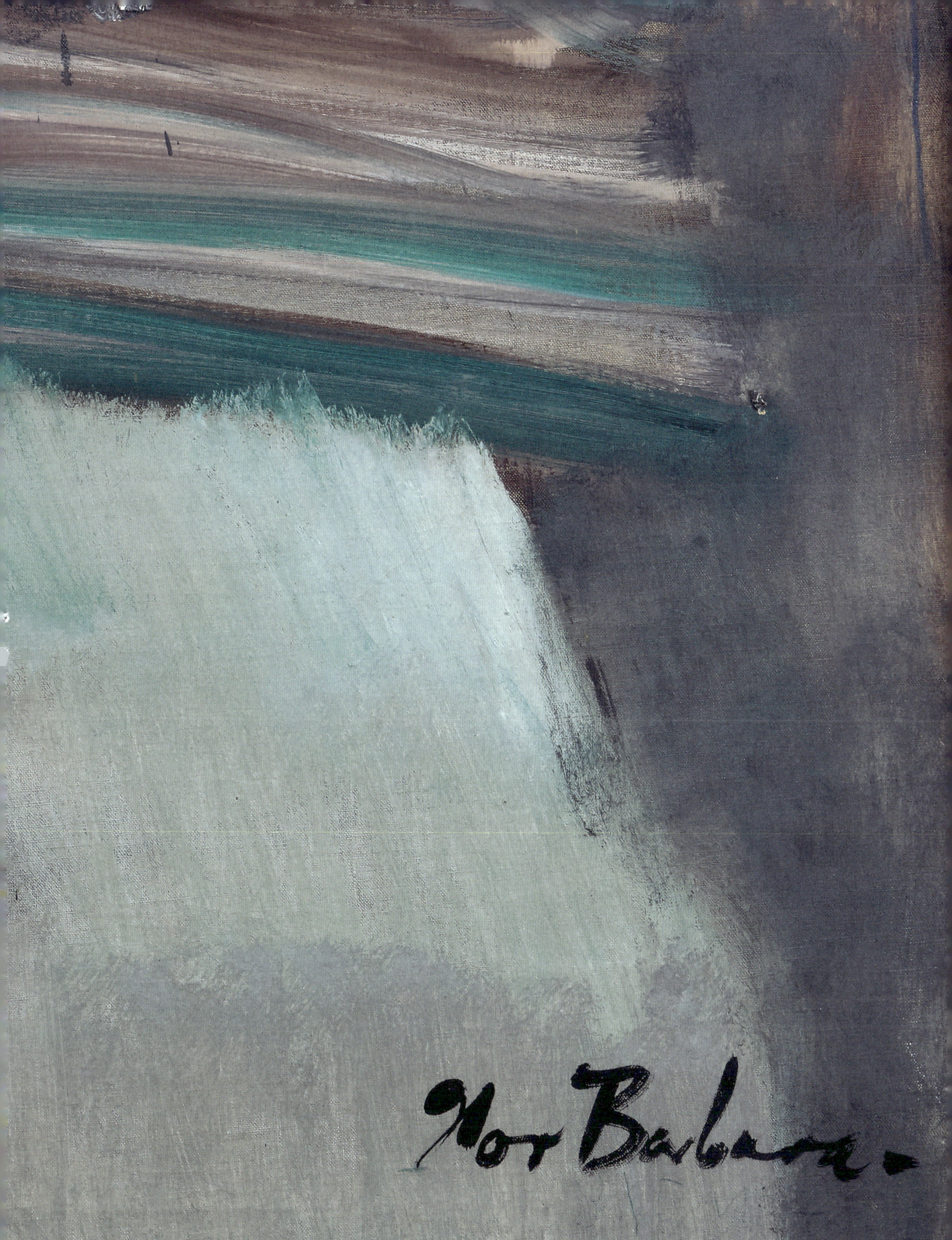
Nor Barbara.

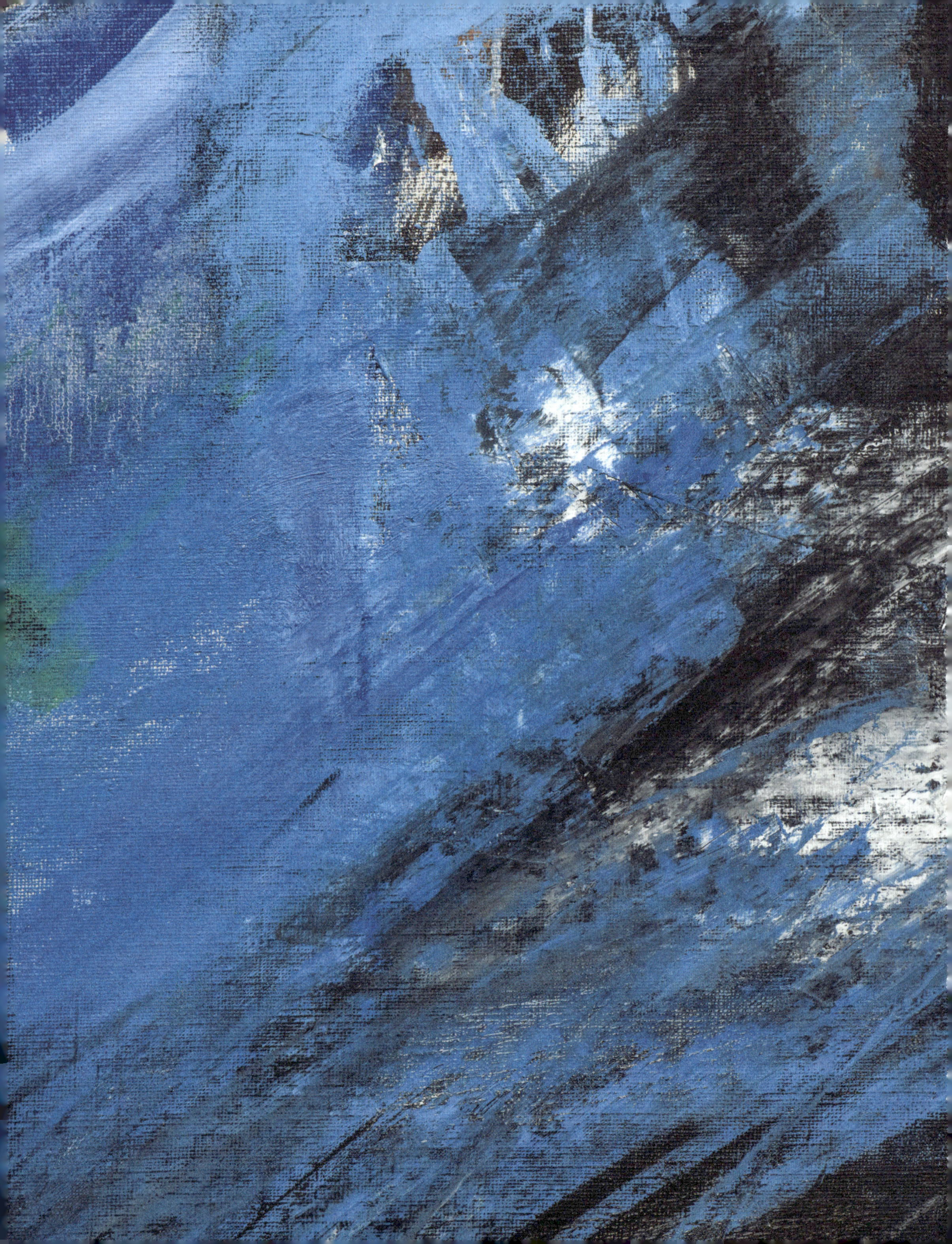